D1426940

Building Faith

Building Faith

A Sociology of Religious Structures

ROBERT BRENNEMAN AND BRIAN J. MILLER

OXFORD
UNIVERSITY PRESS

OXFORD
UNIVERSITY PRESS

Oxford University Press is a department of the University of Oxford. It furthers
the University's objective of excellence in research, scholarship, and education
by publishing worldwide. Oxford is a registered trade mark of Oxford University
Press in the UK and certain other countries.

Published in the United States of America by Oxford University Press
198 Madison Avenue, New York, NY 10016, United States of America.

Library of Congress Cataloging-in-Publication Data
Names: Brenneman, Robert, author. | Miller, Brian J. (Brian Jonathan), author.
Title: Building faith : a sociology of religious structures /
Robert Brenneman and Brian J. Miller.
Description: New York : Oxford University Press, [2020] |
Includes bibliographical references and index.
Identifiers: LCCN 2020003947 (print) | LCCN 2020003948 (ebook) |
ISBN 9780190883447 (hardback) | ISBN 9780190883454 (updf) |
ISBN 9780190883478 (oso) | ISBN 9780190883461 (epub)
Subjects: LCSH: Architecture and society. |
Religious architecture. | Religion and sociology.
Classification: LCC NA2543.S6 B735 2020 (print) | LCC NA2543.S6 (ebook) |
DDC 720.1/03—dc23 LC record available at https://lccn.loc.gov/2020003947
LC ebook record available at https://lccn.loc.gov/2020003948

1 3 5 7 9 8 6 4 2

Printed by Sheridan Books, Inc., United States of America

Contents

Acknowledgments

I wish to thank Brian for believing in this project and for being patient with my fickle ear and sluggish pace of writing. Thanks also to the Society for the Scientific Study of Religion's Jack Shand Research Grant for providing travel funds that made possible multiple trips to Guatemala and to the Midwest. Paul Jones deserves a hearty thanks for encouraging this project at multiple junctures, and for providing an excellent and detailed review of the entire manuscript. In addition, Gerardo Marti and several anonymous reviewers at *Sociology of Religion* read early versions of Chapter 2 and helped us greatly as we hammered out some of the original ideas that would become the seed for the book. Many conference goers at the Society for the Scientific Study of Religion and the Association for the Sociology of Religion also provided important comments and encouragement over the years, and Cynthia Read provided editorial encouragement and guidance. That said, any errors or weaknesses in the manuscript belong to the authors alone.

In Guatemala, Israel Ortiz helped enormously by making contacts and setting up interviews. Karen Ponciano and Maria Victoria García Vettorazzi also deserve a shout out for listening to my early ideas and providing encouragement and advice. In Vermont, Dina Alsaffar was crucial in helping to arrange the meeting with leaders of the Islamic Society of Vermont. Most importantly, I wish to give a special thanks to the many people who gave their time to this project by sitting down with me to discuss how the buildings where they met (or buildings they designed) had come to be and how the same buildings had shaped the experience of their congregations. I continue to be humbled by the willingness of people—particularly in Guatemala but also in the United States—to donate their time to a sociologist armed with a notepad and recorder. The Carrillo family in Xelajú deserves an extra special "*¡Gracias!*" for going above and beyond by providing me with not only interviews, but free meals, friendly conversation, and even a place to sleep. Now that's generosity! To all those who shared their time and thoughts, I hope that we have done justice to your experience.

I wish to thank my tag team of consultant-critics, Nico and Gabo, for their continuing encouragement, their growing interest in the project, and for their good company. To Gaby, I owe a special debt of gratitude. You not only humored me patiently in this multi-year project, but you joined me in a quest to understand how physical space shapes community. *Mil gracias!*

Robert

I thank Bob for his initial idea and willingness to share this project after a productive lunch in Indianapolis. Our conversations regarding the research and writing have been lively and fruitful. I am grateful to the people of Holy Transfiguration, Church of the Resurrection, and the Edge who were willing to share their time and church buildings with me. May your congregations and buildings have long lives. I have had several student research assistants over the course of this project who have helped collect data or organize material. My thanks go to Jessica Mohkami, Samuel Breslin, and Victoria Dobleske. My colleagues, department, and college have provided support and feedback for various portions of the project. I am grateful for their backing. Thanks to Taylor & Francis and Oxford Academic for permission to use previously published articles. In the course of working on this project, my family has grown in number and changed physical structures (translation: we moved). They have endured much conversation about religious buildings. They have also provided many much-needed breaks from thinking about the sociological aspects of structures and places. May we all, especially the younger ones, be shaped in positive ways by religious buildings.

Brian

Prologue

Paris, France: April 17, 2019

Flames licked up the soaring Gothic spire as it leaned precariously to one side, towering nevertheless over the stately buildings of central Paris. "Our Lady" was blushing crimson for the first time in her history. Her glowing spire then bowed more severely before careening out of sight. A few onlookers gasped, but the audio recordings, watched by millions if not billions around the world, seem muted, reverent even, as one of the most famous icons of Western religious culture toppled to the ground. Paris wept and the world watched in shock, hardly capable of believing that a building older than democracy, whose foundations were laid 856 years earlier, could be allowed to catch fire and burn.

But it was only after the flames were doused, when it became clear that Notre-Dame Cathedral had been badly damaged but spared the worst of fates, that the social, political, and cultural importance of this structure began to emerge. French persons of all backgrounds mourned the destruction of "Our Lady," and did so with a genuine sincerity and heartbroken solidarity that could hardly have been imagined just a few weeks earlier. Gone, temporarily at least, were the yellow vests and the protests, and in their place, thousands of French people were singing and praying by candlelight, or just observing the charred building and consoling one another in quiet sadness. The following day provided further insight into the place of the cathedral in the national and global imagination.

"I got up a little early this morning so that I could stop by and see her," said one Jean Houssain, speaking through an interpreter to National Public Radio correspondent Eleanor Beardslee. "I had a visceral need to see her."

Lucie Lemaire, an eighteen-year-old college student, lamented: "I'm super sad. I passed in front of it all the time, but I didn't really pay attention because it was a part of my daily routine. She's so beautiful. And this is an enormous loss. And it'll never be the same now." Even Muslim taxi driver Bashir Arbouuli bemoaned the loss as he told Beardslee: "It's not about religion. It's about 800 years of history of France and the whole world, really. It's a symbol that's even stronger than religion."

Of course, Arbouuli is only half right. Notre-Dame de Paris is a building that is profoundly *about* religion. It is a space that was designed by and for a thoroughly religious community, and it replaced no fewer than four consecutively built churches and possibly a Roman temple before that. But the taxi driver was not so far off if he meant that Notre-Dame is about *more than* religion, worship, or sacred gatherings. It is, after all, a *social* structure through and through, and this fact was perhaps never more on display than when the future of the building—its very existence—was abruptly thrown into question. Christian or Muslim, religious or secular, young or old, Parisians voiced their attachment to a building that seemed to speak to the "we," the *nous,* of being French.

Buildings have a tendency to do this—to "build a we" out of a collection of individuals. But this "*e-pluribus-unum-*function" can be easy to forget until the physical structure is jeopardized. Nor is the unifying tendency restricted to beautiful, stately works of architecture. During an early presentation of the research in this book—which had focused entirely on the constructions, modification, and maintenance of religious buildings of all types—an astute listener offered a suggestion that we as authors ought to pay more attention to what happens to a religious community when a building is *destroyed.* The colleague reminded us of the history of trauma experienced by African-American churches targeted by arsonists in the South—a history that, unfortunately, continues into the present. We took note, and then promptly forgot to incorporate or follow up on the suggestion. Only the Notre-Dame fire and the subsequent outpouring of heartfelt laments and deep-pocketed resources reminded us of the earlier suggestion. In particular, an article in the *New York Times* published the day after the fire reminded us that others were making the connection as well. The *Times* reported that a crowdfunding campaign launched by the Seventh District Baptist Association had been launched almost a week before the Paris fire in an attempt to raise money for the three African-American churches destroyed by an arsonist in the preceding weeks. The campaign had raised only a modest amount of funds—until the fire at Notre-Dame struck. Suddenly, the funds raised went from a mere $93,000 to more than half a million dollars, with donations coming from well-known figures such as Hillary Clinton and CNN anchor Jake Tapper. Apparently, for many Americans, including the authors of this book, watching Notre-Dame burn was a wake-up call—a reminder that the destruction, partial or complete, of a religious building strikes a massive and visceral blow to a whole community. And while our book continues to focus on the building, usage, and maintenance of religious buildings, we would be remiss if we ignored the lessons offered by Notre-Dame and the black churches of Louisiana. Religious buildings, because they grow directly from the imagination and solidarity of a community of people, and because they provide such communities with a physical *home* for interacting, worshipping, eating—for simply *being together*—live dangerously close to our hearts. When they are damaged or broken, we feel the injury as deeply as if it were to our bodies.

What follows is an attempt, using the tools of sociology, to understand how and why such buildings get hold of a community and how communities act in concert (and sometimes in conflict) to build, remodel, and rebuild them—including, in some cases, when the faith (or unfaith) of the *rebuilders* and remodelers takes a very different form than the faith of those who laid the cornerstone.

1

Introduction

Sometime during the last three decades, perhaps as early as the late 1980s, a new coming-of-age ritual became a permanent feature of life for the American middle-class teen: the guided campus tour. Today the ritual is so frequent as to be commonplace. All across the country during the spring and summer months of each year, seventeen-year-olds amble down campus sidewalks, parents in tow, crowding behind their college student tour guide who points out each building, describing not only its academic, residential, or social function, but, assuming they have been properly trained, adding colorful anecdotes about its past or present role in the institution. Following a carefully scripted tour of which buildings to enter (usually the newest and the oldest buildings), and which ones to scrupulously avoid (any building constructed during 1955–1985), the guides ferry their charges across the campus and back to the admissions office, hoping that the experience will have provided them with some useful information about the college, or in any case, something impressive. The teens, and perhaps their parents to an even greater extent, use the opportunity to scrutinize the architecture of the buildings, the landscape, and the cordiality of their guides and wonder to themselves, "Is this place good enough for me (or for my son or daughter)? Does it *fit* who I am or want to be?" Clearly, the buildings can speak only symbolically in answer and they are "heard" differently by different audiences, even if "collegiate Gothic" and "collegiate colonial" seem to be the only "safe choices" for college architects in the twenty-first century. But that they say *something* is beyond doubt, for the buildings are "listened to" over and over again for their potential to answer such questions in the minds of prospective students. Campus tours remind us that buildings *speak*. And at important times and moments, people listen, and listen hard.

If the rise of campus tours gives some inkling of the power of buildings to communicate—to attract and repel even the most unpracticed observer— this book examines another influential set of buildings that are far more numerous: *religious* buildings. Within communities around the world, religious structures are both old and new, some standing for centuries, while

Building Faith. Robert Brenneman and Brian J. Miller, Oxford University Press (2020). © Oxford University Press.
DOI: 10.1093/oso/9780190883447.001.0001

others are new constructions or have undergone renovation by new religious groups. How do they speak to the people and communities who use them and those who live near them? Can it be that the buildings built for religious congregations—from the Beth Sholom Synagogue of Washington, D.C., designed by Frank Lloyd Wright, to the humblest inner-city storefront church—have voices with the power to shape human action? We argue that they do indeed. And we believe that such shaping influence has for too long gone largely unobserved in the social sciences and, in particular, in the sub-field dedicated to the sociology of religion.

But before diving headlong into an exploration of how and why buildings matter, we have decided to share our own pathways into this field in order to give readers a sense of who we are as authors and how we came to this topic, so rarely studied by scholars from our field. As with any good social research, it helps to know where the researchers are coming from and why they care about a particular question or set of questions. The following are a few words in that regard.

Robert's Story

It must have been 1981 because I distinctly remember that I had just finished the first grade and on this particular Sunday morning in June, I was, strange as it may seem, excited to be on the way to church. Sunday morning services were not typically all that memorable—and rarely, if ever, exciting—at North Wayne Mennonite, the tiny rural outpost congregation where I attended with my family throughout my growing-up years in southwest Michigan. But I knew this Sunday would be special. A renovation had just been completed and our little square building had been transformed, updated, and expanded. This was to be the first complete service in the renovated building and I was thrilled to see it, run through the lobby, race up and down the stairs to the basement, and, remarkably even, to sit still in the sanctuary, relishing the formaldehyde smell of the new carpet. I am sure that my excitement came in no small measure from watching my grandfather. As the founding minister of the church, he was the one who had spearheaded this renovation project from start to finish. Grandpa had moved to Michigan from Indiana with his family in the late 1960s in order to purchase an old Methodist church building from the Ladies Aid Society that had kept it from falling into disrepair, and to establish a Mennonite outreach congregation there. Now this little country church building was getting an "update" that included a spacious lobby, proper bathrooms, Sunday School rooms, and even that paragon of modernity—a carport! Though the church still sat on the edge of a cornfield across from an abandoned schoolhouse on a dusty gravel road, the little congregation with which my family identified so closely was looking suddenly modern and respectable—suburban, even, with its drive-up entrance and shiny glass doors. After years of hard work and ministry, our church had at last taken a giant leap into the eighties. We had arrived!

Not that any signs of ostentation were allowed. White aluminum siding and clear, square windows remained the order of the day, and the 100-year-old steeple remained safely stowed away in the attic. My grandfather was, after all, born and raised in the Amish church, and had grown up attending church services in the homes of the faithful. The Amish, who fear any temptation toward pride and excess, believe that having any church building at all invites trouble, opening up the potential that a congregation might try to "make its mark" on the world and thus find itself sidetracked from its spiritual priorities. The conservative Mennonite tradition that Grandpa joined as a young adult, and to which he was eventually called to minister, *allowed* church buildings, but tried its best not to think about them. Steeples were a definite no-no. Nevertheless, by spearheading multiple renovations and expansions to this little church building—and by almost single-handedly funding them with the profits from his successful farm equipment business— Grandpa was betting that for social institutions like a religious congregation, *buildings matter*.

It would take me many years to recognize and absorb this lesson. Remarkably, graduate school in sociology provided little opportunity to think about buildings and how they structure institutions and social interaction. Although professors and students spoke often and with great passion about the importance of *social structures* in human society, rarely ever did we stop to think about *physical structures* and the many and powerful ways in which buildings facilitate and constrain the networks, opportunities, and hierarchies we wished so fervently to understand and explain. Indeed, it was not until I began conducting research on my dissertation that I first began to "notice" buildings and their sociological importance. I was researching religious pathways out of the Central American gangs, and my principal dialogue partners were former members of the gangs who had converted to Evangelical-Pentecostal Christianity. The congregations that had helped to "rescue" them typically met in small, cinder-block boxes with tin roofs and narrow windows. My earlier experiences in Central America had led me to believe that these churches cared little about their buildings. Because of their humble appearance, I had assumed that these congregations focused instead on the spiritual lives of their members.

But gradually I was coming to recognize that my views were mistaken. These religious communities cared an awful lot about the physical structures where they met, prayed, and sang. For example, when I met Danilo, a twenty-eight-year-old former member of the *Mara Salvatrucha*, he was in the middle of sweeping the church building. This act caught my attention, not least because it is enormously rare to find a young man holding a broom in Central America. Sweeping the floor is work that men, as a rule, simply do not do. A broom is a woman's instrument. And yet so excited and involved was he in this new religious life of his, that he had chosen voluntarily to help clean the sanctuary—and on a weekday no less. Nor was Danilo working for cash as a janitor. Since leaving the gang he had been employed as a baker at a local bakery. The building, typical of a Pentecostal church of the barrio, was small and humble, barely much bigger than a small suburban ranch home but with fewer windows. And yet, as I was learning, its members took great pride in it, contributing their hard-earned resources to its continued construction and finishing, and decorating it with streamers for special events. Furthermore, as I continued to study the tiny Pentecostal congregations that ministered to ex-gang members, I was struck by the enormous energy they managed to generate within their walls. During long evening services on weekends, emotional effervescence, to use an apt term from the lexicon of early sociologist Emile Durkheim, literally ricocheted around the walls of the sanctuary in these tiny structures. Thus, both during and after the writing of my dissertation, I began to wonder if and how religious buildings—and not just the stately cathedrals of Europe and the United States—actually matter.

Brian's Story

I have always been interested in places. Perhaps some of this is due to my parents—one grew up in the city, one in the suburbs, and they liked to travel. At a young age, this interest in places manifested itself in multiple ways, including an early interest in geography (which also certainly helped when following sports teams), playing lots of Simcity (where residential zones could automatically convert to a church), and even drawing out my own cities on graph paper. Along the way, I grew up in a suburban church that was rather plain looking: the façade presented an asymmetrical attempt at colonial architecture, the main worship space was a long narrow sanctuary with wooden pews, and numerous spaces in the building offered functional room for a variety of activities. The men of the church largely built the sanctuary, parsonage, gym, and classrooms in the mid-twentieth century. It wasn't until I started playing music in church that I noticed the building more. While in junior high school, I played piano solos a few times during Sunday morning services, but due to nervousness and focusing intently on the music, the interaction of the physical structure with the musical experience completely escaped my attention. In high school, I started playing with a number of music groups at church. It was then that I recognized how the physical characteristics of a space or building could shape a worship experience.

The first time I played with the high school youth group band, we met regularly in a large square room with normal eight-foot ceilings and with scores of chairs arranged around the band in one corner of the room. The room was more functional than anything else, configured and decorated to quickly transition from a site for a wedding shower to a large Sunday school classroom to hosting a lively youth group. This space presented particular challenges; sound didn't travel well, so we had to mount speakers on poles; the band couldn't hear each other very well; many of the attendees couldn't see what was happening with the musicians or the words projected on the wall via overhead due to all standing on the same level; and the lighting was uniformly bland due to overhead fluorescent tubes. The one advantage to such a space was intimacy: the room was nearly completely full of people and the sound, both from the front and from the group, was all encompassing.

These logistical issues—and a growing youth group, perhaps aided by such intimate settings—pushed us to change our venue and meet in the church's sanctuary, where we could take advantage of a superior sound system, targeted lighting, and a platform raised above the audience. As the piano player, having a set of risers that elevated the stage a foot or so off the main floor meant I was by far the most immobile member of the group. Setting up a keyboard helped, as I could be closer to the other musicians and settle into musical grooves that tend to develop in time spent playing together as well as through physical proximity. As we developed as a band, the new space offered a number of advantages in crafting a more polished worship experience even as other aspects of the space—such as fixed pews which offered some attendees the chance to sit as far away as possible—inhibited group togetherness.

Further involvement in these groups also provided more free rein to be in the church before and after hours for matters like setting up or practicing. These duties helped me see the building outside of reverent times of worship. What did the sanctuary feel like in the gathering gloom of a winter evening? How could spaces that were imbued with sacredness on Sunday mornings be so banal at other times in the week? Later involvement in two additional churches as an attendee, volunteer, and musician revealed consistent building issues that congregations face, such as concerns about the mortgage (owning the building outright was considered a laudable goal), maintenance of aging structures (from painting walls to upgrading sound and light systems to enhance worship), and the repurposing of spaces (from youth group dodgeball to formal dinners to trivia nights to spaces of sincere worship). My own process of maturing within churches showed me the importance of the building, even as every congregation I attended likely said, "A church is not a building but rather the people." Whether in playing music or worshipping or fellowshipping, the building played a vital—and often unrecognized—role.

Thus, when I had an opportunity as a sociologist to think about religious buildings as influential structures in their own right, I was immediately intrigued by the possibilities. Particularly in one of my subfields of interest, urban sociology, buildings receive relatively little attention compared to other causal forces. Just how much of the experiences that people and groups have in religious buildings is shaped by the physical setting?

Summing Up

As the preceding stories indicate, both of the authors are "insiders" to religion, having grown up in and around congregations and having chosen for a variety of reasons to remain involved in them, even as we develop and carry out sociological research on religious people and institutions. We don't believe that our position as "insiders" makes us better researchers, but it does give us perhaps a leg up in terms of breadth of anecdotal evidence— in addition to our formal case studies and original data gathering—from which to draw insights. More importantly, our experience in a variety of congregations and denominations in the United States and Central America has allowed us to observe the curious oversight, both inside and outside religious congregations, regarding the buildings in which they meet. Like the conservative Mennonites with their unadorned meetinghouses, many religious people spend a good deal of their time pretending not to notice their buildings. They are there, but their presence and their shaping influence often go unnoticed. All the more surprising, then, that sociologists have paid scant attention to buildings, since we represent the discipline that has insisted from the beginning that those structures are most powerful whose formative influence goes unremarked. In short, we have gotten used to not noticing the buildings that form our communities, our relationships, and our movements. This book is an attempt to bring buildings, particularly religious structures, and their power to shape lives and communities, into the spotlight.

The following chapters examine important aspects of religious buildings for scholars to consider, particularly sociologists of religion. Chapter 2 presents the two broad approaches sociologists and other scholars often take toward buildings—a symbolic interactionist perspective that analyzes the symbolism and meanings communicated by structures, and a conflict perspective that explores the power dynamics of physical structures—and advocates for a third approach that accounts for the influence of buildings on social interactions and behavior, particularly building upon theories of interaction ritual chains. We present four arguments supporting our new approach. After presenting our perspective, the next five chapters develop our argument through research conducted by the authors on different levels and varied parts of the process involving building, renovating, and using religious buildings. We start in Chapter 3 with an emphasis on the process of constructing a religious building through case studies from Guatemala. Utilizing data from various participants—including pastors and laypersons— this chapter looks at competing demands during the construction process with analysis of how the congregation settled into and experienced the new building. Chapter 4 considers the role of zoning in the United States and what happens when American religious groups appeal to local governments to build or renovate structures for religious purposes. Looking at cases from three suburban communities, we find buildings near residences draw more attention from neighbors and officials, as can requests from Muslim groups. Chapter 5 emphasizes the unique role of the church architect, drawing upon interviews with three American professionals who have worked with multiple congregations of varying denominations, while Chapter 6 moves beyond the construction process and discusses how five congregations, two in Guatemala and three in the United States, utilize structures not originally constructed by the current congregation. These congregations altered the physical structures and learned how to worship in unique spaces, even as some desired to make further alterations to their edifice or even construct their own building from scratch. Religious buildings are not ephemeral or transient, but neither are they eternal. Chapter 7 recognizes this fact by considering the long-term fate of religious buildings among four denominations in the Chicago region. Using a unique church directory from the early twentieth century, we ask how many churches are still standing eight decades later, and how do the congregations that still worship in that structure present the building on their website?

Our Conclusion summarizes five key insights gleaned from our research about the influence of religious buildings, especially in regard to the ways they shape religious experiences, and why understanding this shaping influence matters for sociologists and others who study buildings and religion. Ultimately, our goal is to shed light on the way *spaces shape community* by providing insights that stretch beyond the sociology of religion. We wish to contribute to a newly emerging and rapidly expanding sociological literature devoted to understanding the impact of physical structures on human groups as "structures structuring" social action and human collectives. If we are successful, our readers will pay closer attention to the particular buildings that shape their lives and will be equipped with a vocabulary and a set of sensitizing questions for making sense out of this formative and formidable influence. If buildings "speak," our book is an invitation to listen with renewed and sharpened attention.

We began this chapter by calling attention to the way the college campus tour has become a crucial occasion during which prospective students and their parents are invited to "read" buildings as indicators of the academic prestige of an institution and as barometers of the school's financial stability. The oldest and the newest buildings often receive the most attention, perhaps not only because they can attest to the college's prestige—old but well-maintained buildings suggest a college has been around for a while—and its growth—new construction says a college is growing and has resources to spend—but also because these are the buildings most likely to fit a recognizably "academic" neo-colonial or Gothic Revival style (Biemiller 2010). Yet one building that appears prominently on many if not most college campuses—indeed, it often occupies the very center of campus and generally fits the desired architectural pattern—also creates consternation for both tour guide and participants alike. How to explain the college chapel? The secularized, pluralist environment to which most college campuses now aspire requires that campus tour guides receive careful coaching in how to reassure prospective students that the existence of a chapel or church at the center of campus should *not* be read as a theological statement or evangelistic mission of the institution—at least not in the present. Depending on the institution and perhaps on the savvy of its admissions director, the chapel may even be turned into an asset, as an opportunity to describe the religious "roots" of the institution while providing reassurance that such tradition-specific roots are kept mostly in the safety of the past. Nevertheless, the stubborn persistence of college chapels all across American college and university campuses—from Stanford to Princeton—suggest an ongoing spatial home for religion amidst the more secular purposes of the modern university. They also give testimony to the ways in which the "sticks and bricks" of religious buildings—on a serene campus, a busy street, or a country lane—keep talking and acting on the social relations of the present. It is time sociologists paid real attention to them.

2
What Religious Buildings Do

We shape our buildings, and afterward our buildings shape us.
                                        —Winston Churchill (1943)

[B]uildings silently steer us into associations or away from them [yet]
we hardly notice how.
                                        —Thomas Gieryn (2002)

The Significance of Religious Structures

All across the populated regions of the known world—wherever people live, play, and do business—religious buildings mark the landscape.[1] This statement is as true of the "modern" and "secular" West as it is of the supposedly more religious Middle and Far East. For example, google "Santa Fe, New Mexico" and a picture of a church appears. Perhaps that should come as no surprise, since "Santa Fe" is Spanish for "Holy Faith." And yet it is easy to forget, in the hustle-and-bustle of modern urbanity—and in Santa Fe's laid-back Southwest artistic vibe—that even at the outset of the twenty-first century, *religious* buildings remain the key markers of space in a great many of our cities. The case of the church at Santa Fe, the Cathedral Basilica of Saint Francis to be more precise, is especially intriguing. The church is a large Romanesque structure built of ocher-colored stone quarried in the nearby Sangre de Cristo Mountains, which loom like a misty blue stage curtain behind it. Constructed in the latter half of the nineteenth century by Bishop Jean Baptiste Lamy, the church was an ambitious statement by a French-born cleric who had been sent by Rome in 1851 with a mission to organize and re-evangelize a chaotic diocese in the United States' newly annexed New Mexico Territory. In a fictionalized account of Bishop Lamy's planning for the cathedral, the great American writer Willa Cather portrays the graying bishop as pleased with his ministry, but unable to rest until his plans for a new cathedral are underway. Bishop Latour (the fictionalized name Cather gives to

Building Faith. Robert Brenneman and Brian J. Miller, Oxford University Press (2020). © Oxford University Press.
DOI: 10.1093/oso/9780190883447.001.0001

Bishop Lamy) calls his priest friend home from the mission field in Arizona, where he has been hard at work, just for the pleasure of taking his old friend for a ride to show him the place where he hopes to have masons quarry the stone for the cathedral that still exists only in his imagination. "I should like to complete it before I die—if God so wills," the bishop confides in his friend:

> I wish to leave nothing to chance, or to the mercy of American builders.
> I had rather keep the old adobe church we have now than help to build one
> of those horrible structures they are putting up in the Ohio cities. I want a
> plain church, but I want a good one. I shall certainly never lift my hand to
> build a clumsy affair of red brick, like an English coach-house. Our own
> Midi Romanesque is the right style for this country. (Cather 1927:109)

Although this particular monologue came from the fecund imagination of a novelist, it helps us imagine how a Romanesque cathedral came to appear in 1886 on the frontier of the American Southwest, drawing to this day a sharp contrast with the low, simple adobe structures in the historic district around it. Whether or not French Romanesque was a fitting choice for this town matters less than the fact that it has become a landmark today, and a required destination for tourists and travelers from all walks of life. And that it has become thus must be owed in no small part to the fact that a particular religious leader decided his church needed a building adequate in size and grandeur to the growth and reach his diocese was beginning to achieve. Religious buildings, it seems, take shape in our imagination. But when they achieve reality in stone, glass, and brick, they act back on our imagination, placing upon our collective consciousness an imprimatur that can last well beyond the age of the ambitious leaders and funders who helped build them. In some cases, these religious buildings become so well lodged in the imagination of not only the faithful but of the public at large that they become synonymous with a particular place, or even an entire city. Just how they achieve this molding of the imagination is one of the central topics of this book.

And yet religious buildings are more than historic sites—more than famous tourist attractions. Indeed, only a tiny fraction of the myriad religious buildings in the world can make such a claim to public prominence. More central to their usage is the role that religious buildings play in providing a space for the faithful to gather and a materialized blueprint for structuring their worship. In this chapter we seek to explore both the public and religious roles played by religious buildings, using the tools of social theory. Our task remains the same. We wish to explore sociologically what religious buildings "do" for people and communities, and how people and communities interact with these buildings.

Why Buildings Matter

Perhaps more than any other social science, sociology is a discipline that employs the language of *structures*. We discuss social structures, economic structures, superstructures, and structural inertia, to name just a few. Even that most basic term of sociology—"social structure"—gets used in so many vast and varied ways that it is not altogether clear what we mean to say when we use the term. One thing is for certain, though. Sociologists rarely use the word "structure" in its most basic, literal sense. When we talk about a structure, we are hardly ever referring to a *physical* structure.

Throughout this book, and in particular in this chapter, we wish to call into question this practice of talking about "structures" in every sense except the literal one. In fact, we think that by ignoring the way physical structures shape social interaction—particularly in religious settings—we miss a key opportunity to understand the social bodies we seek to explain, and we forfeit one of the richest unexplored data troves currently available. By not seriously considering religious buildings, we fail to grasp how people "experience architecture sensuously, holistically, and, as Benjamin pointed out, habitually and in a state of distraction" (Larson 1993:252). We offer four arguments for engaging in sociological research on religious buildings: they shape and are shaped by religious congregations and other actors; their construction often involves tension and excitement; they provide a venue through which the past can continue to influence the present; and they highlight the need to bring bodies back into the sociological study of religion. Ultimately, religious buildings are material objects created by humans that also interact with and shape social groups in unique ways.

In an attempt to be consistent with the title of our book and in order to avoid confusion from the long tradition of using the word "structures" in a metaphorical sense, we employ the term religious *buildings* and argue that both the way they take shape and the way they act back on the communities that build them together offer a promising and much-needed avenue of new research. While ours is not a wholly new argument, as others have recently called for a renewed emphasis on place and context in sociology (Gieryn

2000) and specifically in the sociology of religion (e.g., Smith et al. 2013), we believe the emphasis on religious buildings offers important new theoretical insights and untapped resources for understanding the formation and evolution of social groups.

Religious Buildings Shape and Are Shaped by Their Congregations

Although we often seem to forget the fact, religious buildings are, by their very nature, social phenomena. Religious buildings are a powerful example of the "social forces" which shape and constrain the formation of groups and the identity of the members belonging to them. For example, the physical building constructed by a congregation communicates particular values and meanings to those who congregate there, as well as to the many who never enter the structure but who nevertheless draw conclusions about its members based on the building's shape, design, and size. Furthermore, religious buildings are themselves subject to social forces insofar as they are always conceived, designed, and built by a group rather than an individual. Whether that group of individuals is a building committee, a pastor and a few elders, or a denominational planning board, virtually every religious building (or renovation) involves input from multiple members—and often non-specialists—of the religious body. Even when an architect drafts the design, as is often, though certainly not always, the case, a religious building reflects in some fashion the hopes and needs of the community that builds it. Not that everyone in the preceding list has equal access to the design table. "Experts" in both religion and in design and construction typically have the most say, along with those whose financial resources allow them to make outsize contributions to the work. Once built, that religious building will influence the behavior of later users, for, while far from eternal, a religious building has a certain level of what Anthony Giddens (1994) has called "fixity." Its materiality means that, whatever happens to the congregation, the structure it erected—much like the cathedral in Santa Fe—is likely to hang around for a while.[2]

In this sense, then, a religious building project is an eminently social production that interacts with local understandings and offers possibilities both for stability and reinterpretation (Berger and Luckmann 1966; Williams 1997; Gieryn 2002). Religious buildings "speak" not only to the community that meets in them, but also to those whose only notion of the congregation is the building itself, and they do this by drawing on the shared vernacular surrounding physical structures in their community. Their size, shape, and symbols represent legible signs to outsiders about the kind of community that worships within them. Well aware of this fact, congregational leaders and building committees, when setting out to build or renovate, labor long and hard to find ways to communicate actively, but also accurately, to their neighbors and potential visitors while also meeting the practical needs of the members and their liturgies.

There is a second sense in which religious buildings are uniquely social. While there are many different uses for religious buildings (the National Congregations Study finds that religious buildings are regularly used by groups not connected to congregations for art exhibits, as art itself, etc.; see Chaves 2004:233), their primary use is typically for corporate worship. In worship, a *group* of people meet together at a certain time to interact in a very particular way, often claiming to interact with the transcendent or divine. Whereas a home provides a place for an individual or a small group to seek rest, shelter, and privacy, and to interact in patterned ways (Bourdieu 1960), in a church, temple, mosque, or synagogue, a group of people, most of whom are typically of no blood relation, gather to do something that can only be accomplished *together*. Other major architectural monuments, such as museums, skyscrapers, or government buildings, may seek to prompt particular attitudes and behaviors for users or attendees—such as museums attempting to shape national identities and historical interpretations (e.g., McLean 1998; Boswell and Evans 1999; Jones 2011; MacLeod 2013)—but these structures do not share with religious buildings the aim of regularly gathering all members for a shared, deeply symbolic interactive ritual with the supernatural or divine. In other words, the corporate, social nature of worship places unique demands upon religious buildings. Indeed, it is this highly social nature of religious experience that helps to explain why the members of ancient religions describe themselves with singular terms such as "the *body* of Christ," "the *light* to the nations," or the Muslim *Ummah*. These terms imply that religious individuals see themselves as belonging to a larger unity that is greater than the sum of its parts. Social scientists who study such phenomena ought to seek every opportunity available to study such *corporate work* of a religious body.

In addition to religious buildings reflecting social groups and providing space for social activity, in their creation and afterward, religious buildings are objects that exert unique pressure on those who utilize the space. They have materiality, even if their design is not fully understood by attendees (Price 2013:183). They are not simply receptacles into which any person entering can impose a new set of meanings and values. The physical structures themselves interact with the social beings within. In a photographic study of religious buildings, New York–based writer and photographer Camilo José Vergara pointed out, "Through its physical features, a building affirms its presence as the house of God, as something permanent, a home for the religious life, a place to articulate beliefs, and a symbol of the identity of the pastor and the congregation" (Vergara 2005:39).

These two dimensions of religious buildings—as social creations as well as material objects—clash with an assumption often underlying what gets published in the sociology of religion: that the impact of religion can best be understood by looking to the individual and without examining the material objects they interact with. Although researching buildings is certainly not the *only* way to study the social production of a social body, this approach could offer a helpful corrective to the overused tendency of interpreting religion through the lens of the individual believer floating free from the influence of physical spaces.

Not everyone has ignored religious buildings. One example of the insights that can emerge from examining religious buildings as material phenomena is illustrated in recent research on American megachurches. While much attention has been paid to the individual experiences in such settings and the theological and cultural shifts present in these large congregations, some of these new churches also aim to present new kinds of religious spaces intended to promote particular behaviors and meanings. In other words, these new types of congregations aren't just new social arrangements, but are also embedded within and influenced by particular buildings and physical configurations. Churches like Willow Creek in the Chicago suburbs view architecture as "an instrument of evangelism" and have worked to create new spaces that do not look much different than corporate office parks or shopping malls (Loveland and Wheeler 2003:127–79) and that are ahistorical in welcoming popular culture (Dickinson 2015). Yet, these new designs are building on previous social histories of church design (Kilde 2002; Eagle 2015). Sociologists Scott Thumma and Dave Travis (2007:30–41) discuss four different types of megachurches and the unique architectural approaches each can take, such as differences in the presence or absence of religious symbols, the choice of luxurious versus minimalistic decor, and the size of sanctuaries. Across these styles and even among the churches with more traditional architecture, there is emphasis on presentation and marketing the congregation to a wide range of people. Such research highlights that understanding megachurches must go beyond paying attention to superstar pastors, competitive religious settings, or promoting a particular kind of feel-good religion; it also should include close study of the spaces themselves and the behaviors and attitudes encouraged by them at the corporate and individual levels.

A second example involves Catholic and Protestant conceptions of space for priests or pastors and laity within religious buildings (Collins 2010). Catholic churches emphasized sacred space, whether around the altar, where only priests could trod, or at the entryway with a set of objects (such as a font of holy water). In contrast, Protestant spaces tend not to feature barriers (like screens or communion railings) and the lack of overt religious objects (except a Bible carried by a pastor) is intended to promote leveling among those present. These physical changes to buildings may have been motivated by increasing the energy generated in rituals—not necessarily motivated by doctrine—but they also became defining features of religious buildings themselves, and these traits influenced later religiosity. Put differently, the design and layout of a religious building "steer" or "routinize" social interaction with powerful and lasting effects on the communities using the space, a point to which we will return later in this chapter.

Religious Buildings Create Energy

Skeptical readers may be thinking, "Sure, some *liturgical* congregations think about and spend a lot of money on their elaborate buildings constructed on prime real estate. But what about the non-liturgical congregations? Don't their tiny, humble worship structures reflect a disdain for 'earthly vessels' like buildings? Aren't these buildings simply a means to an end—a place to meet for worship, gather for meals, or conduct their religious affairs?" While on the one hand it is true that religious groups that emphasize the importance of texts, which are portable (McGreevy 1996; Gamm 1999), at least speak of their building only as "a means to another [i.e.. religious] end," it is far from true that congregations in non-liturgical traditions care little about their buildings. In fact, they care a great deal about their material "meeting place."

One key piece of evidence suggesting that buildings matter a great deal to religious communities of nearly all traditions can be seen in the observation that religious building projects frequently involve a great deal of excitement and enthusiasm, and sometimes result in conflict over the exact size, shape, and décor of the proposed building or renovation. These discussions and the occasional outright conflict can take place at the congregational level or within a denomination or religious tradition (e.g., Price 2013). As will be apparent in Chapter 3 involving religious building projects in Guatemala, when a religious community decides to embark on a major building or renovation campaign, the excitement of gaining a new or refurbished "home" typically comes accompanied with tensions over what and how to build or remodel. The new building can also even be the result of difficulties a church faces (Ammerman 1997:107–29), not just the result of new growth or having acquired more resources. Such excitement and/or tension are not unique to the "high church" or otherwise well-to-do religious groups that engage formal architects and build large, impressive structures at great expense. Denominations that build small, relatively unassuming or unadorned structures can be equally divisive when hammering out plans for a building. After all, in these traditions, such as conservative Mennonite, Brethren, or Baptist congregations as well as Quaker meetings, *not* building ornate houses of worship and *avoiding* certain amenities that might communicate over-attachment to material goods can be just as crucial, just as central to the identity of the believers meeting there as the tall spires of the Catholic cathedral or the large dome of the Orthodox church. Either way, members know that since the building speaks to both insiders and outsiders about the group that meets there, it's important not to send the wrong message.

The very nature of a physical structure, especially one that serves an identifiable community, involves providing a locus of identity for the group that identifies with it. Sociologists working from the "symbolic interactionist" school of thought have pointed out that the architecture of a building provides members of the community identifying with that building an invitation to self-reflection (Smith and Bugni 2006). Just as important, building projects, especially those that serve a voluntary association, involve the mustering of resources from members, including money as well as contributions of folk art or construction skills to urban churches (Vergara 2005). Decisions about the proper size of the foyer and whether or not the basement should include an industrial kitchen—not to mention the decision of which architectural firm, if any, ought to be engaged—require concrete, fundamental decisions about the management of monetary resources usually contributed by members of a voluntary association. Such moments involve delicate diplomacy by leaders who must find a way to help members feel "represented" by the new building and perhaps even excited enough to continue or increase their (typically voluntary) giving, even if ultimate decisions lie within the hands of a relatively small group of leaders.

Finally, decisions about the size and structure of a building can result in significant financial commitments for decades to come. Large and architecturally "interesting" buildings can require significantly more maintenance for future generations. Such is the case for St. Paul's Episcopal Cathedral in Burlington, Vermont. In that congregation, parishioners in the early 1970s responded to the arson that destroyed their nineteenth-century building by launching a national competition that resulted in a contemporary brutalist design. While the innovative modernist building continues to be a source of pride for most members of the church, its concrete-and-glass design requires substantial costs in energy and maintenance for a congregation wrestling with demographic decline due to its location in the "graying" Northeast. In other words, building projects are not merely abstract arguments over doctrine or politics. They involve current and future giving from members whose future presence and participation is never fully guaranteed, particularly in societies with high levels of religious competition. The difference between two proposals put before a congregational building committee can easily reach into the millions of dollars, especially when energy costs and future upkeep are considered. Naturally, such differences can easily create division within a committee and a congregation.

And here is an interesting point of entry for researchers. Sociologists of religion have relatively few opportunities to observe *tension* among community members, in part because religious congregations tend to avoid topics that may involve conflict whenever they can (Moone 2004). Thus, the social process leading to the construction of a new or renovated building provides a unique opportunity to witness the way congregations actually handle tension and allocate resources. As religion scholar Jeanne Kilde suggests, "church buildings and spaces are political places, places in which social power and authority are asserted, tested, and negotiated" (2002:11). Do major givers have more to say in the design process? How do leaders create a sense of ownership in light of the fact that some, even most, design proposals must ultimately be rejected since only one building can be constructed?

The construction of religious buildings also often involves interaction be-tween a religious community and professional architects with whom they may well differ (Zukin 1991; Larson 1993; Jones 2011). We will examine this tension in more depth in Chapter 5, but a few points are worth mentioning here. A number of scholars have examined the role of architects producing iconic buildings within a new global structure. Sociologist Leslie Sklair (2010) argues that while once upon a time religious congregations and the state were the typical clients of major architects, these institutions have been replaced by a global capitalist class operating within a hegemonic system of globalization. In this view, shared by other sociological critics, the crises of capitalism and globalization often lead to "autistic architecture" where large buildings have little in common with their immediate surroundings, are in-tended to attract attention, and have a shorter life cycle (Kaika 2010, 2011).

Nevertheless, the exciting and contentious nature of religious buildings sometimes spills over to the public realm, where a variety of actors—from neighbors, local officials, and a broader public—find themselves getting involved. Recently, a Catholic parish facing declining membership in Burlington, Vermont, floated the idea of selling its building to a developer, only to find resistance from "concerned neighbors" who felt that the disap-pearance of the simple, traditional brick structure might change the look and feel of their community. Few of these neighbors were members of the parish—some were not religious at all—but they had nevertheless grown at-tached to the traditional appeal of the neighborhood and worried that the disappearance of an icon like the church might diminish that traditional vibe. In other cases, religious architecture highlights the otherness of a minority religious group, and these visible symbols can lead to conflict over what is allowed and how the building is interpreted by others (Jones 2011). Think of the tension generated by proposals for mosques in places like New York City, Nashville, Britain, and Switzerland (Biondo 2006; Guggenheim 2010; Jia, Karpen, and Hirt 2011). All of these examples remind us that the phys-ical characteristics of a structure are rarely neutral in the interpretations of a broader community.

Even "familiar" religious architecture and groups can provoke dis-agreement from local residents. One of the authors lives in Wheaton, Illinois, dubbed by some as the "Vatican of Evangelicals" for its collec-tion of churches, a religious college, and religious organizations (Vescey 1978). The city has experienced its share of opposition regarding religious buildings, even though the city seal features a church steeple (among other tall buildings in the community) and the community has a reputation for a large proportion of conservative Protestants. Residents successfully lobbied the city to set guidelines for future construction by several sizable churches near the downtown (Stewart 1989). The city and congregations underwent negotiations (Mehler 1990) and one of the major churches moved to an adjacent suburb in order to get the space they wanted to further their growth (Goldsborough 1999). In this case, the buildings prompted the opposition, not necessarily the social groups involved or their particular values. While religious congregations and organizations can be centers for rallying NIMBY ("not in my backyard") support against unwanted land uses, their architectural decisions can prompt the ire of neighbors who view these buildings as threats. Religious buildings, it seems, both repel and attract.

Buildings Give History Leverage over the Present

If Peter Berger (1963) was right in his insistence that the closest "companion" to the sociologist must be the historian, most sociologists, including those of us who study religion, have, it must be said, all too frequently ignored his advice. In our zeal to explain the "breaking news" in the religious world, we have typically relied on just enough history to provide "context" for explaining the present. Paying attention to religious structures could help steer the subdiscipline of sociology of religion toward a more robust appreciation and a more thorough empirical analysis of the historically situated nature of all religious communities. Indeed, architecture delivers its impact not solely through "discourse and codified practices," but also "artifacts that are useful and can be beautiful" (Larson 1993:16).

Buildings are "time-stamped" in at least two ways. First, the actual dates of commencement and completion of construction on a religious building provide important clues as to the nature of a religious community in a given time and place while speaking to the prevailing religious and architectural social networks (Collins and Guillén 2012), even as historic structures—like Notre-Dame de Paris—are contested and reinterpreted by later generations (Murphy 2011). Within a month of the occasion of the fire at Notre Dame, the *New York Times* reported that dozens of architectural firms from around the world had submitted proposals—from the sublime to the ridiculous—for replacing and/or transforming the destroyed roof of the church (Marshall 2019). In some cases, earlier building features like cornerstones are altered by later religious groups occupying the building (Vergara 2005). Communities that engage in a building project are typically rich in members, resources, or motivation, or a combination of these. Sociologists studying religious buildings can learn about the particular history of a congregation (or even an entire denomination) by merely observing the *dates* of construction of its buildings, let alone other physical aspects of the structure. To put it differently, bricks and stone—two of the more common materials used to build religious buildings in the West—deteriorate slowly, leaving subsequent generations a sort of "paper trail" (etched in stone) revealing the economic capacity and drive of a particular religious group in a particular time and place.

Even more important, though, is the fact that religious buildings from the past continue to exert influence on later social groups. The structures don't just sit benignly; their materiality affects groups using the buildings and those in the neighborhood. Three examples suffice here. The first is taken from a study of state buildings, the second from urban churches in the Chicago region, the third from a study of religious buildings in Guatemala.

Paul Jones (2011), a British sociologist of architecture, notes that the state building projects of nineteenth-century Europe helped to cultivate an intensive period of nation-building in which major state architectural projects became key moments of debate in a vociferous struggle over how to situate the nation with regard to the past. When the British government embarked on a rebuilding of the House of Westminster in the 1830s, a "Battle of the Styles" ensued that pitted proponents of the Gothic style against supporters of neo-classical architecture. At stake was not an aesthetic preference, but rather a momentous debate over whether the growing British Empire was to be a new kind of Holy Roman Empire—profoundly religious and Christian—or an enlightened republic in the Greco-Roman tradition. (The Gothic proponents won the battle over Westminster, but later projects initiated the neo-classical style that ultimately won the war.) As this example clearly shows, the symbolic dimensions of buildings extend well beyond the religious sphere. Whenever a major building is built with an aim to "represent" a group—be it an organization, a congregation, or a nation—excitement, tension, and probably conflict are likely to ensue, especially since the physical durability of the structure adds lasting impact to the material symbolism embodied in the building. Thus, government capitol buildings embody historical winners for later generations to see and experience, even as the outcomes of these historical contingencies continue to affect nations and social groups. Not that such representations are static or eternal. One has merely to tour Cuba's

"Museum of the Revolution"—a neo-Gothic structure originally built as the "Presidential Palace" prior to the revolution—in order to realize that interpretations of official buildings can change with major swings in power and ideology. Religious buildings, meanwhile, add the unique dimension of representing a relationship not only to the wider society (or world) but also to the Divine. The vast interior and soaring verticality of the European cathedrals communicate not only the cultural hegemony of Christianity during the late Middle Ages. They communicate to the worshipper (both then and now) the grandeur of God—a God whose vast magnificence reminds the adherent of her relative smallness by comparison.

In the numerous neighborhoods of Chicago, older church buildings abound, though many of these structures house new religious groups or have been retrofitted for altogether new uses. Numerous buildings from mainline Protestant denominations or Jewish synagogues (Cutler 1996; Kieckhefer 2004) have since been purchased or used by black or new immigrant churches, particularly in neighborhoods where white flight after World War II turned over communities from ethnic whites to new groups. In contrast, Catholic parishes had a different relationship with their building and sense of place. Middle-class Catholic congregants left for the suburbs and new parishes were built there, but the older urban buildings remained and often became home to newer waves of Catholic worshippers (McGreevy 1996; Gamm 1999). These older buildings then shape what is possible for worship and social gatherings by later users.

Many Protestant buildings tell a different story. In Cicero, a working-class suburb of Chicago, a church built by Presbyterians in the early twentieth century was purchased and occupied in the first decade of the 2000s by Comunidad Cristiana Vida Abundante, a large and growing Latino congregation. The large windows, designed to maximize natural light, were kept mostly covered during worship in order to allow for the utilization of video and overhead projection screens, as well as to allow for enhanced artificial lighting of those on stage. Meanwhile, ushers kept strict control of seating, generally moving congregants as close as possible to the altar/stage. When the congregation outgrew the space and built its own worship center in 2012, no windows were used in the new sanctuary, and arena-style seating brought worshippers closer to an enlarged, artificially lit stage.

Data regarding the ongoing historical influence of religious buildings also abounds outside of the United States. For example, during a trip to Guatemala in 2014, I (Robert) was given a tour of two "new" religious building projects with sharply contrasting visual cues about the past. On the outskirts of Guatemala City, the Casa de Dios (House of God) church has built a sprawling new church sanctuary and campus including multiple parking garages and separate structures for education and recreation. The campus, somewhat unselfconsciously christened "Ciudad de Dios" (City of God), was finished and dedicated in 2013. The project involved a capital campaign of US$55 million and the finished construction has been paid for in full, thanks to the donations and "faith promises" of thousands of members of the church. The central sanctuary building—there are multiple buildings on the campus as well as a multilevel parking garage—seats several thousand and is thoroughly "modern" in the sense that it does not contain traditional elements of "ecclesial" architectural design. Resembling a basketball arena from the outside and a theater in the main sanctuary, the building is intentionally absent of easily recognizable religious symbolism except insofar as the "footprint" of the building resembles a dove when seen from the vantage point of an airplane. Thus, viewed from the ground, the shape and décor of the building do not call to mind the historical Christian church. It is abstract and contains no steeple or spire. When I spoke with the architect, she informed me that the design process was directed entirely by a four-member committee including the lead pastor, the architect, the builder (who happens to be the father of the architect), and one other church leader. For inspiration, the committee visited two other structures: Rev. Joel Osteen's Lakewood Church in Houston, Texas, which meets in the remodeled Compaq Center that was formerly home to the Houston Rockets, and the Cirque du Soleil in Las Vegas, Nevada.

A few days later, in San Juan, Atitlán, a thriving indigenous Mayan village on the shores of Lake Atitlán, I had the opportunity to tour a new Catholic church building being constructed on the town square. A smaller community worships here than worships at Ciudad de Dios, but the church is similarly proud of its ongoing building project—a full description of which appears in Chapter 3—and has received contributions of money and time from many of its parishioners. In this instance, not only did the "new" sanctuary keep the "traditional" 1:5 rectangular dimensions of a Catholic church, the new building was being built in the same style as the original and with the same locally quarried volcanic stone that was used in the original building. Furthermore, the congregation had decided to preserve the original façade of the much smaller sanctuary that was mostly demolished to make way for the new building. Completed in 2017, the "new" church incorporated the façade of the building originally constructed at the behest of Spanish priests more than a century earlier.

Taken together, these two building projects revealed starkly opposing orientations toward the past, both palpably present in the religious landscape of Guatemala today. At Ciudad de Dios, as well as at several other large mega-church structures in Guatemala City, religious symbolism was avoided almost entirely. Such a design suggests that what is emerging at these congregations is something new and distinct from the Christian past. Neither the tradition-ally Roman Catholic cruciform shape nor the recognizable Protestant rec-tangular shape is utilized, and no cross or steeple is present. Meanwhile, at La Iglesia de San Juan, due to the preservation of the locally quarried vol-canic stone, the building expresses the congregation's embeddedness in its own local history and landscape. A fundraising campaign for adding a large bell tower suggests that the congregation continues to value traditional de-sign. As these examples visibly illustrate, religious buildings themselves exert historical influence by providing crucial opportunities for congregations to communicate to their members and their surrounding community in ways that embrace important elements from the past, or that draw a contrast to the past. The religious building is thus part of an ongoing conversation involving congregants and the community that materially invokes both pre-sent and past—even more modern church buildings "react" to earlier church structures—on a regular basis.

Buildings Shape and Constrain Embodied Interaction

It is relatively easy to understand the "symbolic" importance of religious buildings. But buildings do much more than merely provide a "legible symbol" to onlookers. Religious buildings have *walls*—both interior and exterior—and these walls shape and constrain the gathering of real bodies in space and time. They provide attendees both position and location (Griswold, Mangione, and McDonnell 2013) as they make meaning of the event in which they are participating.

In his fascinating study of the planning, design, construction, and occu-pation of a research building on the campus of Cornell University, sociol-ogist Thomas Gieryn explored the way buildings, in both their design and their usage, can shape a social institution such as a university and even a dis-cipline, such as biotechnology. Drawing on Le Corbusier's notorious (and highly controversial) definition of a house as "a machine for living in," Gieryn (2002:53) notes that an academic building, like the Cornell Biotechnology

Building, can be thought of as "a machine for manufacturing biotechnology." After all, the initiative and the resources for building a $38 million biotech building—one that ultimately included not a single classroom or dedicated teaching lab—emerged from college administrators and state legislators who worried that the university and the state of New York might be left behind in the race to promote and monetize research and design in the growing biotech industry. By drawing together professors and researchers from fields that might otherwise see little of each other on a large university campus—disciplines such as molecular biology, genetics, and biochemistry were given offices and lab space, while microbiologists and undergraduate teaching faculty were left out—and by providing them with a gleaming new structure near the center of campus, the builders hoped to spur the kind of research that would generate payoff in the form of industry-funded grants and lucrative patents. Thus, according to Gieryn (2002:60), "The building stabilizes the designers' vision of biotechnology, as it structures (fixes, routinizes) the social practices that will come to mark this new science. Decisions of inclusion and exclusion, for example, are now accomplished through the allocation of square footage and the distribution of keys: the social structure of Cornell biotechnology is built-in." One way to think of an academic building like the Cornell Biotechnology Building, then, is as a piece of *technology*—one that makes a powerful statement about the future of the university. When an academic building need not include space for classrooms or teaching labs—indeed, space was allocated in the plans for "visiting industrial scientists" who, it was hoped, would be given leave from their posts at pharmaceutical and other biotech companies in order to spend time researching alongside university researchers—we can be fairly certain that a shift in the nature and mission of the university is, quite literally, *taking shape* under our feet and over our heads.

Gieryn's larger point is that the physical construction of a building encodes certain practices and routines into the social structure of a community, group, or institution. Applying this insight to the study of religious buildings is a key goal of this chapter. Thus, when an Orthodox Jewish congregation builds or remodels a synagogue, designers must decide where to put the *mechitza*, or physical barrier separating the seating for men and women, since leaving it out would make it impossible for the congregation to be a part of the Orthodox Union, at least in the Orthodox Union of the twenty-first century. Meanwhile, the separation of the sexes in Orthodox congregations (as well as congregations in Muslim and certain Christian traditions) structures male-female relationships and shapes identities as well as the social structure of gender relations within Orthodox households.

But there are other, more subtle forms of "encoding" social structure that occur when a religious building is built and occupied. For example, when a congregation from the "high church" tradition of Christianity opts to include a choir loft and space for a pipe organ into its floor plan, it makes an important statement about its relationship to traditional liturgy, all but guaranteeing the continuation of more choral music and the need to hire a formally trained minister of music. Meanwhile, the congregation that forgoes these more traditional elements of design, but includes a dedicated sound booth, makes electronic music (which can be led with or without a professional director) virtually a given.

Finally, in matters as seemingly "straightforward" as how to organize the space for seating vis-à-vis the actions of the clergy and worship leaders, designers also play a role in structuring the *experience* of worship. Mexican architect and Pentecostal theologian Daniel Chiquete (2006) has shown with his research that Mexican Pentecostal churches of the Sinaloa region tend to construct their sanctuaries according to a 1:1.5 ratio, rather than the more typical elongated rectangular ratio of 1:4 or 1:5 used by Catholic churches in the same region. In other words, rather than a long, "stretched-out" rectangle, perhaps with perpendicular wings made possible by the cruciform shape, the typical Pentecostal sanctuary of the Sinaloa region resembles a "fat rectangle," often with the stage jutting into the seating itself. Uniting worshippers in a tighter "knot" and bringing them closer to the leaders or performers on stage are moves that call to mind social theorist Randall Collins's (2013) description of the phalanx formation. Collins argues that the physical organization of the phalanx, by bringing soldiers into closer proximity, capitalized on positive feedback loops of emotional energy, and in so doing reduced the frequency of desertion while allowing generals to bring their troops into direct confrontation with the enemy despite the overwhelming tension and fear of experiencing physical harm. We believe Pentecostal congregations have used the tighter proximity of worshippers provided by their worship spaces in order to enhance their success at creating positive feedback loops of emotional energy that (a) can be carried into future encounters, (b) builds a collective sense of solidarity, and (c) keeps parishioners coming back. After all, desertion constitutes an existential threat to both the army battalion and the religious congregation. Discouraging desertion in both the short term (because the service is emotionally rewarding, not boring), and the long term (due to shared solidarity with the group and the desire to return frequently to an emotionally engaging experience) must be a high priority for religious congregations, especially in an era marked by secularization and digital distractions. A physical arrangement of bodies in space that amplifies the emotional energy experienced by all (or most) of those present can be an important asset in fighting boredom and alienation.

One of the more exciting possibilities opened up by the study of religious buildings involves the potential for linking up to the theory of interaction ritual chains in fresh and productive ways. In this emerging social theory, most prominently articulated by Randall Collins (2004), the proximity of physical bodies, coupled with elements such as "barriers to outsiders," "shared mood," and "mutual entrainment," combine to create powerful catalysts of emotional energy within a co-present group of persons. As discussed in Chapter 1, Robert's own research among small Pentecostal congregations in Central America—most of which worshipped in unadorned, even homely buildings in poor neighborhoods—provided the inspiration to examine the possibility that physical structures matter immensely and that Collins's theory provided tools for understanding the dynamics behind Weber's (1978) "charisma" and Durkheim's (1995 [1912]) "collective effervescence." In such congregations, the smallish structures, combined with the utilization of well-amplified electronic instruments, appear to provide effective "maximizers" of emotional energy for the congregants who meet in them. Or, to put it differently, the financial limitations that compel neighborhood Pentecostal churches to build or inhabit modest structures counterintuitively enhance the emotional effect of their frequent worship services by making it easier to regularly fill a sanctuary with bodies and sound.

The capacity for amplifying emotional energy by simply filling a space with bodies was on the mind of Winston Churchill when he delivered his now famous speech to the House of Commons in 1943. The Commons had been partially destroyed by German bombing earlier in the war, and in the debate over how to rebuild the chamber, Churchill had sided with those proposing to build it according to the same smallish proportions upon which it had been built one hundred years earlier. Tiered benches (for those siding with the reigning government versus those siding with the opposition) sat facing each other directly, rather than in a horseshoe or semi-circle around a speaker, and the benches did not even have enough space for every elected member. Nevertheless, Churchill believed that both the small size and its "oppositional" design had helped give rise to the rowdy, boisterous democratic culture for which the Commons had become famous, commenting that "[w]e shape our buildings, and afterwards, our buildings shape us."

The importance of including bodies in the study of religiosity is underscored in recent research regarding the privatization of faith in the United States. The famous example of "Sheilaism" in *Habits of the Heart* (Bellah et al. 1985) suggested a new kind of spirituality that is notable in part because it can be done solo, without the traditional religious congregation or community or building. The rise of the "spiritual but not religious" coincides with an increasing number of Americans living alone (Klinenberg 2012). How exactly does disembodied religion, separate from religious buildings and congregations, operate? Have recently constructed sanctuaries changed their architecture to better accommodate a more private religious experience? Indeed, some have argued that the Protestant meeting-house design employed from the Reformation onward emphasizes a specific interaction between attendee and preacher (e.g., Kilde 2002; Loveland and Wheeler 2003), whereas more communal architecture—say with open seating in the round (Kieckhafer 2004)—promotes more interaction between attendees. One congregation in northern Indiana, a small but growing conservative Presbyterian congregation founded in the early 1990s, met for about a decade in a rented space using stackable chairs. When the congregation finally built its own space, however, the congregational leaders opted to purchase pews rather than movable chairs. By doing so, the congregation was able to provide visual links to religious tradition while also adding durability to a particular arrangement of bodies in the space—that of bodies facing forward toward a minister located the far end of a space.

Even understanding what a social space like a religious building means often requires embodied interactions. As Kieckhefer (2004:9) notes, "Response to a church is learned . . . the lesson is learned gradually, through experience of liturgy and by life within community, and by absorbing principles of interpretation learned from others." Part of the process of joining a religious group includes becoming accustomed not just to practices and meanings (Luhrman 2012), but also to its spaces and regular behavior therein. Given the different worship practices of religious traditions and denominations (Chaves 2004), some of this variation might be attributed to, or at least reinforced by, unique spaces that influence bodies.

Conclusion

What do religious buildings do? We think they do a lot, and we have used this chapter to lay out at least four ways in which religious buildings can be understood to play an active role in the religious and social life of a community. First, religious buildings *grow* out of social relations. By emphasizing their indebtedness to the social group that imagined, designed, funded, and built them, we mean to underscore that religious buildings are both products of and ongoing contributors to a community. Second, religious buildings *carry meaning*. This "communicative capacity" is of course true of any building, but it is especially true of religious buildings, whose religious symbols (or lack thereof) give outsiders an indication of the cultural and even ethnic traditions esteemed and cultivated by their members. Moreover, such communicative capacity does not merely identify the values of a congregation—it is also expressive of power and authority. Steeples point heavenward (to what matters), but by their size, materials, and, most importantly, their height, they also demonstrate the financial capacity of their patrons. Thus, in our "reading" of religious buildings we need to be attentive not only to religious symbols but to the size, building materials, and location of a particular building. Does it sit on the central plaza or on a side street? Does it rise above its surroundings or is it dwarfed by comparison?

Third, religious buildings *create and maintain a particular relationship to the past*. As was visible from the example of two very different congregations in Guatemala, religious building projects provide a particularly powerful opportunity for a religious group to define its position vis-à-vis a religious past. Even if that "relationship" to the past is one of distinction from, rather than connection with the past, the relationship is no less important. Fourth, religious buildings *exert material force on the patterned interactions of a religious group*. In saying this, we mean to emphasize the importance of walls—both interior and exterior—as powerful shapers of interactive rituals in time and space. For while it can be important and valuable to pay attention to the appearance, décor, and symbolism of a religious building, it is equally important to note the way the actual physical layout of the building contributes to the patterning of regular interactive rituals conducted within that structure. In order to do this, we believe interactive ritual chain theory can be an important theoretical tool for generating new insights on how and why space matters within a religious building.

The preceding four arguments together help provide a rough map for the empirical chapters that follow. In addition to emphasizing the social nature of religious buildings, we pay close attention to the "expressive" character of these buildings—expression that includes the capacity to express power relationships and a connection to or disjuncture with the past. And we will remember that religious buildings shape and constrain embodied interactions, with important consequences for the ongoing existence of the group that meets there. In short, when sociologists and other scholars discuss religious structures, they should include the physical structures in conjunction with the social structures that shape social life. As Thomas Gieryn (2002:65) suggests, "In buildings, and through them, sociologists can find social structures in the process of becoming."

The present chapter began with a description of a 130-year-old Catholic cathedral in the American Southwest and included an account of a visit to a brand new Protestant megachurch on the outskirts of Guatemala City. In these two major religious buildings one can glimpse some of the most important features of the ways religious buildings work. Both buildings "grew" out of the vision of an ambitious and successful religious leader. Both buildings communicate symbolically and forcefully in their size, their location, and their design; that is, they carry meanings as well as power. Both buildings tell a story about each congregation's relationship to the past. In Santa Fe, a French bishop sought to direct attention to the Roman roots of his tradition. In Guatemala City, a telegenic pastor directed his architect to avoid any visual references to Christian tradition. Additionally, both buildings were constructed in order to facilitate a particular mode of gathering and worship—and these building designs continue to shape the worship of the faithful who meet within their walls today. In the church at Santa Fe, built long before the reforms of Vatican II, abundant natural lighting illuminates a soaring nave, which draws the attention of worshippers to the artwork above, in front, and all around them, including, among other images and portraits, the Stations of the Cross, gorgeously rendered in Santero mission style. Meanwhile, at Ciudad de Dios in Guatemala, the interior of the sanctuary is built and lit in such a way as to direct the full attention of every worshipper, and at all times, to the stage, for this is the place where all the action takes place. No symbols, beyond the logo of the church itself, grace the walls.

In what follows we will pay attention to more than landmark religious buildings, historic or contemporary. For it is certainly the case that "humble" buildings are "active" in the very same ways as imposing structures. But we hope that by examining these projects, we have provided a sense of the possibilities for understanding how religious buildings work. We now turn our attention to an examination of the extraordinary *energies* unleashed when a congregation embarks on a quest to build a new structure.

3

Ours until Jesus Comes!

In December 2016, the Seventh-day Adventist church in the community of Alioto, on the outskirts of Guatemala City, faced a problem: they were running out of space. The congregation of approximately one hundred worshippers called a meeting to discuss the situation in their small cement building located on a corner lot. Later, they contacted an architect, who drew up plans for a renovation that would involve adding a second story and using the vertical space to incorporate stadium-style seating. After all, building "up" was the only way the church could add space, given that the current building occupied every inch of the tiny lot on which it sat. And even in far-flung, lower-income satellite towns like Alioto, land doesn't come cheap. But price estimates for such a venture sounded steep. Within a few weeks, several "commuter" families who attended the church from neighboring Mártires del Pueblo—a community within walking distance, further up the hill—decided to break away and form their own congregation. Permission was obtained from denominational leaders and shortly afterward, a group of about forty worshippers, nearly half of whom belonged to one extended family, began meeting for Saturday morning worship in the garage of one of its members. Iglesia Adventista del Septimo Día Mártires del Pueblo (Martyrs of the People Seventh-day Adventist Church) was born and soon began dreaming of a place to call "home."

I (Robert) learned of the off-shoot church in the spring of 2017, during an interview with Ursula, an older Guatemalan friend of mine.[1] Ursula is a grandmother who works in the kitchen at a seminary in the capital. I was interviewing her for a different research project related to security and gangs. Mártires del Pueblo is one of many so-called squatter settlements surrounding the city, many of which were formed in the 1980s and 1990s with the help of progressive clerics and university students. Like so many other communities formed of land refugees, what began as a united, organized effort had, over time, given way to newcomers, land speculators, overcrowded schools, an overabundance of youth with little hope of finding paid work and, eventually, youth gangs. A couple of years ago, a young man was shot and

Building Faith. Robert Brenneman and Brian J. Miller, Oxford University Press (2020). © Oxford University Press.
DOI: 10.1093/oso/9780190883447.001.0001

killed by the gang just steps from Ursula's front door, and less than a block away from her home is an abandoned lot that has been used by local gangs on multiple occasions as a place to deposit the lifeless body of an enemy. That the community itself is named "Martyrs of the People" is an oddly ironic reality that says much about how security and risk are distributed in Central America.

Still, for thousands of poor and working-class Guatemalans, Mártires, with or without the irony, is home. And when the Adventist commuters from Mártires saw the opportunity to have a congregation of their own, they leapt at it. The fact that they had no space of their own was not a barrier to meeting regularly for worship, at least not at first. A minister designated by the denomination would conduct the Saturday morning services and the congregation would do the rest. But it would only be a matter of months before the little band of worshippers began dreaming about a designated meeting space. That possibility began to materialize shortly before my interview with Ursula when a member of the congregation learned that a neighboring family, after having been victimized by the gangs, had packed up their belongings and moved back to the rural province that they had fled years earlier. The family had seen enough of life at the urban margins. Seizing on the rare prospect of a nearby piece land becoming available, the congregation's leaders contacted the owners and began negotiating to buy a small vacant lot adjoining the home of the former neighbors. It wasn't cheap. The owners wanted 60,000 quetzals, or approximately US$8,300 for the 7 x 15 meter (23 x 49 ft.) weed lot, a rectangle only slightly larger than the typical college classroom. And that was the cost of the land only. Still, the community was excited and within a few weeks, money was raised for a US$1,200 down payment and terms drawn up for a loan. So great in fact was the commotion about having a church building of their own that even the children were getting excited. During our interview, Ursula indulged me in a story of her own granddaughter's enthusiasm for the project.

"Grandma, for how long will the church building be *ours*?" said the six-year-old, who lives in her grandmother's home along with her father (a lay leader), her mother, and three siblings.

"Well, it's going to be ours permanently," replied her grandmother.

"You mean ours until Jesus comes?!" said the granddaughter?

"Yes, ours all the way 'til Jesus comes!" laughed her grandmother.

Ursula's granddaughter's palpable excitement at the prospect of worshipping with her family in "our" building illustrates a key insight offered in the preceding chapter: religious building projects tend to generate enthusiasm. In this chapter, we will refer to the excitement at the prospect of a new or renovated religious building as *building energy*, and we will explore some of the reasons that such dynamism is generated by a building project. Along the way we will explore three related questions: Why are there so many religious building projects in Guatemala? What do Guatemalan congregations hope to gain from a new building or renovation? What are some of the most obvious ways congregations are socially impacted by a new or renovated building?

Interviews and observations carried out in person by Robert, with occasional help from Guatemalan sociologist Israel Ortíz, among four different Guatemalan congregations in the midst of, or having recently completed a major building project, provide the principal data for exploring these questions. The interviews and field observations were conducted in 2017. The key aim of this particular leg of the research project was to identify congregations in the process of a build (or having recently completed one) and to ask their leaders and parishioners what they hoped to gain from a new or renovated space. We wanted to know (a) why congregations embark on such a venture, and (b) what they expect the new building will do for them.

Building Energy

Religious building projects create emotional energy. In fact, one of our primary concerns in writing this book is to explain and explore a phenomenon that we are calling *building energy*. The term is intended to describe the emotional energy that arises out of the decision to embark on a building project. For a religious congregation, a building project is a cooperative undertaking that involves shared sacrifice and risk, but also shared payoff in the form of material results that are visible and that possess both symbolic value and use value. In introducing this term, we are borrowing from the interactionist tradition of sociology, which argues that certain situations arrange individuals in a group in such a way that both the group as a whole and each individual member of the group experience a heightened mood and a sense of empowerment. Whether at a football game or a birthday party, both the context and the sense of sharing in something larger than the self give rise to excitement, some of which will be carried away from the event itself (Durkheim 1995

[1903]; Collins 2004). New beginnings are especially ripe for the experience of new emotional energy. For example, the sociologist of immigration Guillermina Jasso and her colleagues have used the term "migrant energy" to describe the heightened energy exhibited by first-generation immigrants and their children, who tend to achieve more than their socioeconomic status would otherwise predict (Jasso et al. 2005). For our purposes, *building energy* is quite simply a term that helps us describe and explore the notable injection of excitement and enthusiasm occurring in congregations that take on a building project.

It would be difficult to think of a better place to study building energy than Guatemala. Deeply religious, relatively free of building code regulations, and home to the explosive growth of both traditional and "neo-"Pentecostal groups, Guatemala is home to what amounts to a national *blitz build* of houses of worship. Although detailed statistics are difficult to come by, the Guatemalan Evangelical Alliance, which provides an umbrella organization for the vast and varied denominations of the country's Protestant community, estimates that there are approximately 41,000 Protestant congregations in the country—or ninety-six Protestant churches for every single Catholic parish—and this number continues to grow (Villagrán 2016). Even the most casual visitor will notice after spending a few days in the country that religious buildings are *everywhere* and that many of these structures are new or still under construction. Just as remarkable is the *scale* of some of the largest new religious buildings. Some of these buildings, like Mega-Frater, with a sanctuary that seats over 12,000 worshippers and is home to the charismatic congregation Fraternidad Cristiana, are among the largest buildings in the region and attract tourists and admirers (most of them Evangelicals and Pentecostals) from throughout the region. Indeed, it may be true that in most of Western society, religious groups long ago ceded to industrialists the reputation for commissioning their cities' largest, most expensive new buildings (Sklair 2017). But in Guatemala, congregations still compete to build some of their cities' largest new structures. For example, as mentioned in the preceding chapter, Iglesia Casa de Dios completed work on a US$55 million sanctuary and building complex in 2013. Just as impressive, the congregation moved into its remarkable, sparkling white sanctuary that same year without owing a penny toward its construction.[2] Nor are these two well-known landmarks the only major religious building projects in the country. Religious building energy is everywhere.

But what is behind this energy? One obvious driver is the population growth that creates growth opportunities for all of Guatemala's institutions, not just its religious organizations. In a country that has consistently posted a population growth rate of over 2 percent annually—the highest in the region—many congregations, not to mention schools, hospitals, and government agencies, are practically bursting at the seams (Estadística 2018). A total population that stood at 10 million in 1995 had already grown to an estimated 16 million by 2015. One can scarcely imagine the kind of building frenzy that would need to occur if the population of the United States were to increase by 60% in a single generation.

Just as important a factor in the mushrooming of the religious built environment is Guatemala's vibrant religious culture. More than nine out of every ten Guatemalans affiliate with a religious tradition, almost exclusively Catholic or Protestant. The growth of Protestantism in Guatemala—which grew rapidly in the 1980s and 1990s, garnering 40 percent of the population by 2013—has been well documented in academic circles (Smith 1991; Stoll 1991; Cleary 1992; Garrard-Burnett 1998; Gooren 2001; Pew 2006). Their tendency to divide and multiply with great frequency—what Guatemalan missionary and communications scholar Dennis Smith (1991) has called "the amoeba school of church growth"—has contributed to the spread of small, unassuming cinder-block structures across the Guatemalan landscape. Less frequently noted, however, is the fact that the numeric declines among Guatemalan Catholics have been relatively modest, especially when compared with Catholic losses in other Central American countries in recent decades. Guatemalan Catholic parishes have generally remained strong and as of 2013, 47 percent of Guatemalans self-identified as Catholic—a proportion that is still higher than those identifying as Protestant (Latinbarómetro 2014). Guatemalan Catholics also tend to be quite active, with higher levels of religious engagement when compared with Catholics in most of Latin America and the United States (Pew Research Center 2014). As in the case of the Catholic church in San Juan la Laguna described later in this chapter, Pentecostal congregations are not the only religious communities building or expanding their worship spaces.

It would be a mistake to argue that the need to provide more physical space for an increasing number of bodies is the sole factor driving religious building projects in Guatemala. Were space the only factor, we could expect to see larger buildings, but not necessarily more of them. Nor would we be likely to see renovation projects aimed at improving and beautifying religious buildings, a trend that is also quite visible among congregations large and small. And yet, as borne out by each of the cases in this chapter, religious buildings provide an ideal occasion for a congregation seeking—*needing*—to define itself and establish its social and religious identity in a highly competitive religious marketplace.

Building Energy in Martyrs

Less than a month after my initial conversation with Ursula, when I learned of the new congregation's plans to purchase a piece of land, I was invited to attend an informal groundbreaking for a new building on the site. But just getting to the community proved a great deal more difficult than I had expected. Mártires sits on a steep hillside far from the center of Villa Nueva, a mushrooming metropolis that has itself expanded with the ranks of poor and working-class Guatemalans unable to afford the high rents of Guatemala City proper. Fortunately, the community had chosen to break ground on a Sunday morning (Saturday being the day of rest and worship for Adventists) when traffic is at its lowest, and I was eventually able to find my way past the industrial parks, the congested open-air Sunday markets, and through the older, more established squatter settlements like Alioto, up to the community itself. The streets in Mártires (see Figure 3.1) are mostly unpaved and heavily rutted and despite the attention it attracted, I was glad to be driving an SUV on this occasion.

When I arrived, I counted eight men and women working on the site. Children wandered in and out, sometimes grabbing a pick axe or a hammer to break rocks alongside the adults. Women participated in the heavy work until later in the day, when they turned their attention to the preparation of a communal lunch. I was surprised at first by how informally the process seemed to proceed. Later I learned that what was being erected on this day was simply a temporary structure that would be used for the moment, until the congregation had raised enough money to build a formal structure. Since the congregation relies on an assigned, traveling minister for ministerial support, its day-to-day leadership comes from its lay leaders. Abel and Edson, two of these leaders elected by the congregation, negotiated a variety of decisions needing to be made, such as when the ground was level enough, where rocks needed to be broken down further, and what sort of lean-to might be appropriate for the coming weeks of services. There was also the

Figure 3.1. A typical street in Mártires del Pueblo.
Photo: Robert Brenneman.

question of where to place the bathroom and how much space it should occupy. Abel felt that a small area would suffice, and proceeded to mark out on
the gravel an area of about 5 feet by 5 feet. Someone else ventured that this
space was too small for a bathroom. One of the older women, who happened
to have a wide girth, stopped swinging her pick axe long enough to point out
that the appropriate size of a bathroom depends on the size of the rear end
using said bathroom. This comment was met with uproarious laughter and
more teasing.

In fact, humor was a staple of the interactions among adults and youth
throughout the day. While Guatemalans are always fond of humor and
teasing, I was struck by how continuous and contagious the joking was on
this particular occasion. The good-natured ribbing seemed to indicate the
close, trusting nature of the relationships among these *hermanos y hermanas*
(brothers and sisters in the faith), as well as the excitement flowing from the
prospect of working together to create something that could be used by all.
Although there were not enough tools for everyone to pitch in physically,
those who didn't have a tool waited their turn and made observations from
the sidelines, often remarking on the speed or agility—or lack thereof—of the
persons they were watching. Since the space was walled in, with a makeshift

Figure 3.2. Members of the Mártires del Pueblo Seventh-day Adventist Church level the ground in preparation for a temporary sanctuary.
Photo: Robert Brenneman.

corrugated metal "gate" at the entrance, I was able to keep a rough count of the number of people on site (see Figure 3.2) at a given time. As we neared lunch time, I counted twenty-five people on the site, many of them children and youth. More would appear when the food was served. Some were clearly drawn by the prospect of a sturdy lunch, but others arrived bringing building materials, many of which were repurposed from the community. For example, most of the 4 x 12 sheets of corrugated metal roofing were purchased from a building site no longer in need of them, and all of the lumber (for holding up the roof) showed the nail-marks of prior use.

Earlier in the day I had quietly donated about $50 toward lunch in gratitude for having been invited to participate in the event. As the day wore on and more and more children, youth, and adults began arriving, I wondered why I had given so little. Nevertheless, Ursula left and reappeared around 1:00 p.m. with several pounds of raw steak. My field notes describe the occasion of the potluck.

> *Food seemed to appear out of nowhere. One moment the charcoal was being lit and it seemed like just a short time later, meat was being taken off the grill*

and children were being invited to wash their hands and get a plate. The plates were piled high with steak, black beans, rice, chirmol *(a mild sauce made of grilled tomatoes), a spicy salad, and large, piping hot corn tortillas. . . . A makeshift counter/table was made and the men, and then, finally, the women ate, and all ate well. A light rain began to fall and a makeshift lean-to roof was quickly prepared so that children and some adults could stay dry, but the rest of us simply continued eating under the falling rain. . . . Soon after we'd finished eating, Abel closed the day with a word of thanks to all and Edson reminded everyone that, as he had said the day before, no one would receive money for the work they'd done today. Rather, they were making a deposit in a celestial bank account and that was a deposit that could be collected later. Shortly afterward, people began to file out of the space.*

Not long afterward, I joined Ursula and her son, Abel, for *cafecito* (late afternoon coffee break) in their home just a short walk from the building site. Wanting to know what sort of space their congregation hoped to create, I asked Abel if there were any "non-negotiable features" that the permanent structure would need to possess. He could think of only one—multiple rooms. This requirement seemed odd to me, not least because of how small the entire plot of land was to begin with. Dividing it even further seemed doomed to leave little space for worship. When I pressed him further, he explained that *ambientes multiples* (multiple spaces) were necessary in order to make it possible to hold separate Sabbath school instruction for children and adults. In fact, the long-term vision of the community was to create a two-story building with worship space on the first floor and Sabbath school and youth group classrooms on the second floor. Doing so would allow separate classes covering about two to three grades per class, and this division would make it possible to provide age-appropriate instruction. Like many if not most adults in this congregation, Abel himself does not possess even a high school diploma, but age-appropriate theological education is important to him and to the community. It seems likely that this desire for partitioned educational spaces is related to the theological identity of the Seventh-day Adventists—a tradition built upon a special understanding of biblical prophecy. Our conversation thus reminded me that religious buildings created for religious groups that value a particular body of knowledge have instructional needs that must be balanced with worship and experiential ones.

Such a building will not come cheap. Indeed, even without a second story, building a permanent, four-walled, two-room building will likely cost the congregation about US$20,000. Added to the cost of the land itself, the entire "first phase" (one-story) project is likely to require about US$30,000 according to estimates by the congregation's leaders. And this figure assumes that much, if not most, of the labor will be donated. Although the congregation has received a few small donations from other Adventist congregations wanting to help, most of the cost of the building will likely come from the congregation itself. In fact, assuming that the congregation retains its current size, each of the of approximately seven families actively involved in the church will likely spend upward of US$4,000 on the project. This figure becomes even more startling given that a typical income for a household in a community like Mártires might be in the neighborhood of US$450 per month. Thus, while much of the attention, and frequent criticism, regarding new religious buildings in Guatemala centers on the massive structures built by megachurches, it is quite possible—likely even—that the tiny, unassuming church buildings dotting Guatemala's urban and rural landscape require at least as significant a financial sacrifice from their membership. Building energy—the feeling of efficacy and solidarity that emerges when a group of people share a common goal and take on a common risk in order to realize it in stone, wood, and mortar—is surely a motivational resource that spurs a congregation to begin a building and provides the congregation with rewards during the effort and when they finish.

Bringing Beauty within Reach at Revival Pentecostal

Standing on the street in front of the congregation's brand new building, it may be difficult for a middle-class North American visitor to appreciate the beauty that Pastor Octavio sees in the corrugated steel structure that houses Iglesia Evangélica Pentecostés Avivamiento y Unción del Espíritu Santo (Evangelical Pentecostal Church of Revival and Anointing of the Spirit, hereafter Revival Pentecostal). Completed in February 2017, the small, rectangular building, painted a bright hue of blue (see Figure 3.3), sits on *rented* land across from a Shell service station on a busy road on the northern rim of Greater Guatemala City.

"You've probably noticed that the work that we've done, we have done well (*bonito*)" said Pastor Octavio with a note of satisfaction in his voice. "Unfortunately, when the landowner says 'Time's up!' we will have to leave it here and go somewhere else."

Figure 3.3. A photograph of Revival Pentecostal taken from the street.
Photo: Robert Brenneman.

I interviewed Pastor Octavio on a Thursday evening in November, about nine months after the building had been completed. He arrived around six in the evening, ready to be interviewed prior to evening worship. Like many Pentecostal churches in Central America, Revival Pentecostal meets for worship almost every day of the week, usually in the evenings. Having spent nearly fifteen years meeting in homes and then in a rented space, the congregation was glad to have the opportunity to have a building of their own, even if that meant building it on someone else's property and paying Q1,000 (about $125) per month for permission to build it there. Pastor Octavio admitted that the congregation had resisted the temptation to create something that looked or felt makeshift. Although the land around the building was hard-packed dirt, inside was a sparkling white ceramic tile floor. "In our last building [also located on rented land] we put down a cement floor, but when we came over here, God blessed us with a floor like this."

In working-class Guatemala City contexts, white ceramic tile floor is emblematic of having achieved a certain degree of status and sophistication. And indeed, stepping inside the building from the rough concrete stair leading into the sanctuary, the bright tile floor (reflecting the sharp fluorescent tube lighting) makes an impact, providing an impression of cleanliness and order. The ceramic tiles, with a price tag of about $800, were a gift from a friend of the congregation who attends only occasionally, and the members themselves installed the flooring.

> We were going to leave it just like that, a packed dirt floor, but we always strive for the best because people come, and when we have visitors, maybe a friend, a potential soul for the Lord, we want the best for them, right? Anyway, we spent the money and God will pay back all that we've done. In other words, God will return our expenses because this material, looking at it one way, someone could say that it's a big loss because who knows how many thousands [of quetzals] but looking at it spiritually, God blesses us because when we were at the other site, we put down a cement floor even though the land wasn't ours and now we're here and God has blessed us with a floor like this.

In other words, for Pastor Octavio and his parishioners, the ceramic tile floor and other special comforts beyond the absolutely necessary are a spiritual investment that helps the church attract and keep visitors, and thus, constitute a means of evangelization. By offering a clean, polished white floor, the congregation helps its congregants as well as its visitors—few of whom may be able to afford ceramic tile floor in their own home—feel special and well attended to. Nor is a tile floor the only embellishment inside the sanctuary. At the far end of the sanctuary, behind the slightly raised altar area, a wall-to-wall mural-fresco painting greets worshippers with a bucolic landscape featuring waterfalls, evergreens, and a dove (representing the Holy Spirit) in flight. The mural, visible in Figure 3.4, is so wide it partially wraps around the altar area and is a source of pride for the pastor and his congregation.

> In the same way, we didn't want to just leave [the backdrop] as plain drywall or metal. Instead I wanted something nice [bonito]. So we bought some plywood and a brother who likes carpentry said, "How much do you need? . . . I am going to contact a brother who paints landscapes. . . ." So he said, "When you have it ready, paint it white and I will make sure the landscape gets painted." Thanks to God, lots of people have come and said things like, "Wow, that's first-rate!" and "How did you do that?!"

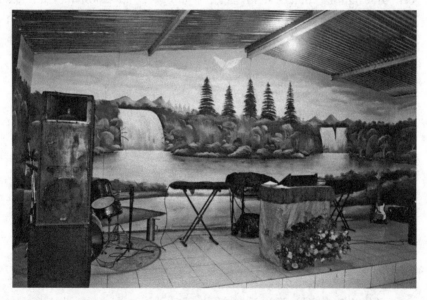

Figure 3.4. A dove, symbolizing the presence of the Holy Spirit, alights at the top of a mural wrapping around the altar area at Revival Pentecostal. Note the large loudspeakers at the left.

Photo: Robert Brenneman.

In effect, the painted landscape and (comparatively) upscale flooring put beauty within the reach of parishioners at Revival Pentecostal. Furthermore, feeling proud of their church building and the worship atmosphere that it provides undoubtedly makes congregants more confident in inviting friends or family members to visit a service and worship with them. After all, a clean, polished, attractive space that is also brand new communicates to non-members that even this small gathering of worshippers has momentum and is going places.

But there is one more feature of the congregation that figures heavily into the congregation's financial sacrifices aimed at attracting visitors, especially young visitors: the PA system. Arranged on the raised platform at the front of the sanctuary is a music and audio system with gigantic loudspeakers that, for the uninitiated, seem far too big for this small space of approximately 1,200 square feet, or only slightly larger than a typical high school classroom. Such equipment represents an enormous investment for a congregation of this size and social class, yet the vast majority of Pentecostal congregations, no matter how small, put significant time and energy into acquiring them. In addition to using income from the offerings and from pledge drives, Revival Pentecostal employed fundraisers to purchase their first sound system for the current building, selling tamales on Saturday mornings to make $50–$100 for a weekend of cooking and selling. Eventually, the congregation was able to raise enough funds to purchase a state-of-the-art sound system including amplifiers, mixing console, multiple keyboards, and loudspeakers. Unfortunately for the congregation, within months of acquiring the equipment, thieves broke into the church by cutting a hole in the corrugated metal wall. Approximately $3,000 in sound equipment and instruments were stolen. "We have receipts," said Pastor Octavio, as if to underscore how much the loss hurt. Police were contacted but declined to investigate the crime scene after learning that the minister had been inside the building after the crime. Thus, the congregation resumed their fundraising while using a borrowed PA system. Eventually, new equipment was purchased, but this time, parishioners are not taking their chances. In order to avoid further thefts, Pastor Octavio and several members of the congregation take turns spending the night at the church in order to deter thieves from returning to steal the new equipment. I asked Pastor Octavio why his congregation puts such significant resources into its audio equipment: "You know, that's a question that many people always ask us. We're looking for talent, right? For example, if you were a musician and you liked to play the keyboard, the drums.

You're not going to play alone. You need other people—another person to play the keyboard, someone else to play the bass. Pretty soon you have a group."

In other words, having an excellent (or at least a high-wattage) sound system makes the congregation more attractive to musicians, making it easier for the congregation to put together a tight worship band. Pastor Octavio further explained to me the special draw that audio equipment has for young males. Although young women provide vocals for the worship band, the boys and young men play the instruments and run the sound system. Furthermore, worship bands often get invited to play revival meetings, accompanying the minister to remote towns and villages far beyond the city. Much like a rock band's tour, these events provide youth—including "helpers" who act much like band roadies or groupies—with rare opportunities to travel outside the city. For example, on the weekend after our interview, Pastor Octavio and the worship band had accepted an invitation to conduct revival meetings at a village on the Northwest coast. They planned to pay a driver $170 to transport the pastor, the band, and all of the band's equipment six hours each way by pick-up truck.

I asked Pastor Octavio if he didn't find such marathon trips exhausting:

That's our vision. Not to make money, because when they ask us what we charge, we say "Nothing." Our vision is to see more souls, or to show that young people can do it. Because we have boys that take care of the sound. So it's their way of showing that young people can do it [sí se puede]. There are those (youth) who say that "I'm not good at anything," or "I'm useless" and sometimes we don't value them. . . . [But] by way of the music—maybe they don't pray or preach, but by way of the music, they do the work.

Thus, an expensive sound system figures heavily into the congregation's attempt to attract others—especially youth—both inside the church and while "on tour." That this congregation of approximately sixty lower-income and working-class members was willing to spend $3,000 to purchase audio equipment not once but *twice* is even more startling when considering the fact that the entire building cost the congregation an estimated $4,000 (not including donated labor), according to Pastor Octavio. Put simply, even congregations with severely limited resources and lacking in a deep tradition of religious liturgy or architecture are often willing to spend relatively large sums of self-raised funds in order to create a visual and aural experience that attracts visitors of all ages and communicates to them that the members of this congregation care deeply about the worship experience.

Negotiating Conflict at San Juan Bautista

Tile flooring also played a role in the new sanctuary built at San Juan Bautista, the church for the village of San Juan La Laguna, which lies on the coast of Guatemala's beautiful Lake Atitlán, located about two hours northeast of Guatemala City in the Department of Sololá. An indigenous town of about 10,000 residents, almost all of whom speak the Mayan language of Tz'utujil as their maternal tongue, San Juan's centuries-old Catholic church, located prominently on the town's center square, was already in desperate need of more space by the mid-1990s. A building committee was formed in 1998 and construction began in the early 2010s. According to Alvaro, a local indigenous leader, business owner, and former chair of the building committee, the congregation weathered several conflicts over the course of their multi-year building project, not least of which was the decision regarding which flooring material would be installed in the altar area at the front of the large sanctuary. Alvaro, along with other committee members, felt that the flooring for this area should be extra special. "It's just that [the altar] is something *special*. For me, it's *sacred*," Alvaro told me, emphasizing the words "special" and "sacred."

When it came time to purchase the altar flooring, Alvaro recalled that committee members had made a special trip to the city of Quetzaltenango, about a three-hour drive away, in order to see and quote marble flooring for the altar. The committee felt that only marble would do justice to this most sacred of places. But the parish priest failed to see it this way. On the morning when work was supposed to begin, the priest put his foot down according to Alvaro, adamantly opposing the high price tag of such a material. Eventually, a compromise was brokered and workers installed a higher-end, shiny ceramic tile flooring that contrasted less dramatically from the tile used in the rest of the sanctuary. Alvaro indicated that although the compromise headed off a major conflict, neither side was completely satisfied with the end result.

Nor was flooring the only occasion for disagreement. Indeed, from the beginning, the building project was steeped in conflict. When the project began, the congregation had been without a parish priest for two decades, and indigenous leaders who provided the lay leadership of the congregation found little support from the local bishop for their project of building a new church building. Undeterred, the lay leaders found a bishop from a different region of the country who was receptive to their desire to build, and that bishop took the idea all the way to the papal nuncio (the representative of the pope's office in Guatemala), who was able to pressure the designated bishop into signing his approval. Afterward, the project hit more roadblocks. Upon hearing about the plan to raze the old church and build a new one, representatives from the Ministry of Sports and Culture—whom Alvaro consistently referred to as "the anthropologists"—arrived to carry out a site study and later asked the congregation to refrain from any building until the site could be fully assessed for its cultural and historical value. Some committee members saw this prohibition as unfair and wanted to proceed anyway, but Alvaro, who had spent several years studying at the university in Guatemala City, argued for patience. Eventually, according to Alvaro, the Ministry of Sports and Culture gave its approval for the building of a new church, with one stipulation: the façade of the old church, with its volcanic stonework, needed to be preserved. A local (non-indigenous) architect was subsequently hired who drew up plans for a structure that not only integrated the old façade, but called for the incorporation of the same volcanic stone in the construction of the building, shown in Figure 3.5.

Figure 3.5. The façades of the new and old churches of San Juan Bautista.
Photo: Robert Brenneman.

By 2005, the building committee had reorganized itself, and fundraising for the new project began in earnest. Although he was quite candid about the many conflicts that occurred, Alvaro remembered this period as a time of great energy and excitement: "All this led to a new era in the diocese," he recalled. A priest was assigned to the parish (after decades of having to share a priest with another town) and some money was raised from foreign sources, including a German foundation that gave about 15,000 euros. But the lion's share of the money and labor came from local donations. There were raffles and special fundraisers, as well as thousands of small donations from the town's residents and even from residents of nearby San Pedro La Laguna. Additionally, every single Catholic household in San Juan was asked to provide one day of work every thirty days so that there were twenty-five workers available each day. This schedule was created after the building committee conducted a census of the town.

I asked Alvaro if any evangelicals had helped in the project, and he reported, "The evangelicals contributed. They would come and provide lunch. Others would pay for someone else to take their turn. They didn't want anyone to see them there." Some of these non-Catholics contributed, according to Alvaro, because they supported the project, while others did so because a son or daughter had married into a Catholic family, causing them to feel a sense of connection or duty to the Catholic church. In any event, such evangelical support for a visibly Catholic building project is surprising given the long-standing competition between Catholics and evangelical Protestants in Guatemala. It suggests that in religious contexts, building energy can spread beyond even the community of members, generating excitement and unity, as well as moments of tension and conflict, within the ranks of those making decisions about what the structure should look like.

In all, Alvaro reported that about five million quetzals (or about US$666,000) were raised for the building, in addition to the thousands of donated work hours. Furthermore, every Catholic family was asked to provide five to ten sacks of *piedrín* (a sandy building material that can be excavated with a shovel from the earthen walls next to highways and construction sites) for making cement, and many residents helped bring volcanic stone from a large hill on the other side of the lake, taking hundreds of trips by small fishing boats. Local artists also contributed to the project. In order to prominently incorporate the town's widely celebrated artistic tradition, the building committee sought help from local artists who organized to divide up the Stations of the Cross and assign one to each of fourteen painters.

While some of the Stations seem to draw inspiration from European naturalism, others incorporate the bright colors of their own signature style. *Station XII: Jesus Dies on the Cross* depicts a crucified Jesus and his mourners, rendered in traditional Tz'utujil clothing as they conduct a Mayan ceremony. An elder dressed in Mayan priestly attire blows on a conch shell while a pair of indigenous women offer incense and light candles at the foot of the cross, with the volcanoes of Sololá looming in the background. Such artistic contributions provide further evidence of the communal, indigenous nature of the effort.

The large, main entrance doors were carved from a single piece of solid wood by a local carpenter and feature low relief scenes and symbols from the life of John the Baptist. But the elaborate, hand-carved doors proved expensive. In an effort to finish the project, the committee, with support from the parish priest, opted to buy the second set of doors from a woodworking shop in Antigua. Rather than being carved from a single piece of wood, these doors incorporate separate panels. Both the fact that the doors were not carved from solid wood, as well as the fact that they were not made by a local artisan, irked Alvaro. Eventually, feeling that the priest and other committee members were sacrificing quality in order to move the project toward completion, he had resigned from his post on the committee, just before the inauguration and blessing of the building in 2015. Nevertheless, he remained a regular worshipper and was generally pleased with the outcome, as well as proud of the congregation's visible accomplishments. "In short, we ended in conflict. But I am satisfied because the church is 95% finished." By 2019, the church of San Juan Bautista had embarked on yet another building campaign, this one aimed at erecting a large bell tower adjacent to the new church. For now, the building energy at this congregation continues unabated.

Discovering Talent at Codesh Ministries

Among the most interesting aspects of the San Juan Bautista building project is the extent to which local indigenous leaders like Alvaro conceived of the project and carried it forward. This fact is no small matter, given centuries of historic racism and discrimination toward indigenous Mayans from colonial rulers and then mestizo leaders and politicians (Pelaez 1998 [1970]; Taracena et al. 2002). Indeed, it was not until the 1990s that the first generation of university-trained indigenous leaders began to emerge. And yet, as we have seen, religious building projects have the capacity to generate not just conflict, but a great deal of excitement, enthusiasm, and solidarity as well. Even before the first footers are dug, congregations like Mártires del Pueblo and San Juan Bautista were experiencing an energized membership, eager to commence a major project that would help to define the congregation and its place in the community. Such projects require considerable organization and planning. Both the increase in emotional energy and the need for clear decision-making processes allowed leaders to emerge, and in the process, to discover their capacity to organize their co-parishioners and delegate responsibilities of all kinds. That most, if not all, of the leaders to emerge were men should not be too surprising given the patriarchal nature of contemporary Guatemalan society.

Not all of the skills and abilities that emerge or are discovered during the process of a communal building project, such as a new church building, involve leadership or administration. In the case of Codesh Ministries, an evangelical church located on the outskirts of Quetzaltenango, Guatemala's "second city," the process of building a new sanctuary, followed by a second addition a decade later, helped some of its youth to discover and solidify their careers. Juan and David Carrillo were in their twenties and were heavily involved in the church's youth and worship ministries when the congregation decided to buy a piece of property and build a formal sanctuary. Prior to that time, the congregation, a non-denominational church of about ninety worshipers identifying with Presbyterian theology, had been worshipping in a modified garage attached to the home of its minister. Inquiring with an architect, the congregation was told that the price tag for a construction company to design and construct the building they were hoping to build would be approximately $300,000. They thus decided to do the work themselves, little by little, purchasing the materials as they were able. This do-it-yourself approach saved the congregation about two-thirds of the total cost. According to the estimate of Pastor Josué, the price for the sanctuary that was eventually built, mostly by the youth of the congregation, was about $100,000. Yet by doing the work themselves, the congregation got more than a building. Juan reported that participating in the construction, along with his brother and other youth, led him to discover his love for building and architecture:

We did the labor ourselves. . . . I had just returned from Canada when the building began. I had other ideas at the time. I wanted to go back to Canada so I enrolled in INTECAP [a vocational school] where I could learn things like carpentry, structures, welding and electricity because I saw the potential that it would have [back in Canada] without knowing that God would use it so that I could apply it for the church.

Asked what he had learned from the construction, Juan replied,

For one thing, although we had become accustomed to paying for everything, we learned that we could do things ourselves. In reality, we didn't have the economic capacity to produce a building of this size because we didn't have that many members. The majority of members were youth and children. Adult members were maybe twenty or thirty and we didn't have the economic means to generate that kind of construction. We dreamed of having a building, we had talked to a builder, but the cost was too high.

To save money, the congregation hired an architect who would draw up the design and advise a small number of youth to perform the work. The congregation paid four youth, including Juan and his brother, David, a modest income of about $50 per week, or approximately the amount paid for a day laborer. Additionally, the architect helped the congregation find other ways to economize. For example, rather than purchasing expensive trusses to hold up the relatively large roof, the builder taught the youth how to build their own steel girders by welding together pieces of steel. Such labor-intensive practices stretched out the time it took to complete the project, but saved on the cost of materials. In Juan's words:

When there were big projects like lifting large structures, we would ask other youth from the church or adult members to help us because it was very heavy and four of us weren't enough. It was a year of great blessing in which we were able to serve the Lord by building a structure. We put up the roof, did the electrical work, put in a drop ceiling, built the benches, windows, and doors.

Meanwhile, Juan and David were learning the trade of construction and simple engineering. Having purchased some tools and having worked on all aspects of the church building, they were finding that they not only *could* do much of the work themselves—they also enjoyed it.

We liked all of this and we had a friend who was an architect, and the architect who had designed the church would tell us, "Look, the resistance is this much, the slope for this needs to be this much." They would give us instructions and we would do it. We were the labor. Then I went back to the university and God gave us the opportunity to do some work for a cooperative, and after that, once they saw our work, they hired us to build a whole bunch of small structures. So we bought some larger machinery and put together a workshop and now that's what I do: construction. I'm not an architect yet, just an apprentice, but I do the technical work, structures and all that.

Thus, the work that Juan and his brother put into erecting a sanctuary allowed them to discover their own capacities in construction, which led to founding a small business in metalwork and carpentry. Juan also returned to the university with a clearer vision of what he wanted to study. After having abandoned a structural engineering major in order to spend a year in Canada, he returned to Guatemala and resumed his university studies, this time studying architecture. When I interviewed him in 2017, he continued to take subcontracting jobs in metalwork and carpentry, but was also working on his thesis project in architecture. The project involved building a large addition to the church sanctuary with a kitchen and dining area, as well as classrooms for Sunday school and vacation Bible school. But this time, Juan is the architect. Having managed to convince his thesis supervisor to allow him to propose the church addition as a community project—which meets the requirement of the public university that all students perform a community project prior to graduation—means that his supervisor provides oversight, reviews the plans, and stops by occasionally to consult with Juan and review the building's progress.

But assigning the design to a young architectural student, brimming with excitement from his university training, can cut both ways; the ideas of the architect may collide with those of members regarding what a church and its sanctuary should look like. During the current phase of construction, a decision was made to replace the original, homemade windows from the first phase. But some members saw no reason for windows at all, while Juan proposed vinyl windows because of their energy savings.

The majority of churches—I recently did a tour of Mega-Fráter and Casa de Dios—keep their sanctuaries dark so that they can control lighting. This was a dilemma because some of the brothers and sisters wanted the church to be dark in order to place our own lighting, which is warmer, during times of adoration. But I helped them to see—I like very much ecology and the fewer energy costs we can generate, the better—that artificial lighting is good but how much does that kind of lighting cost? The costs start to add up and there's nothing like natural light. In architecture, they teach us that natural light relaxes us and helps us generate emotional aspects far better than an LED light or a neon gas light.

In the end, the architects—Juan and his professor—won out. The church would replace the windows, rather than bricking them up as some of the members had wanted.

Learning from Guatemala's Religious Buildingscape

The main purpose of this book is to improve our understanding of the way buildings shape community, and we began this chapter by asking why so many religious buildings are going up in Guatemala. The answer to that question seems to be that a combination of surging population, strong religious devotion, and denominational splintering have given rise to a religious buildingscape that is constantly growing and multiplying. But in reviewing the four case studies in this chapter, it also seems clear that religious building projects don't just capture the vitality of a religious organization—they catalyze it. In each of the congregations where Robert visited and spoke with leaders, reports of renewed or revived excitement in the congregation during a building project were described with phrases like "entering a new era" and "a year of great blessing." One could even argue that the veritable "blitz build" of religious structures currently underway in Guatemala is itself part of the cause for Guatemala's continuing religious vitality. After all, religious building projects provide an occasion for a congregation to develop and hone a vision, organize its members, and produce a visible, material structure that will help to define that congregation in the wider community.

Nor should we overlook the fact that in a great many religious building projects in Guatemala, the members themselves provide much of the construction labor, working together toward a goal in which progress and the fruits of their labor quite literally *materialize* before the congregation's very eyes. Indeed, although it was by no means a factor in the selection of these cases, in all four of the building projects studied closely for this chapter, members of the congregation provided the lion's share of the physical labor to erect and finish the structure. By allowing members themselves to participate in the construction in a hands-on way, these congregations democratized participation, allowing persons with little or no religious training to have the opportunity to contribute directly to the identity of their congregation. And while Guatemala's traditionally gendered division of labor means that men were typically more involved in the actual construction than women, many women also participated, either by providing food for the workers, raising money, or, as in the case of Mártires del Pueblo, by joining in the physical labor.

Second, in answer to the question of what Guatemalan congregations hope to gain from a religious building, it seems clear that many congregations hope that a new building will help them attract new members by putting beauty within their reach and by attending to their needs. In congregations large and small, finding ways to incorporate beauty into a structure was a constant. At Revival Pentecostal, a hand-painted mural covering the back-drop of the raised altar was a means of communicating tranquility and the presence of the Holy Spirit, while at San Juan Bautista, the individually commissioned Stations of the Cross and the hand-carved wooden entrance doors provided visitors with clear evidence of the community's care for their church and for their commitment to the local artistic scene. Meanwhile, at both congregations, spending extra on flooring was important enough to warrant significant financial sacrifice. At Revival Pentecostal, paying extra for flooring was described as a way of attracting members, while at San Juan, it was a means of distinguishing the sacredness of a particular area of the altar—a space reserved for clergy and lay leaders involved in the mass.

In response to how congregations are impacted by a building project, we have seen that both energy and tensions can result. San Juan Bautista saw mul-tiple conflicts throughout both the planning and carrying out of its building project. But the project was also able to provide the community with an op-portunity to organize itself, selecting local indigenous leaders and giving them the chance to work together with authorities both locally and nation-ally. At Codesh Ministries, a small congregation with both indigenous and non-indigenous members from the working and lower middle classes, youths who had yet to find and solidify their career goals found in their church's building projects an opportunity to identify and cultivate their own profes-sional goals. Put another way, the research for this chapter makes clear that religious building projects do more than simply produce a new or enhanced material structure. They define, contribute, and reshape such communities in important ways. After all, it's worth remembering that the term "building" is a noun created from a verb. It is both a thing and an action—an object and a process, one which alters the community that embarked upon the journey.

Thomas Gieryn's insight on physical structures as instruments of *technology* has particular relevance here. Gieryn (2006) observes that, whatever else they do, buildings structure communal life and routines in such a way as to encode a set of practices into the social structure of an institution. Since our study is not longitudinal, we are limited in what we can say with confidence about the long-term impact of design choices by the congregations engaged in the construction projects we observed. Nevertheless, the cases profiled in this chapter reveal an intentionality of design that will undoubtedly have an impact. When Mártires del Pueblo made the decision to set aside space for a classroom for children's instruction, reducing an already small worship space, the congregation virtually ensured the continuation of child-focused Sabbath school as a central aspect of its communal life. The decision to retain the large windows in the sanctuary at Codesh Ministries will make it less likely that the congregation will follow the trend—very popular in Guatemalan Protestant congregations—toward restructuring the worship service to resemble a performance. Natural lighting works well for the congregation's current worship style, incorporating traditional hymn-singing, prayer, and "congregational sharing," which involves passing the mic around the sanctuary for the sharing of prayer requests. Incorporating plenty of windows into its sanctuary helps Iglesia San Juan Bautista, a Catholic church, keep its doors open during the day for the many tourists and worshippers who visit, thereby helping the church facilitate the practice of daily prayer by the faithful while also helping to fuse the artistic, cultural, and religious identity of this indigenous town. Revival Pentecostal's decision to direct a significant portion of its budget toward a high-wattage sound system will help solidify its ability to attract young musicians and tech-minded boys. In short, although it might sound overly crude, we can think of these buildings as "machines" for cultivating religious community. For it seems altogether likely that the buildings, together with the technological and artistic artifacts inside them, will have an important impact on the lives—religious and otherwise—of their members and beyond.

Finally, our examination of the preceding case studies makes clear the key role played by *conflict* in the process of identity formation within religious congregations embarking on a building project. From choosing which grade of flooring to install, to deciding upon the presence or absence of windows, and the shape of the entire structure, aesthetic and design decisions require that communities come to an agreement about matters that impact both current and future budgets, and these decisions often divide a congregation right down the middle. In some cases, as in San Juan Bautista, the conflicts can even divide the congregation between parishioners and clergy. Such battles over design and budget are hardly unique to congregations. In their fascinating analysis of the controversies surrounding the design and construction of London's Olympic Stadium, Yavena and Heaphy (2012) point out that municipal and national building projects often become sites for both cooperation *and* conflict among actors (both individuals and institutions) whose interaction becomes the basis of identity construction and reconstruction. In the design and construction of the Olympic Stadium, Londoners saw an opportunity to shape the future of their city, and East London in particular—not that all Londoners had an equal seat at the negotiating table. Certain actors, such as Mayor Boris Johnson and the Royal Institute of British Architects, had both a greater investment in the stakes and a heightened ability to shape the outcome. For these actors, the controversies surrounding how to build (and eventually, transform) the stadium became opportunities not only for shaping the building, but also for crafting their own reputations in the world of politics and architecture. Although we did not have access to the data that could demonstrate the particular contributions and motives of actors in the religious building projects described here, we can only assume that similar dynamics are in play in these cases. In summary, communal building projects provide opportunities for identity construction not only for the group as a whole, but also for the many actors involved in the project. Much like Durkheim's "collective effervescence," building energy, it turns out, benefits both the community and the individual actor.

However, the contributions made by a building project to a community and its members, while significant, are not eternal. New buildings often shed their novelty and become normal, routine aspects of the landscape, and building energy tends to dissipate in the process. In Chapter 7 we will turn our attention to a religious buildingscape erected during a flurry of activity in the early 1900s in order to explore the lingering effects of an earlier century's building energy. But before we explore the long-term impact of a "blitz build" on a religious landscape, it is worth acknowledging that not everyone who is impacted by a new religious building shares the same enthusiasm for the project. In the following chapter, we will explore a crucial step in the building process that must be faced by congregations in the United States, a particularly tricky one in urban and suburban communities that adhere to careful planning protocols before approving a new structure of any significance. Prior to building or renovating, a congregation must submit its plans to local officials for approval.

4

Religious Buildings Need Not Apply

The Naperville Planning and Zoning Commission, a group whose work typically attracts little public attention, held a lively public hearing on October 5, 2011.[1] The meeting involved discussion of a proposal from the Islamic Center of Naperville that asked the suburb of Naperville to annex fourteen acres of land on its southwestern border and then zone that new city land as R1 residential property. The group, with nearly two decades in Naperville, did not submit plans for a new religious building; rather, they wished to use the single-family home on the property for meetings and suggested they would look into constructing a new edifice within five to ten years. A city employee summarized the case, a lawyer spoke on the behalf of the Islamic Center of Naperville, and members of the Planning and Zoning Commission asked about six different issues. Then, twenty-nine residents spoke on the record regarding the proposal, interspersed with several responses from the petitioning group. While several residents supported the request from the Islamic Center (including the former pastor of the Church of Christ congregation who was selling the land), the majority opposed the annexation plans and represented the interests of single-family homeowners who lived adjacent to the property in question. Neighbors lodged multiple complaints: vague plans for the future of the property, a threat to property values, unease about the construction of a large building, increased traffic, a wish for homes to be built on the site. One resident's comment recorded in the official minutes stood out: "Would prefer a trailer park to a large structure due to the congestion and traffic that results from religious use." Given the wealth and status of Naperville, a thriving suburb of over 140,000 residents with high-paying jobs, educated residents, and a median household income over $100,000, it is hard to believe residents would truly prefer a trailer park near their home over a religious building. What would lead residents to make such statements? How might we explain opposition to the construction of religious buildings?

We have been arguing throughout this book that religious buildings *matter*. But so far, most of our arguments have addressed the ways in which

Building Faith. Robert Brenneman and Brian J. Miller, Oxford University Press (2020). © Oxford University Press.
DOI: 10.1093/oso/9780190883447.001.0001

buildings matter to the communities that fund their construction and make use of them. The previous chapter explored how multiple congregations in Guatemala navigated largely internal challenges in constructing their own buildings. Yet, religious buildings also matter to people who never set foot inside them. Neighbors see the structure on a daily basis and may be affected by the activities that take place inside and outside the nearby religious building. Going further, some neighbors and local officials might view efforts by religious groups to construct a new building or alter an existing one as a threat to the neighborhood or community. The cases from this chapter flip the lens from religious insiders participating in building projects to the views and reactions of locals responding to building projects involving religious groups. By investigating the process of building and zoning proposals by religious communities in suburban Chicago, this chapter provides examples of how non-members view the appearance of a religious building in their midst.

When a religious group in the United States wants to use a building for worship and gathering, they must make sure that the building in which they want to move can accommodate religious uses under zoning laws. The proposal, design, construction, and use of religious buildings takes place within a larger regulatory structure (Imrie and Street 2009) that may often go unnoticed in most communities until conflict arises. If a religious group wants to use a structure located in a zoned area that does not allow religious uses, they must apply for a variance or for the zoning to be changed. To illustrate, a religious group gathering in a home in a neighborhood of single-family homes may run into difficulty as neighbors and communities expect that homes will not be used regularly by large groups of people. To alter an existing religious building, a religious group must apply for permits ranging from approval of construction and/or demolition, to consideration of changes to the property, to concerns about alterations to historical structures (depending on the local zoning guidelines). Furthermore, neighbors of the property can comment on the plans of the religious group, often in public meetings where representatives of the religious group and local officials both present and hear from the community. Such meetings can influence the actions of local officials. Even as religion in the United States is marked by religious competition due to the lack of a state religion and the separation of church and state (e.g., Iannaccone 1991; Finke and Stark 2005) and religious pluralism is common due to the aforementioned factors as well as waves of immigration, the development of new religions, and diversity within religious tradition (e.g., Chaves and Gorski 2001; Putnam and Campbell 2010), religious groups often require the approval of neighbors and communities to use land and buildings for worship and other religious purposes. While congregations, even those that are a part of more hierarchical denominations, may appear to select their sites according to economic concerns (Zelinsky and Matthews 2011:66), neighbors and communities can either support or turn down requests from religious groups regarding land and buildings. In other words, even in a society like the United States, which expresses strong values of religious freedom, congregations are not completely free and unfettered in where they worship or in the details of the physical structure in which they meet.

The primary mechanism by which religious groups can or cannot use land and buildings involves zoning guidelines developed by communities. Local governments have designated land within their boundaries for particular uses. For example, zoning typically separates residential and industrial uses with the idea that few residents would want to live near industrial facilities. In the eyes of residents, religious buildings can generate similar problems to industry or commerce: increased traffic, noise, lights, and a disruption of neighborhood character. Zoning laws in the United States tend to privilege single-family homes (Fischel 2004; Hirt 2014). Thus, the concerns of neighbors can be consequential as public officials weigh the merits of proposals. Suburban homeowners and communities believe zoning can help uphold important features of their community: property values (e.g., Gans 1967; Blakely 2006:201; Anacker and Morrow-Jones 2008; Albright, Derickson, and Massey 2013), as quality of life is perceived to be tied to higher values; exclusivity, often defined in terms of race and social class (e.g., Low 2003; Self 2005; Freund 2007); better fiscal health (Hendrick 2004); and a "cohesive spatial vision" that includes the factors of race, gender, and class (Purcell 2001). Suburban homeowners rarely greet change to land near them with open arms. When they purchase homes, they often expect the surrounding area to remain similar or improve compared to when they moved in. Additionally, they hope their property values stay level or increase. Suburban residents can be generally resistant to new development (Baldassare 1986) and may generate more opposition when new developments are located next to single-family housing or when the process involves more permits and stages of approval (Pendall 1999). As scholar Nancy Eiesland (2000) found in a study of a growing Atlanta exurb, a new religious building can indicate that larger changes are underway in the community.

Communities can also use zoning to limit the access of certain groups to land because of race and ethnicity and/or social class (Danielson 1976; Bogart 1993; Clingermayer 1996, 2004; Ihlanfeldt 2004; Schmidt and Paulsen 2009; Rothwell and Massey 2010; Massey et al. 2013; Rugh and Massey 2014). Researchers looking at Asian communities in southern California note how new residents of different racial and ethnic groups can bring new religious congregations (Li 2009:75–76, 95; Padoongpatt 2015). For example, neighbors of a large Buddhist temple in southern California where Thais worshipped used local regulations to oppose gatherings that disturbed their "suburban ideal" (Padoongpatt 2015:84). As summed up by sociologists Anne Shlay and Peter Rossi (1981:717), "Zoning is an important, local, political method for shaping the housing and population composition of metropolitan neighborhoods."

Additionally, communities may prefer land and buildings that generate revenue. Religious uses do not generate money for the community through their property. Businesses bring in tax revenues through both property taxes and sales taxes (Wiggins 2003; Moreno 2006; Hackworth and Stein 2012). However, religious institutions are exempt from paying property taxes (Cragun, Yeager, and Vega 2012).

When religious groups make decisions in how to use buildings, they do so under the watchful eyes of neighbors and communities who may disagree with them on the best use of the land. As Hackworth and Stein (2012:58) note, "Building a church or mosque is only partially a matter of religious or cultural will. It is a process that is managed by institutions and practices that are poorly understood within the existing secularization literature." In most cases, appointed and/or elected local officials quietly make decisions about altering or constructing religious buildings by weighing the concerns of neighbors, municipal guidelines, and how they understand or envision their own community.

At the same time, public and government discussions of proposals from religious groups can occasionally become rancorous. The cases of mosques and Islamic Centers after the events of September 11, 2001, and the antipathy Americans have for Muslims (Pew Research Center 2017) illustrate how zoning decisions can become contentious in multiple communities. A 2012 report (Pew Research Center's Forum on Religion & Public Life 2012) detailed fifty-three cases where local residents and/or governments opposed proposals from Muslim groups. The majority of the cases occurred in major metropolitan areas, with many cases located in suburbs outside the central city. Two major objections from those opposed to the mosques or Islamic Centers included quality of life concerns (such as traffic, water, parking, noise, and property values) and fears about Islam (such as violence and connections to radical groups). Pew did state, "many mosques and Islamic centers have been built in recent years with little or no opposition" (Pew Research Center's Forum on Religion & Public Life 2012), yet several high-profile cases have attracted national attention. The proposed Islamic community center (Park51) near Ground Zero in Manhattan became national news, even as local officials said that local regulations allowed the use of the space by the Islamic group (Ruez 2013; DeFoster 2015). Similarly, a proposed mosque in suburban Murfreesboro, Tennessee, stirred up debate, vandalism, threatened violence, and a lawsuit and efforts from locals to block construction (Green and Sjlk 2011; Brown and Hauser 2012). Such disputes over buildings are not just limited to national discussions in the United States; Michael Guggenheim (2010) discusses nationwide conversations about Muslim groups seeking to add minarets to structures in Switzerland.

Most local zoning disputes do not draw national or even regional attention. Yet, disagreements between religious groups and local governments can lead to court cases. Keetch and Richards (1999) found that minority religious groups are disproportionately represented in such legal activity. Legislative action by the US Congress—the Religious Freedom and Restoration Act (RFRA) of 1994 and the Religious Land Use and Institutionalized Persons Act (RLUIPA) of 2000—established guidelines for zoning cases involving religious groups. In the latter act, Congress suggested communities cannot discriminate against religious groups seeking buildings in which to worship (e.g., Hamilton 2005; Giamo and Lucero 2009; Laycock and Goodrich 2011).

Curious to know whether zoning laws in the Chicago area impact the building and placement of new religious structures or the acquisition and use of existing buildings for religious purposes, I (Brian) examined forty proposals from religious groups for land and/or buildings in three Chicago area suburban governments between 2010 and 2014. I had three primary questions regarding religious groups and zoning. First, are certain religious groups singled out for zoning scrutiny? Given hostility toward Muslims in the United States (Pew 2017), fifty-three cases of opposition to mosques discussed in a 2012 report (Pew Research Center's Forum on Religion & Public Life 2012), and a number of cases in this data that involve Muslim groups, I look at whether Islamic groups have a more difficult time obtaining permission to build or use buildings. Furthermore, with the changing population of suburbs in terms of race and ethnicity (Frey 2015), immigrants (Singer, Hardwick, and Brettell 2008), social class (Kneebone and Berube 2013), and religious groups (Numrich and Wedam 2015), could decisions about religious buildings exclude or discourage certain suburban residents from settling in a community (as suggested by Keetch and Richards 1999)? Being able to worship in their own space in the suburbs would suggest that the religious group is now part of mainstream American society. Second, what are the outcomes for proposals from religious groups regarding building or altering buildings for their purposes? While I do not have data on how many proposals local governments approve or deny for non-religious uses, a comparison across three sizable suburban communities provides insights into how common it is for religious groups to face opposition and/ or a denial of their requests. Third, when opposition to proposals does arise, what are common concerns raised by local officials and neighbors? Do they object to traits of the religious groups, or do they raise concerns that could be leveled in response to any new nearby development?

Forty Suburban Religious Zoning Petitions

Answering these three questions involves investigating the actions of three Chicago suburban governments in response to requests from religious groups to alter, purchase, or use a building. Looking at a five-year period between January 2010 and December 2014 yielded forty proposals brought to three local governments. Details of each case are in the minutes of the local government bodies, with these documents available for reading and download online. The minutes available online have varying levels of detail across the three government bodies but offer enough detail to track key elements of each proposal, questions posed by local officials, comments from the public (though the DuPage County Zoning Board of Appeals does not reveal any public comments), and votes from the committees. I supplement the three case studies following the discussion of the broad patterns with local newspaper coverage from the *Aurora Beacon-News*, *Chicago Tribune*, *Daily Herald*, and *Naperville Sun*.

How do religious groups go about proposing a new building in a suburban setting? Typically, when a religious group wants to build or use a building, they first present their request to the Planning Commission or Zoning Board. This appointed or elected group hears from the religious group, which is often represented by a lawyer or clergy member, considers the opinions of the community's planning professionals, listens to the public at both regularly scheduled meetings and the occasional public hearing, and votes on a recommendation to send to the highest governing body for that community. After a positive recommendation, the City Council or County Board then considers the planning group's vote and makes a final decision. This final stage is contingent on whether or not the petitioner decides to move forward to this final decision stage.

Examining cases in three related yet diverse suburban communities presents numerous benefits. This part of the Chicago region has common demographic shifts, operates under the same laws and regulations from the State of Illinois, is part of a rich religious landscape in the suburbs (Zelinsky and Matthews 2011; Numrich and Wedam 2015), and has experienced several recent high-profile suburban cases of Muslim groups seeking to expand or construct buildings (e.g., Daniels and Gregory 2011; Schmadeke 2013; Blackburn 2014; Carlman 2015a). The Chicago area has many non-Christian buildings, including one of the largest Hindu temples in the country, built in the first decade of the 2000s in unincorporated DuPage County, and an Aurora Hindu temple that expanded its facilities to serve more worshippers (Holt 1998; Yates 2001; Cilella 2012). Islamic centers and mosques are plentiful: Zelinsky and Matthews (2011:224, 236) show forty-six mosques in Cook County in 1990 and twelve mosques in suburban Cook County by the first decade of the 2000s; Numrich and Wedam (2015) profile several notable suburban mosques and education centers; and Howe (2018) examines a DuPage County Muslim foundation bringing together Islamic teachings and American culture.

At the same time, the three local governments preside over three diverse communities. Aurora is roughly forty miles southwest of Chicago. Identified as an industrial satellite city in the early 1900s (Taylor 1915), the city sits on the Fox River. Its population more than doubled between 1990 and the present. Today, Aurora has an estimated 201,110 residents (2016 estimate), a median household income of nearly $64,000 (2016 estimate), and is roughly 40% white, 41% Latino, and 10% black (2010 counts).

Naperville too has experienced significant population growth, though it was a farming community until the postwar era rather than an industrial suburb. The community, which lies roughly thirty miles west of Chicago, experienced over 50% population growth for every decade between 1950 and 2000 (Lang and Lefurgy 2007; Miller 2016) and now has 147,122 residents (2016 estimate). The residents are relatively wealthy—a median household income of \$110,676 (2016 estimate)—and mostly white. Compared to Aurora, Naperville is whiter and has different minority groups: 68% of residents reported being white, 18% Asian, and nearly 6% Latino (2017 estimate). Naperville is now known as a wealthy edge city, defined as having a lot of office and retail space as well as numerous jobs (Garreau 1991; Numrich 1998; Numrich 2000a) and has a reputation for a vibrant downtown and high-performing schools.

DuPage County became its own unit in 1839 when it separated from Cook County. As suburbanization occurred in the twentieth century, the county built its reputation with population growth, wealth, and Republicanism. Today, it is the second most populous county in the Chicago metropolitan region (after Cook County) with 929,368 estimated residents in 2016. The median household income is \$81,521 (2016 estimate), in between that of Aurora and Naperville. Similarly, the percent of residents of different racial and ethnic groups is between the figures for Naperville and Aurora. According to 2016 estimates of race and ethnicity, DuPage County is just over two-thirds white, 14% Latino, 12% Asian, and 5% black. While suburban governments oversee much of the land in the county, the DuPage County government is responsible for planning and zoning issues in unincorporated areas scattered throughout the county. County-level data show that Catholics are by far the largest religious tradition in DuPage County, with significant minorities of evangelical Protestants, Other, and mainline Protestant traditions (Association of Statisticians of American Religious Bodies 2010). Naperville is largely contained in DuPage County (with other parts in Will County), and Aurora is largely in Kane County (with portions in DuPage, Will, and Kendall counties).

Patterns in the Responses to Building Proposals

To look for patterns across these dozens of proposals in front of three suburban governments, I coded the minutes involving proposals for religious buildings for several important variables for each case: Did a Christian or non-Christian group submit the proposal? Did the proposal ask to construct a new building, alter an existing religious building owned by the group, or convert an existing building to a religious structure? Was there at least one negative comment or question from a member of the public at a meeting of the government group? If there were public comments, to what did residents and neighbors object? Did the proposal receive a positive vote (and a unanimous vote) from the government body? Google Street View showed whether the property was adjacent to residences on the same side or across the street.

Religious groups brought a total of forty separate proposals to these three suburban governments between January 2010 and December 2014. Petitioners did not bring all requests to the City Council or County Board: the Planning and Zoning groups evaluated thirty-nine proposals, while the Councils and Board combined reviewed thirty-one proposals.

The local government bodies approved the majority of proposals. Of the forty final decisions, thirty-five involved approvals. Across all the cases, eight involved a denial at some stage: six by the Planning and Zoning bodies and two total from the City Councils and County Board. A majority of the approved requests went forward smoothly as the planning group approved the request, sometimes with particular conditions, and then the final deliberating body, either the City Council or the County Board, approved the request with little discussion or unanimous approval via a consent agenda.

Christian groups made the largest portion of these requests, accounting for twenty-nine of the forty total cases. All but one of the remaining cases involved Muslim groups. Each suburban government made decisions about at least two non-Christian groups. Proportionally, DuPage County considered requests from more non-Christian groups, as they accounted for more than half of the cases.

The religious groups made a variety of requests involving land and/or buildings. The largest number of cases—nineteen—involved changes to existing buildings. Such requests could involve adding to a structure, consolidating lots, or making changes to the grounds. Members of the public made comments opposing six of these cases. The next largest set of requests asked to convert an existing non-religious building, whether a commercial structure, an industrial property, or a house, to a religious building (13 of 40). Four of these cases received opposition—all in Aurora—and only two were voted down, both by the DuPage County Zoning Board of Appeals and involving requests by Muslim groups to convert homes into worship spaces. Less common were requests to use new land to construct a religious structure: of these eight petitions, six involved non-Christian groups (all under the jurisdiction of DuPage County) and three received a "no" vote.

When residents made public comments regarding proposals, the proposals involved buildings and land near residences, and they expressed concerns about how the building could affect their quality of life. Most of the cases, thirty-three of forty, involved properties adjacent to residential properties. A location near or away from residences affected whether the proposal drew opposition. The local government groups approved all seven proposals not adjacent to residences, and the public did not oppose these in public comments. In contrast, proposals involving a location near residences drew increased scrutiny. This was a large enough issue that in 2010 the DuPage County Board considered a regulatory change "that would prevent religious organizations from opening facilities in unincorporated residential areas" (Smith 2010; Ruzich 2010b). Board members and residents argued the change was not motivated by religion, though Muslim groups disagreed (Goldsborough 2010a, 2010b) and a *Chicago Tribune* editorial urged the Board to reconsider (Chicago Tribune Editorial 2011).

Not all proposals involving properties near residences prompted opposition. Of the sixty-five total public meetings with available online minutes for these forty cases, only twenty-three, just over one-third, attracted public comment. The number of comments varied: among the six Aurora cases with public comments, one attracted eight comments (seven positive) and the others had one to three comments; the majority of the eleven Naperville cases with public comments had two or fewer comments, another petition drew four, and the most controversial attracted forty-two; and the three cases before the DuPage County Board with comments involved twenty-five, fifty-one, and sixty-four comments. The comments were not always negative, and some community members expressed support. Unfortunately, the DuPage County minutes do not contain the details of whether the comments supported or opposed the petitions.

Residents raised a wide range of issues regarding religious buildings. The most frequently raised issues did not involve the particular religious beliefs or ties of those bringing forward the proposal. Instead, the concerns included the following: more time needed for residents and others to consider and address the proposal; proposals without enough detail for local residents to feel comfortable; increased or problematic traffic flows; concerns about sufficient parking and parking lots; residents did not want a large religious structure nearby; they preferred single-family homes for the property; water/stormwater/sewer issues; and property values.

The one Naperville case that attracted forty-two public commenters (the case discussed to open this chapter, as well as further in a case study in the following discussion) likely skews this commenting data. At the same time, these categories provide some insight into what concerned neighbors. These concerns could summed up as quality of life issues where residents disliked perceived threats to their existing properties.

Three Case Studies

To better understand these broad patterns across three suburban governments, I go into more detail with one case each from Aurora, DuPage County, and Naperville. These case studies help show how local officials interacted with concerns expressed with residents. In each case, the local government approved the request from the religious groups, even though the concerns slowed down the approval process.

Islamic Center of Naperville

Returning to the example from the beginning of the chapter, the request by the Islamic Center of Naperville provides an example of how neighbors can respond negatively even when the group is known in the suburb and they did not plan to erect a structure for a decade or so. Several years after the group's founding in 1992 (Temkin 2001), in 1996 neighbors expressed worries about expansion plans as well as parking on Friday afternoons outside the center's first Naperville location (Bils 1996; Chicago Tribune 1996; Gregory 1996). In 2011, a request made by the group to add a gymnasium to its second facility drew one public comment—a neighbor supported the proposal while also wanting to make sure the gym would not be used for religious meetings— and was unanimously approved by the two Naperville bodies.

In October 2011, the Islamic Center requested that the city annex fourteen acres near the southwestern edge of the city to R1 (Low Density Single Family Residential) with the intent of constructing a new religious structure in the future. The previous owner of the property was Hope United Church of Christ. They had used the single-family home on the property and considered building a larger structure. According to the 2011 Planning and Zoning Commission minutes, this particular land had been subject to numerous public hearings in the previous eleven years: Will County converted the land to R1 with no public comment in 2000, and eight hearings between January 2006 and March 2007 involving possible residential development led numerous neighbors to express their wish that the land remain for religious use. Residents had opposed an earlier proposal to construct a building for the Islamic Center of Naperville on a nearby property (Chicago Tribune 2005).

Twenty-nine residents spoke at the public hearing held by the Naperville Planning and Zoning Commission on October 5, 2011, after a presentation from a city employee and a lawyer representing the Islamic Center. The majority opposed a large religious structure. Afterward, for a short time, signs opposing the annexation appeared near the property (Swasko 2011). A month later, at another public hearing, thirteen residents spoke about the proposal and there was a more even mix of support and opposition. At the end of this hearing, the Planning and Zoning Commission unanimously approved the annexation and R1 zoning.

The City Council took up the matter on December 19, 2011, and, with four public comments raising concerns and two public comments in support, approved the annexation 9–0. Council members said placing more restrictions on the property was unnecessary since the petitioner said a future religious building was five to twenty years in the future (Jenco 2011).

This case and three others involving Muslim groups seeking buildings in unincorporated areas of DuPage County helped inspire a fictional theater production titled "Mosque Alert" that considered what might happen if a Muslim group moved to open a facility in a historic building in downtown Naperville (Carlman 2015a, 2015b).

MECCA

A little before the annexation request brought by the Islamic Center of Naperville, DuPage County considered a request from a Muslim group in the southeastern corner of the county. The Muslim Educational Cultural Center of America (MECCA) asked to construct a tall mosque and eventually a school in unincorporated Willowbrook. The County held four public hearings in late 2010. Neighbors raised flooding and traffic concerns (Ruzich 2010a). When the DuPage County Zoning Board of Appeals discussed the petition on January 13, 2011, board members raised multiple issues in voting down the proposal: using too much of the property for the religious structure and parking lot (roughly 65% of the land), extra traffic on a two-lane road (91st Street), potential changes to the character of the nearby neighborhood, and possible problems with flooding. Additionally, one Zoning Board member said the petition would oversaturate the area with religious groups, which included nearby Christian, Buddhist, and Hindu organizations within several blocks (Ruzich 2011).

Before reaching the next DuPage County Board meeting, the Board's Community Development Committee heard from "dozens on both sides of the proposal" before voting 5–1 to approve the proposal (Daniels 2011a). On March 12, 2011, the full County Board approved part of the proposal but not all of it. They voted down a motion to send it back to the Zoning Board and instead approved (by a 13–5 margin) the proposal for a 47,000-square-foot building that could accommodate 597 worshippers and included space for a weekend school and gymnasium. Yet, the height of the structure raised concerns: the zoning allowed a maximum height of 36 feet, but MECCA requested a dome 69 feet tall and a minaret of 79 feet. The Board denied the height request (Goldsborough 2012).

MECCA reduced the height of the dome to 50 feet and the minaret to 60 feet, and the building height issue came back to the County Board on March 13, 2012. The lawyer representing MECCA said the structure could not be under 36 feet if it were to "be functional and true to religious custom" (Goldsborough 2012). In the Board discussion, one member noted that other religious buildings had higher peaks (though this possibly occurred under old regulations), another said he "didn't appreciate the threats and bullying" and felt that the neighbors in the adjacent subdivision should have a say, and a Board member said the group did not have the proper setback for the minaret to meet October 2011 changes to zoning allowing certain religious elements to reach to 72 feet. The Board denied the height variation 14–4 (Sanchez 2012). Around the same time, the County Board denied another request for a mosque to exceed 36 feet for a dome. Just to the west of Lombard and with less opposition from neighbors compared to the MECCA case, the County denied the proposed height for the Pin Oak Community Center (Goldsborough 2011b).

The construction of the MECCA facility took several years. There was some disagreement about extending a construction permit in mid-2012 as the group needed to demolish the single house standing on the property (Placek 2012). The website for the center tracked the progress of construction: by August 2015 the site had experienced tree removal, site grading, utility installation, and the construction of foundations. As of August 2018, the MECCA website included a front page with images of the center under construction alongside mentions of the center's grand opening (described elsewhere on the website as having occurred April 22, 2017).

Kingdom Impact Center

While the first two case studies involved converting land to religious uses or constructing a new religious building, this third case involved renovating an existing structure. While few petitions from religious groups in Aurora attracted much negative public attention, this case did, even though it involved fixing up a dilapidated structure.

In 2014, Kingdom Impact Center asked to renovate a rundown building constructed in 1957 and formerly serving as a church building. The property was on the west side of Aurora in a largely residential area and was bank owned and "in somewhat of a deteriorated state" after sitting vacant for roughly ten years. This group describes itself as "a Christian, apostolic, and prophetic church" and appears to be a white Pentecostal congregation (Kingdom Impact Center 2016). The members of the commission asked numerous questions about the soundness of the building and the feasibility of rehab.

Despite the negative condition of the building, three nearby residents all raised concerns about renovating the building and using it as a church. The residents discussed concerns including stormwater issues, parking and traffic problems, and the length of the rehab and whether the petitioner had the resources to complete the job. In contrast to the problems raised, one commission member said, "I can empathize with the neighbors having to look at that building and living across from that, but I can also appreciate that if the building is not going away I'd rather see it occupied and improved." Another commission member concluded, "If you improve the property, it is bound to improve the values of the properties around it." The Plan Commission approved the petition 7–0 and the City Council approved the request on April 22, 2014, through the unanimous consent agenda.

A press release from the real estate consultant for the petitioner noted that the religious group looked forward to completing "dramatic top to bottom renovations" (RECI 2014). Additionally, the purchaser spent $80,000 on curb, gutter, and sidewalk improvements. This outlay led the alderman in Ward 5 of Aurora to initiate a loan program for up to $15,000 a year for property work that would benefit the larger community (Lord 2015a). The city of Aurora acknowledged the level of improvements to the property in late 2015 (Lord 2015b).

Proposals, Zoning, and Community Relations

Across forty proposals from religious groups involving buildings and/ or land over a five-year span in three suburban communities, conflict between religious groups, neighbors, and local officials did occasionally arise. Local governments approved a majority of building requests from religious groups. Reservations brought forward by neighbors and officials, often related to quality of life issues, did not automatically lead to a final denial. Non-Christian groups, primarily Muslims in this geographic area and time frame, made successful requests to use buildings and acquire land.

However, certain features of the proposal made by a religious group could lead to more opposition and a more difficult process for the petitioners. A location next to residential properties led to more public comments, and all of the five denials shared this feature. It mattered which suburban government considered the proposal: DuPage County had more opposition to non-Christian groups, four of the five denied cases at the final stage occurred here, and six of the eight total denials occurred here. Non-Christian groups often had lengthy processes or encountered more opposition (a common factor in three of the five final stage denials). Even though DuPage County eventually approved four prominent mosque cases (Carlman 2015b) and approved multiple mosques in commercial areas (Daniels 2011b; Goldsborough 2011a), opposition to Muslim groups was conspicuously strong (with one case including claims of connections to Iranian groups; see Smith 2009) and the process of approval lengthy (and sometimes requiring court involvement; see Manchir 2012; Schmadeke 2013; Blackburn 2014). DuPage County had past issues with limited minority populations sharing in postwar suburban growth alongside issues of limited housing for low-income residents (Freedman and McNamee 1979; Goff and Miller 1986), exclusionary zoning (Gillespie 1982; Fegelman 1984), and possible sundown towns where blacks and other non-white groups were not allowed (Loewen 2005).

These forty suburban cases shed light on four important themes in this book as we have traced the process of building or altering and using a building for religious purposes. First, building energy can be thwarted by neighbors and local officials. Congregations are often very excited to acquire and/or renovate property to make it their own, but such energy is not necessarily shared by the neighbors or local officials. Communities can be welcoming toward new religious buildings or changes to religious structures. Yet, even if local officials approve the process, the time span can drag on and the process made more difficult by opposition. It is not clear from these suburban cases if there are lingering consequences of a more acrimonious or lengthy process involving religious groups and local officials and neighbors. Would religious groups experience decreased building energy as they await approval, or would difficulties rally the congregation to more or extended energy?

Second, religious groups often feel that certain features of a building are necessary for an optimal worship experience. While they may not always be able to meet these aspirations due to budgets and what buildings and land are available, a local government and neighbors can restrict what the religious group can do with a building. The case study of MECCA described earlier is instructive: while the Muslim group said a dome of a certain height was part of "religious custom," neighbors and officials felt 36 feet was sufficient in a residential area. This difference in height affects both the interior and exterior experience of the building. It does not allow the religious group using the building to fully shape the structure they are constructing in a way that they desire. The local restrictions on height also hint at the changing societal expectations about religious buildings. Certainly centuries and maybe even just decades ago, a spire or steeple of a church may have conveyed status for the community and a congregation. Today, such a feature is less desirable among both congregations—for example, megachurches that may want to eschew traditional church architecture—as well as communities where a towering religious structure is viewed as a nuisance or threat to homeowners.

Third, religious groups may largely see their building efforts as an internal affair, but the necessity of approval from local governments and minimal opposition from neighbors highlights that religious buildings are also a part of neighborhoods and communities. At the least, nearby residents in the cases in this chapter do not want the building to be a threat to a quiet suburban way of life. Even some increased traffic a few times a week can be viewed as problematic for nearby residents. More perniciously, neighbors may not want certain groups to be visibly present. The opening or construction of a religious building for a new, lesser-known group may be too strong a sign that the new group is here to stay. Or, a religious group with ties to larger social discussions or concerns can prompt more scrutiny at a local level, even when the local religious group has provided little reason for concern. The creation or altering of religious buildings always takes place in a social context that may be more or less favorable toward the requests of the religious group.

Fourth, religious buildings are always under negotiation from those who use the structure, as well as those who interact with the religious structure in their neighborhood and community. The zoning process can represent the beginning stages of negotiation between the religious group and the community, or it can be part of later negotiations when established groups work with buildings and/or land. As Michael Guggenheim argues (2010), local governments and regulations may have difficulty keeping up with and mediating changing ideas about architecture, buildings, and land use. Truly incorporating religious buildings and congregations into a community extends far beyond zoning regulations, even if such legal hurdles are necessary to overcome in an American context.

New religious groups in suburban areas might face less local scrutiny if they are willing to use existing non-residential buildings, purchase existing religious buildings, and/or select new locations some distance from residential areas. Making a request to use TV studios, strip malls and shopping centers, industrial properties, and a building abandoned for ten years (though the case of the Kingdom Impact Center suggests that renovating an abandoned structure can still raise concerns) for religious purposes can find receptive ears, as multiple Protestant groups in Aurora and Naperville during this time period could attest. Additionally, the proposals from Christian groups during this period to renovate or add to existing structures attracted minor opposition, if they attracted much comment at all. The Islamic Center of Naperville's 2011 request to add a gymnasium and office space to a structure near a busy commercial intersection led to no negative comments. Still, their request that same year to buy fourteen acres surrounded by houses prompted fierce opposition. Of course, finding a non-religious building to use or worshipping in a structure that is less than ideal might require extra effort on the part of religious groups. Moreover, certain religious traditions may be more able to use a variety of structures.

Ultimately, religious congregations want an edifice in which to worship and build and maintain community, but negative suburban reactions to a building proposal may be influenced by both local particularities and larger concerns such as development, immigration, and different racial/ethnic groups and social classes. Ecological models of urban growth or religious activity—such as that advanced by Robert Park and the Chicago School (Park 1925)—might suggest religious groups simply need to find a cheaper plot of land. Encounter opposition? Move to a cheaper and/or more accom-modating location. The religious markets approach might suggest religious groups are free of obstacles as they try to get ahead, a process that could also involve finding a suitable building. Since American legal and political structures provide accommodations for religious groups, including legisla-tion like RLUIPA, congregations should be confident in pursuing locations.

We suggest the reality on the ground in the United States is more compli-cated. Religious buildings and land are a community concern as well as an as-piration of a religious congregation. Regulatory scrutiny from local officials and neighbors, even if the petition of the religious group is approved or the group and the local government come to a compromise, can make it more difficult for some religious suburbanites to fit in. Achieving acceptance and integration in the American suburbs goes beyond residences and includes physical structures for religious activity. Erecting a religious place of worship or converting an existing building—especially if that building provides visual cues to the religious tradition itself—in the suburbs is, in effect, a means for ethnic and religious minorities to "punch their ticket" of acceptance into mainstream American culture. Recognizing this fact, some neighbors may see such buildings as a threat to their community. To some degree, religious groups can prepare for adverse reactions from the community and work to build positive relationships. However, some of these reactions might be too difficult to overcome and the extra work may amount to a tax on cer-tain groups. While the "American Dream" may involve finding a private sub-urban space, choosing a suburban location that a group desires, and avoiding open suburban conflict (Baumgartner 1988; Archer 2005), the buildings of American religious groups are not solely their own.

The next chapter considers how architects operate within a different set of constraints. Even as architects do operate within legal parameters and regulations (Imrie and Street 2011), we discuss how architects navigate be-tween their own training and aesthetic values alongside the desires of reli-gious congregations. When religious groups build or renovate buildings, what is the role of the architect, and what are the long-lasting consequences for the physical structure and religious congregation of involving a professional?

5

Architects, Community, and Transcendence

A story is told about Sir Christopher Wren, the prolific English architect who helped rebuild London in the years after the Great Fire. Legend has it that Sir Wren decided one day to visit the construction site of St. Paul's Cathedral, a building that would become his crowning achievement. Unrecognized among the laborers, the architect asked a stonemason what he was doing. The mason replied, "I am cutting stone." A second inquiry with another laborer brought the reply, "I am earning a day's wages." But when the architect put the question to a third man, he received a different response. The laborer stopped what he was doing, stood tall, and, straightening his shoulders, replied, "I am helping Sir Christopher Wren build a beautiful cathedral."

The story serves as a fine example of the contagious nature of building energy, which can infect even those who, it would seem, have little to gain from the construction of a new building. Like the members of the newly formed Adventist church in Mártires, Guatemala, the stonemason in this legend found the prospect of collaborating in the building of a new religious structure to be a thrilling endeavor. But the legend also says something about architects, and so it is fitting that I first heard the story during an interview with LeRoy Troyer, AIA. A founder and former senior partner of Troyer Associates in South Bend, Indiana, Troyer, was eighty years old and had only recently retired when I interviewed him in his home. He would pass away several months later, leaving behind a legacy as a key Habitat for Humanity promoter and a designer of hundreds of religious buildings across the Midwest and beyond.[1] Troyer was one of the three veteran architects of religious buildings who shared their time with me in a lengthy interview as I prepared to write this chapter, the goal of which is to improve our understanding of the unique role of the architect in the process of constructing and using *religious* buildings. Other conversations with architects and students of architecture in less formal contexts in Guatemala and the United States proved helpful, but formal interviews with the three architects profiled in the following form the backbone of the research for this chapter.

Building Faith. Robert Brenneman and Brian J. Miller, Oxford University Press (2020). © Oxford University Press.
DOI: 10.1093/oso/9780190883447.001.0001

Troyer's anecdote about Christopher Wren reminds us that architects—including and perhaps especially those who design religious buildings—hold a special place in the public imagination. From Leonardo da Vinci to Frank Lloyd Wright, to Frank Gehry, the great architects of history have typically had an easier time capturing the public's attention than, say, sociologists or theologians. Perhaps this capacity to arrest the notice of the masses comes from the architect's ability to engage in material creation—that is, to design and direct a coordinated effort to make something concrete and material appear. No wonder theologians as diverse as Thomas Aquinas and John Calvin have borrowed the image of an *architect* to imagine the God they worshipped. For these theologians and others, it seemed obvious that something so magnificent, diverse, and complex as the natural world could only be designed and built by a "Divine Architect."

At the same time, a few architects, though themselves mere mortals, have achieved god-like status due to their ability to design and carry out building projects that shape and reshape the landscape in unforgettable ways. Some of the prominence of such figures—most, though not all, of whom are men—comes from the fact that they sit at the pinnacle of a (patriarchal) field that thrives on competition and hierarchy. Indeed, the sociologist Garry Stevens argued in a withering critique of the profession (2002) that prestige is a key commodity—perhaps *the* key commodity—that architects have to offer and for which the most notable are in such high demand. In Stevens's view, "great" architects design buildings that are unique and stand out visibly precisely because their fundamental "task" is to help a person, family, or company distinguish themselves as being one of a very small circle of elites who can afford "great architecture." Stevens makes a useful point, and one to which we will return later, and yet it would be difficult to deny the feeling of awe that a great work of architecture—ancient or contemporary—can evoke when we encounter it. From the Great Pyramid of Giza to the Taj Mahal and all the way to Falling Water, monumental works of architectural beauty and technical sophistication call us to wonder at the creative minds that conceived them, and it is surely in part because of such achievements that the architectural profession continues to enjoy a reputation for producing larger-than-life virtuosos whose brilliance occupies the unique intersection of artistic and technical genius. Of course, international fame has not been the primary objective of the vast majority of architects, past or present. In truth, only a tiny minority of elite architects jockey for international prestige by producing innovative design "statements." Outside this "favored circle," the key concerns of most architects involve regularly acquiring and completing commissions to design practical, functional structures that will be understood and appreciated by the corporations that can pay for them, rather than privileging aesthetics (Larson 1993; Stevens 2002; Sklair 2017).

But what is the specific role of the architect—including the vast company of professionals who do not occupy the rarefied air of the "starchitects" of fame—in helping religious communities realize their goals for a new or remodeled religious building? This chapter begins with an attempt to define the role of the architect in general, and proceeds to narrow in on the role of the architect of religious buildings. The larger objective is to identify what, if anything, is unique about the challenge of designing spaces for religious practice and worship. Since architects of religious spaces have considerable experience in this endeavor, I (Robert) use research from a variety of resources developed by and for architects of religious spaces, and I borrow from several conversations with architects of religious spaces in the United States and Guatemala.

The Role of an Architect

The act of creating architecture, then, is a problem-solving or design process. The first phase of any design process is the recognition of a problematic condition and the decision to find a solution to it.

—Ching (1979:10)

Many formal definitions exist for the term *architect*, which seems to have arisen from the Greek terms *arkhi* ("chief") and *tekton* ("builder"). At the most basic level, architects make plans for a physical structure, usually at the request of an individual or group, and then see to it that those plans are carried out. But at a more fundamental level, the architect, as revealed in the preceding quote by noted professor of architecture Frank Ching, is a professional problem-solver whose tools belong to both the aesthetic and the technical realms, and whose medium is space. Put simply, the task of the architect involves *using space to solve problems of a human dimension*. If this definition sounds too pragmatic or mundane, consider the vast array of problems faced by persons and groups across history—persons and groups who sought the help of architects for a solution to their varied problems.

For example, Mayan leaders of the priestly caste needed architects to solve problems related to authority. During the first millennium of the Common Era, before the invention of the telescope, they commissioned the construction of a complex of pyramids, the placement of which allowed these priestly astronomers to predict the movements of the heavens with what must have seemed like supernatural accuracy. A wizard-like knowledge of the planets helped them to solve, albeit temporarily, the problem of the tendency for the dominated to eventually lose faith in the authority and capacity of their leaders.

Or consider a slightly more recent example from what is now India: in 1631, the Mughal emperor Shah Jahan, stricken with grief at the death of his beloved wife, Princess Mumtaz Mahal, faced the problem of needing a resting place that would do justice to the memory of the princess. History suggests that the Shah ultimately conscripted the help of the architect Ustad Ahmad Lahori in order to build the Taj Mahal, a structure that has succeeded spectacularly in keeping the memory of the princess—not to mention the architect and the Shah himself—alive all the way to the present.

Of course, most of the "problems" brought to the studios of architects are of a decidedly more practical nature, and the available means of addressing those problems are similarly modest in scope. A more down-to-earth example of architectural problem-solving from closer to home involves a man by the name of A. V. Keeney, who needed a modest home in which to live and raise a family. In 1915, he sought the services of one Ernest W. Young, an award-winning architect from Kansas City who had moved to South Bend in time for the building boom of the early 1900s. With meticulous precision, Young designed and directed the construction of an 1,100-square-foot bungalow on the northwest side of South Bend, Indiana. That home, small by today's standards, was built at a cost of $2,500 and would house several families over the course of its first 100 years, including my (Robert's) own. Mr. Young, as it turns out, managed to solve problems of space, shelter, affordability, and beauty for persons and families he would never meet.

In short, the "problems" faced by architects and their clients run the gamut from symbolic, to political, to practical. By relying on a conceptually expansive understanding of architecture as an attempt to "solve problems with space," we gain a conciseness that is useful in its flexibility since it leaves open the question of just what sort of problem an architect must solve in a given situation. The residential architect must help a person or family solve problems related to the need for shelter, privacy, safety, and a perhaps a degree of prestige. The corporate architect must help a manufacturer solve problems related to safety and efficiency in the production of value for clients. The architect of civic buildings must solve problems for city officials and residents related to history and memory. And in each case, the problems to be solved are rarely singular or unitary, but rather multiple and complex. Architects who help their clients overcome those problems in a balanced way—or that, in any event, leave them with the impression that they have done so—develop a positive reputation in their field and in the local market of clients.

But what sorts of "problems" confront religious communities, and what kinds of solutions can architects of religious buildings offer? This is the question to which we now turn. In what follows, we explore religious architecture by way of conversations with three US architects, each of whom has considerable experience designing buildings for religious congregations. These three architects, one of whom had retired shortly before our interview, were chosen on the basis of convenience—Troyer is a distant relative of mine (Robert's), and Vivian became known to me through a shared acquaintance—but also with an eye toward providing a breadth of philosophy and approach. Each architect hails from a distinct religious background and at least two (Troyer and Stroik) described clearly diverging perspectives on what religious buildings ought to do for their congregations. While illustrations of religious buildings from the work of each architect can be quickly found on the Internet, we include here a single photograph of a religious project from each one that can help provide a clue to the kind of buildings they have designed.

Ann Vivian: Designing for an Experience

Ann Vivian, AIA, NCARB, is a licensed architect and partner at the office of GVV Architects in Burlington, Vermont. Her father taught architecture at MIT in the 1950s and 1960s and collaborated with the likes of I. M. Pei at a time when architectural schools were rife with experimentation and idealism. Watching her father, as well as observing and experiencing the modernist buildings that were emerging on the campus, Vivian found herself caught up in the excitement and became fascinated with architectural design. "That whole conversation, the buildings going up, the old Prudential Center, Kresge Auditorium at MIT—there's a lot of structural adventures with some of those things, and that just kind of engaged me." Not even the male predominance of the field could keep her from pursuing a dream to study architecture.

> My parents were wonderful in that they never said I couldn't do something or that I wouldn't be able to do that. So many of the women of that era ran up against "Oh women don't do that," or whatever. They never said anything like that so I went through school assuming this would be what I would do. So I applied pretty much exclusively to architecture programs coming out of high school.

Although she began her studies in Colorado, she returned to the East Coast after a couple of years and graduated from the Rhode Island School of Design. Today she is one of three partners in her firm and the only member of her team who specializes in designing spaces for worship and in helping congregations find ways to preserve and adapt their existing structures for a changing world. Her interest in religious projects, she admits, comes at least in part from growing up in a Congregational church and from her continuing participation in a congregation of the same denomination. But she also credits her involvement in the design of religious spaces to her participation in a group called the Interfaith Forum on Religion, Art, and Architecture of the United Church of Christ (UCC) to which she was invited in the 1990s. A loose fellowship of architects interested in buildings used for worship, the group stimulated her curiosity and led to her involvement in one project after another, eventually totaling nearly two dozen projects with religious groups from Protestant to Roman Catholic, to a Zen Meditation Center. The fellowship "was an opportunity to think about the evolution of sacred space and how it relates to theology," according to Vivian.

> They [the UCC] were looking at something like 80 percent of the buildings that churches were in were more than 150 years old—this was thirty years ago now—but they were reaching the point of congregations, even at that time, reducing in size. How they managed these older buildings and what was important was [sic] their main concern. One of our conversations was trying to understand what made a building a sacred space in the denominations especially that didn't rely on symbolism.

In other words, for an architect of religious buildings in northern New England, knowing how to help a graying congregation preserve, update, and adapt its aging building is paramount. But working with New

England congregations, especially those steeped in a participatory tradition of congregationalism and lay leadership, also means finding ways to help the whole membership feel that they are involved. When working with Congregationalists and other mainline Protestants, Vivian conducts multiple workshops, with participation from the entire congregation:

It's working with the whole congregation that's important, and I'm showing them examples of a big range of styles of churches, eras of church buildings. But [I also] talk a lot about the experience of worship and how their expression of liturgy is really important to the design of the space. And a little bit about where they see that going. Because liturgy evolves just like everything else.

Not every tradition is as open to contributions from the laity about where they "see the liturgy going," and Vivian admits that in her work with Catholic congregations it is usually the priest who gives most, if not all, of the direction for design: "It's almost always the priest and really usually you want to do one or two presentations to the whole congregations but it's really already a *fait accompli.*" As we will see in the following, not all Catholic congregations fit this mold—indeed, Vivian's experience may well be a product of the fact that much of her work has been in northern New England, where Catholic congregations tend to be smaller. Nevertheless, it should not be too surprising to learn that in congregations that place significant value on their particular tradition, lay members look to the clergy for guidance on how to design or renovate their gathering spaces in ways that accommodate or enhance that tradition. For example, in designing a significant addition for the Vermont Zen Center shown in Figure 5.1, which included a zendo (meditation room), reception room, and dorms, Vivian reported working exclusively with the sensei. "I didn't encounter the community at all in that [project]. [They're] using a lot of tradition, so she's the interpreter of the tradition. The tradition's coming from another culture into ours and the sensei is basically interpreting it. So you take the traditional elements from Japanese practice and you bring them into this culture."

When I asked Vivian what she believes to be the principal task of the architect, her first response emphasized context:

I think pretty much across the board, [your task] is to listen, and understand the needs of the client, whatever that client is, and then interpret that

Figure 5.1. Interior of the zendo designed by Ann Vivian for the Vermont Zen Center.
Used with permission.

into a space that's going to serve their needs as well as making it beautiful and as energy efficient as possible. . . . Beauty is not so important for some clients as it is for other types of clients. Context is always really important. And maybe it's just from being here in Vermont, but there's always been an emphasis on contextualism. Things can be new, but not offend. (Laughs).

Stated differently, the task of the architect, as Vivian describes it, depends almost entirely on the needs of the client. Or to put it in the language used earlier, the task of the architect is to help her or his clients solve whatever problem they define as needing solution. But what about the specific role of the architect of religious buildings? Do religious congregations share any similar "problems" across traditions? Vivian seems to think so.

[Designing for] liturgy is a little different than designing for process. Like, if you're working for a manufacturing client, for example. You're worried about getting a product in the door and out the other. Whereas churches, you're really designing for experience. And you know, you hope you end up with sacred space, or space that's sacred to some. But it's not like I have some big secret for how to make a space sacred. It's really a function of what's going to give an experience that gives a glimpse of the Divine as people encounter it.

In other words, the way a particular religious tradition defines what is sacred shapes what modes of experience it prescribes for bringing people to the doorstop of sacred encounter, and these prescriptions call for one kind of space versus another. Whereas a zendo utilizes a minimalist palette to reduce distractions and thus aid the adherent in her practice of meditation, a megachurch in the Pentecostal tradition, drawing on its tradition of prioritizing an outpouring of the Holy Spirit, may call for arena seating and high-tech acoustical and lighting engineering that can help to *focus* the attention of worshippers on a minister or a musical performance. During my interview with Vivian, I mentioned my research in Guatemala, which includes megachurches that spend enormous sums of money on acoustic design and state-of-the-art PA systems aimed at creating a particular sonic experience. The architect found this anecdote interesting but not surprising:

> The emotion is wrapped up in the sound and spending. The sound is filling the volume and spinning. . . . Even though it's speaker-driven, it's a similar kind of thing. . . . You know that's what the church has offered from the beginnings, right? It's an experience that's different from the everyday. That it's something grand or greater. You know, that glimpse of the Divine because it's not something that humans can create in their own small [space]. They have to be able to come together in a space that allows that kind of thing. A liturgy. . . . It's a totally different thing that whole idea that there's something other, something beyond you.

Asked if she had any favorite religious buildings, Vivian mentioned structures as diverse as Lincoln Cathedral, a gigantic medieval English church, as well as the MIT Chapel, an austere, modernist structure built in the 1950s. What these seemingly contrasting structures have in common is their ability to help create and enhance a sonic experience. Lincoln Cathedral houses an enormous nineteenth-century organ which was built in the center of the worship space rather than at the front or back. The church, then, is a notable example of religious buildings that act as a kind of "speaker box" for the organ, enhancing and magnifying the sound for everyone inside. At MIT, the chapel is part of a group of buildings built with what was at the time an emerging new science of acoustic design—when some architects were getting "geeky" with acoustics. Thus, for Vivian, raised in a tradition rich with instrumental and vocal music, religious buildings that offer participants an exceptional aural experience are among her favorites, for these are the structures that she has found the most moving in her own religious experience. "I think it so often comes down to light and sound and community. And then the practice over and over of worshipping with a community that you're a part of."

LeRoy Troyer: *People* Are the Church

LeRoy Troyer, AIA, was born and raised in an Amish family on the plains of northern Indiana—hardly a likely beginning for someone from a profession that prides itself in cultural sophistication and a thorough knowledge of the latest technological advancements. But despite growing up in a home with no electricity and no tradition of (nor need for) going to high school or college, Troyer discovered his calling early:

> I wanted to be an architect since the fourth grade. The teacher, Jean Miller, taught careers and sent me to the principal's office to get the drawings in order to see what architects did. So that's what I wanted to do. I helped my Amish father build some buildings on the farm and helped the neighbors when their barn came down. I never had my high school so I worked for Yutzy Construction, doing drawings in the evenings, and during the day I would go out and help build the buildings. An architect from South Bend heard about me [and] offered me a drafting job. . . . That's how we ended up in South Bend.

By this time, Troyer, who was already a married father, had opted with his new family to leave the Amish community and join instead a small Mennonite congregation that met in the South Bend area. In fact, the first project Troyer designed and oversaw was a sanctuary for this small band of Mennonite and former Amish families, which, at the time, called themselves Kern Road Chapel. Troyer accepted the challenge, despite the fact that he still had no formal training, having attended public schools until the eighth grade before leaving school to work on the farm. Designing the building, shown in Figure 5.2 along with a Troyer-designed annex, was a moonlighting labor of love. Troyer reports that, using a homemade drafting table and T-square, he designed the building even while working for a local builder: "It was really stressful and wore me out. I spent so many hours on it—evenings, during the day, at noontime, extra hours." Since the tiny congregation was made up largely of young teachers and recent college graduates, the church relied heavily on volunteer brigades from other congregations in the region, who came to support the building of a church that was in many ways a mission outreach for the denomination. "There were only six families when we built it. I began to really realize that Christ wants to live *in us*. He doesn't want to live in buildings. It's really not—there's no such thing as any sacred space. God created *us* in his image."

Despite his decidedly non-materialist theology, Troyer nevertheless believed fiercely in his calling to be an architect. Upon inquiring at Notre Dame's School of Architecture, he learned that the college would make a special exception allowing him to enroll in its program even though he had not graduated from high school, as long as he could show evidence of an ability to complete college coursework. After succeeding in courses in math and science at the local public university, Troyer returned with his transcript to Notre Dame and was admitted to the School of Architecture, receiving his license in 1971, and founding in that same year the Troyer Group,

Figure 5.2. Kern Road Mennonite Church. Troyer designed the original sanctuary on the far left in 1962, as well as the large new sanctuary addition on the right in 1997.
Photo: Janice Sutter.

a firm that would design hundreds of structures for religious groups, from congregations to colleges, to faith-based nonprofits.

Among Troyer's most well-known projects have been designing a master plan for Nazareth Village, a village in Palestine recreating for visitors from around the world first-century life around the time of Jesus, and, more recently, designing a gigantic replica-museum of Noah's ark. The ark project, a curious conclusion to a career aimed at helping congregations and corporations build practical, energy-efficient structures (long before such solutions were popular), only makes sense when viewed in light of Troyer's Amish upbringing and his abiding interest in wooden post-and-beam structures. Curious about just how "biblical" the structure was, I asked Troyer if the building was made of "gopher wood" as the Hebrew Scriptures indicate. He couldn't resist a joke on the word "gopher":

> Yeah, we *went for* a lot of wood. . . . We had to use cypress and also cedar. They thought they had to build a steel structure because it was so big. We used the Egyptian and the Hebrew cubit which is 20.4 inches, from here to here (signals elbow to fingertip). We made the ark 510 feet long, 85 feet wide. So that's a big structure. A lot of wind. We designed it 10 percent stronger than the code required [because] it's like a big sail.

Clearly, Troyer, who, at eighty, had recently retired and sold his family business, loved a challenge—especially a challenge of, literally, biblical proportions. Whether or not the ark, owned and operated by the fundamentalist Christian group Answers in Genesis, manages to make believers out of biblical skeptics—a key goal of the project (Bielo 2018)—remains to be seen, but Troyer expressed hope that his contribution might help the project inspire belief and wonder.

Nevertheless, far more frequent than arks or model villages in Troyer's portfolio of religious projects were the expansions, renovations, or new design projects for Christian places of worship. Already by the early twenty-first century, a decade before his retirement, Troyer's firm could boast having consulted for or designed over three hundred religious building projects, including sanctuaries for congregations ranging from Pentecostal to Catholic to Greek Orthodox. Undoubtedly, Troyer's warnings to congregational leaders not to get too wrapped up in their buildings, but to instead maintain a focus on carrying out their spiritual and social mission, helped to endear him to budget-conscious religious leaders who might have wondered if they could trust an architect. In fact, Troyer reports having had to remind more than one pastor of his central vocation with the rhetorical question, "Do you want to be a pastor of the people or of a building?" Such advice resonated especially with ministers and lay leaders in Mennonite, evangelical, and other less liturgically formal congregations in which buildings often represent, at best, a means to a religious end, but are not supposed to be an end in themselves.

But by the late 1970s even Catholic congregations were seeking Troyer's services. By then, a document produced by the National Conference of Catholic Bishops was circulating among US Catholic congregations contemplating building or renovating their worship space. *Environment and Art in Catholic Worship*, a fifty-page pamphlet incorporating photographs of interiors of newly designed religious buildings and advice about designing new buildings, offered the lament, "Many local churches must use spaces designed and built in a former period, spaces which may now be unsuitable for the liturgy" (Bishops' Committee on the Liturgy 1978:15). The implication for many readers of the document was that more traditional buildings were not appropriate to the new Post–Vatican II reality of the church, and that a growing church needed new buildings that also *looked* new and up-to-date. The fact that all of the photographs of church interiors included in the pamphlet depicted distinctly minimalist, modernist designs contributed to such perceptions. Additionally, the document encouraged Catholic congregations to consider the needs of the "assembly of believers" as the "primary demand" of any new or renovated Catholic worship space. Such emphasis on the needs of "the assembly," as opposed to the needs of tradition or of individual prayer, fit well with the emphases at Troyer Group, which, at the invitation of the Chicago diocese, developed a 200-page "Building and Renovation Kit for Places of Catholic Worship." The document, which contained a wealth of information from practical know-how to theological reflection, included a full reprint of the *Environment and Art in Catholic Worship*, often referred to with the acronym EACW. The themes in that document seemed to fit well with the Troyer Group's tendency to design buildings that were clean, spare, and, energy efficient, and which boasted an acoustical design tuned for music.

The Troyer Group, of course, was hardly the only architectural firm helping Catholic congregations to design contemporary, minimalist worship spaces. Across the country, many Catholic congregations were outgrowing their worship spaces, and the EACW was providing guidance not only with its text, but with illustrations of sleek, modernist sanctuaries obviously influenced by the architectural modernism of the mid-twentieth century. Much like Troyer, who emphasized the church *as a body of people*, the EACW encouraged congregations to think of the gathered community as the starting point for renovation: "[W]e have to begin with ourselves—we who are the Church, the baptized, the initiated." For the framers of the EACW, a worship space *becomes* sacred through the gathering of the assembly of believers, for "such a space acquires sacredness from the sacred action of the faith community which uses it" (Bishops' Committee on the Liturgy:23). While the document does not go as far as Troyer in asserting that "there is no such thing as any sacred space," it comes surprisingly close to doing so by defining as dangerous "the historical problem of the church as a place attaining a dominance over the faith community" (1978:23).

Nor was the Conference of US Catholic Bishops alone in promoting a more human-centered approach to designing religious spaces. As religious historian Richard Kieckhefer (2008) has shown, religious architecture in the West shifted toward sanctuaries that aimed attention toward the gathered assembly itself and away from the altar and the pulpit. This more human-centered arrangement led to the creation of many sanctuaries with an open design, flexible seating, and "worship-in-the-round." A great many of the sanctuaries designed by Troyer's firm reflect these same design moves. They also feature practical functionality and efficiency.

One way to think about the EACW and Troyer's more human-centric design preference is to place them within the context of the larger debate over modernism in architecture. Modernist architects of the mid-twentieth century believed that new technology had made it possible for them to address human needs for shelter, space, and community in radically new ways. Sweeping away traditional elements of classical style, symmetry, and ornament, apostles of modern architecture such as Le Corbusier designed rational, technologically advanced but stylistically nondescript buildings in an attempt to meet the demand in rapidly growing cities for not only housing but also "social uplift" to masses of poor and working-class families. In many cases, most dramatically with the dynamiting of the Pruitt-Igoe residential projects in St. Louis in 1972, these experiments in "social architecture" failed to deliver on their promised benefits, and sometimes the buildings even worsened the conditions of the poor (Crawford 1991), such that by the late 1970s, a backlash had materialized, and modernist architecture, including and especially its social aims, had more critics than advocates (Sorkin 1991). The preference in EACW and in many of Troyer's designs for clean,

ornament-free interiors, along with their human-centric focus and an ecumenical disdain for tradition and local symbolic vernacular, all resonated
with modernist preferences in architecture, despite the fact that modernism
was about to undergo a time of soul-searching and criticism from within and
without. As we will see in the following, a backlash against modernist architecture would soon emerge within the Catholic church that would mirror
and extend some of the criticisms already being leveled from the broader
field of architectural criticism.

For his part, however, Troyer was less interested in architectural trends
or movements than in solving practical problems of space and light for his
clients. When I asked Troyer to name a particularly memorable religious
building project, he named a Mennonite church in Normal, Illinois, where
in the late 1970s he designed, after consulting with the congregation, a multi-
purpose space which could be used as both a foyer and an educational space.
The worship space itself can be rearranged using mobile planter-dividers on
wheels, allowing greater flexibility for different kinds of events.

> They also wanted to have recreation, so we worked with them. I left it up
> to the people. Rather than just come up with ideas. I think the best ideas
> come out of people if you engage the community. . . . It's a very multiple
> use building and they built it themselves, mostly college students with an
> industrial arts teacher. They also wanted an energy-efficient building so we
> put a skylight in the center. . . . The skylight was like sixty feet long—white,
> natural light in the whole building.

For Troyer, the best church buildings are those that bring people face-to-
face in a worship encounter, and that make practical, efficient use of available
resources while providing access to nature in the form of plants and natural light. Such views may seem benign or even obvious to some. For those
steeped in a different kind of liturgical tradition, they represent a reckless departure from the symbolic vocabulary of an ancient and venerable tradition.

Duncan Stroik: Church Buildings as Sacred Signs

Duncan Stroik, AIA, joined the faculty of the University of Notre Dame's
School of Architecture in the early 1990s, at the same time that the school
was reorienting itself to become a leader in classical architecture. Having

recently completed his architectural studies at Yale University, Stroik quickly developed a reputation as a designer of classical structures. Already in 1995, a *New York Times* article titled "Architecture's Young Old Fogies" cited Stroik as one of a handful of "Young Turks" who were quietly reintroducing Beaux Arts and classical Greek and Roman designs long thought to be passé by architects of the mainstream. Some architects scoffed at the revival as "backward" and "right wing," while others lauded its promoters as "young radicals." "At their best," the author of the piece opined, "the new classicists seek to combine graceful proportions and ornamentation with affordable materials and an almost Shakerlike simplicity" (Brown 1995:49). Although classical buildings can be expensive due to the incorporation of more traditional materials and craftsmanship, the proponents of the movement argued that their work would be more enduring, making it both environmentally and socially responsible.

When I asked Stroik what attracted him to the field of architecture, he readily admitted that, as the son of an architect father, he was exposed early to the profession. But he was also drawn to the profession as a vocation, believing that architects have a higher calling than simply winning commissions and designing structures: "Architects, at their best, want to participate in the life of the community. Good architecture should ennoble people." Asked how a classicist like himself could graduate from Yale School of Architecture—a program famous for its campus home in Rudolph Hall, a "brutalist" tribute to modernity—Stroik laughed and reported that at Yale, in contrast to many other schools of architecture, faculty still retained a respect for history and expected students to acquire a basic grasp of history and of the history of architecture. Additionally, an "anything goes" approach to debating design meant that even a style as "far out" as classicalism in the 1980s could get a hearing.[2] "They would let anyone get in the ring" he reported, while hastening to add, "I got beat up a few times."

Perhaps not surprisingly, Stroik is also Catholic, having grown up in a Catholic home and embraced the religious tradition of his roots. This combination of being a practicing Catholic and a classicist with a deep regard for the high and "noble" calling of architecture as a contributor to the public has helped Stroik to become a leader in a movement of theologians and architects who are critical of modernist church buildings—especially Catholic buildings. Furthermore, Stroik has become a particularly vociferous critic of the EACW. The EACW's emphasis on building and renovating churches *for the assembly* struck Catholic theologians and architects like

Stroik as a curious, and even misguided, invention. After all, there are many uses to which Catholic religious buildings have been put that do not involve a gathering of people assembled in order to celebrate the mass. From providing a site for individuals to practice daily prayer, to offering a space for the veneration of saints or the safekeeping of relics, to providing a religious backdrop for traditional holidays and celebrations, Catholic church buildings have played a multifaceted role in the life of the Catholic community, and critics of the EACW cite the focus on weekly worship services as an unnecessary acculturation toward Protestantism.

From his post as editor of the journal *Sacred Architecture* and as director of the Institute for Sacred Architecture, Stroik has helped to assemble a gathering of critics who have lobbied hard against what they see as a movement toward modernist, minimalist religious buildings that deviate from Roman Catholic tradition. Stroik and others argue that when Roman Catholic church buildings were built or renovated in the spirit of the EACW, they were frequently denuded of their statues and images—save for the requisite images of American Catholicism, Jesus, Mary, and Joseph—and emptied of their capacity to cultivate the *imagination* of the Catholic Christian. In a head-on critique of the bishops' statement titled "Environment and Art in Catholic Worship: A Critique," Stroik (1999b:9) worried that the document came dangerously close to iconoclasm, since "[t]he ability of the church building to symbolize the Christian community and her belief in Christ, through domes, spires, bells, generous portals, atriums, gardens, and iconography is ignored [in the EACW]. This is problematic, since the exterior is the first image of the Church with which people come in contact." In short, Stroik contends that the framers of the EACW could see worship spaces only as the *domus ecclesiae*, and failed to recognize that a church building is also the *domus dei*, the "house of God" (Stroik 2009).

Other Catholic intellectuals have provided similar critiques. The well-known Catholic sociologist and priest/writer Andrew Greeley, while avoiding specific mention of the EACW, was even less restrained in his criticism of late-twentieth-century modifications to Catholic church buildings. In his socio-religious work *The Catholic Imagination*, Greeley argued that Catholic church buildings, including the massive structures built in medieval Europe, have excelled at the task of shaping the imagination—and therefore the identity and practice—of millions of Europeans, including those who have inherited the culture but not the beliefs of the Catholic faith:

In a time of widespread literacy when religion courses, textbooks, and how-to manuals can reach out to the whole population, the churches are still treasure houses of stories, save in some sterile modern churches with which architects and clergy, in a burst of mistaken ecumenism, have tried to placate the Protestant suspicion that Catholic churches hoard idols. A rule of thumb: if there are no votive candles in it, a church really isn't Catholic. (Greeley 2001b:26)

For Greeley, a church building that does not act as a "forest" of metaphors and stories cultivating the imagination of every visitor—whether tourist or worshipper—is not worthy of the name "Catholic." Austerity and minimalism in religious buildings may have been necessary in certain times and places of need, Greeley argued, but they were hardly worth replicating in the midst of modern American prosperity. In a magazine essay titled "A Cloak of Many Colors: The End of Beige Catholicism," Greeley contended that

Whatever might be said of past practices—the Irish built schools and used the school hall for Mass—there is no longer an excuse for omitting beauty from our sacramental life. We need to elevate the functional with the kind of transcendent beauty that tears a hole in the fabric of ordinary life and allows grace to pour in. The minimalism of beige Catholicism desires only the commonplace. (Greeley 2001a:12)

The idea that architectural minimalism has no place in the Catholic tradition is debatable at best, given the long history of architectural simplicity in the monastic orders, especially the Cistercians (Kinder 2002). Nevertheless, by the end of the twentieth century, recognizing the controversy produced by the 1978 statement, the National Conference of Catholic Bishops set about developing a new statement on the matter of how to design and renovate churches. In 2000, the bishops released a new, expanded set of guidelines titled *Built of Living Stones: Art, Architecture, and Worship*. The document acknowledges in the preface that EACW "has had a profound impact on the building and renovation of parish churches in the United States" and somewhat diplomatically proposes "a new document on church art and architecture that builds on and replaces" the earlier statement (USCCB 2000:3). But while *Built of Living Stones* does go further in paying tribute to the variety of devotional activities that take place in a Catholic church building, it does not go far enough for the traditionalists at *Sacred Architecture*. For example, in an essay for the Fall 2015 issue, the theologian Aidan Nichols (2015) argued that while *Built of Living Stones* represents an improvement over the EACW, it fails to adequately appreciate the potential for a religious building to speak *even when no one is inside it.* For Nichols, a Catholic church building should speak in much the same way an icon communicates—that is, as a portal or window that *points toward* divine truth. Such a view places the architect of a church in a prominent position as an interpreter of a theological tradition. It is a view that Stroik (1999a:2) clearly shares when he argues that "[d]esigning a church can be likened to painting an icon, which is a spiritual act, done with prayer and fasting."

The responses of Stroik and others to the EACW and *Built of Living Stones* are instructive because they illustrate the way physical structures and their design can become lightning rods for debate over how to embody a religious tradition in a changing world. Nor were such controversies over church architecture limited to the Catholic community in the United States. Within this community, however, Stroik is confident that his work to mobilize critics has paid off. Not only was the EACW replaced with a significantly less "iconoclastic" revision, the influence of the earlier document, and the modernism it seemed to promote in its text and photographs, seems to have waned, at least in the United States. "We have defeated it," Stroik dryly remarks of the document. Furthermore, his own work as an architect, such as the Chapel of the Holy Cross shown in Figure 5.3, points to the resurgence in more traditional styles. Asked how he approaches the task of helping a congregation build a new church building, the architect responds: "I'm trying to help them with their *charism.* . . . How do you show that this is God's house as well as your house?"

Architects as Guides

One goal of this chapter has been to develop a sense of the range of approaches to religious building design that are employed by architects of religious buildings. While on the one hand, these three architects barely allow us to scratch the surface of design possibilities, since all of them have worked primarily, though not exclusively, with congregations in the Christian tradition, some clear distinctions have emerged. For example, although all three architects spoke of the importance of listening carefully to a congregation before developing a design plan, Ann Vivian seemed to be considerably more

Figure 5.3. Chapel of the Holy Cross at Jesuit High School, Tampa, Florida. Designed by Stroik and dedicated on August 7, 2018.
Used with permission.

open to a wide range of styles. Stroik, for his part, works only with those religious communities (mostly, though not exclusively Catholic) who share his enthusiasm for traditional building designs. Thus, his influence is exercised at the point of choosing his clients. Meanwhile, Troyer, who worked with a wide range of styles and who also advocated for carefully listening to a congregation before developing a design, clearly had his limits when it came to certain design decisions. For example, when a large Mennonite congregation in Indiana asked him to design a sanctuary for them that was absent any windows (thus allowing them to use artificial lighting in order to control the atmosphere), Troyer threatened to resign from the project. "They wanted to sing off the wall [using an overhead projector and screen]. I said, 'Let's put in at least *some* windows. You're out in the countryside.'" Only when the minister begged Troyer not to resign, fearing that it would split the congregation, did Troyer relent, reluctantly designing a windowless sanctuary for one of the largest congregations in the denomination. Nor was it the only time Troyer would take on the leadership of a church, making strong suggestions that reflected his own theological and architectural proclivities. At a Mennonite congregation in Harrisonburg, Virginia, Troyer recalled being asked to take an uncharacteristic step for a Mennonite church. "They had a lot of professors and they wanted stained glass. 'Why would you want that?' I said. 'Well, we like to have the symbolism.' So I said, 'Well, I'll give you stained glass. You have the Massanutten Mountain range to the East.'" This time Troyer won the debate. The congregation installed clear glass windows overlooking the iconic ridge of Mt. Massanutten.

As these conversations clearly indicate, architects play a crucial role in the development of the material structures that represent the physical presence of a congregation and even a tradition. That some architects play a more proactive role than others in making "suggestions" or decisions about design should not obscure the fact that all architects draw on their own professional formation, as well as religious and/or philosophical commitments, in "guiding" a congregation and its building energy toward a material structure.

Distinction, Community, and Transcendence

The goal of this book is decidedly *not* that of settling the question of what a religious building "should" look like, and similarly, the objective of the current chapter cannot involve taking a position on the matter of how architects of religious spaces ought to go about designing or renovating such buildings. Instead, the goal has been to discover some of the variety of perspectives that guide architects of religious buildings as they advise communities of faith in navigating building projects and to discern if any convergences exist between such perspectives. If anything is clear from getting to know the perspectives of the three architects profiled here, it is that even within the Christian tradition, the particular religious formation of the architects themselves tends to shape how they think about their task.

For Vivian, raised in a Congregationalist church, the experience of music, both instrumental and vocal, is a driving concern, but equally important is the *inclusion*, to the greatest extent possible, of the voices of as many members of the community as possible. For Troyer, raised Amish and later an active member in a Mennonite church—a tradition that began by meeting in the homes of members and only much later started to construct simple "meetinghouses" for worship—the point of a church building is primarily to facilitate a gathering of the faithful, and to do so without "getting in the way" of the more important business of carrying out the mission of the faith community. "Sacred space" as such does not exist for Troyer. But for Stroik, a Catholic with a professed preference for the language and practice of tradition, the role of the architect of religious buildings is precisely that of helping a congregation to build a sacred space since "the crucial issue in church architecture today is the development of the theological understanding of the *church as a sacred place*" (2009:13).

So what, if anything, is unique about the role of the architect of religious spaces? Here it is worth framing the question as introduced at the beginning of this chapter—that of defining the kinds of *problems* faced by architects of religious buildings. It should be obvious from this chapter and from earlier chapters that architects of religious buildings must address many of the same problems faced by those of non-religious. For example, religious communities face problems of size and scale. Working in the Midwest, LeRoy Troyer helped many congregations expand their facilities in order to keep up with surging demographic and ecclesial growth in the 1980s and 1990s, while Ann Vivian has often had to help smaller mainline Protestant congregations in northern New England adjust their facilities in ways that better suit demographic decline and a "graying" membership. Furthermore, both architects have worked hard to provide efficient, environmentally responsible buildings that do not lock congregations into long-term energy expenses. In this sense as well, their "problems" are no different than those faced by architects of non-religious spaces.

But apart from practical considerations, we would be naïve if we ignored the fact that architects of religious spaces—just like architects designing a home, a museum, or a college library—must also deal with the demand from their clients for material indicators of taste that define the social class of the members of the congregation. Undeniably, architects of churches, mosques, and synagogues are often hired with an eye toward solving the "problem" of a community that has come to be embarrassed by the presence of a nondescript, "boring" (i.e., undistinguished) building—that is, a building that is not in keeping with the social class of many of the members of the congregation.

The fact that architects of religious buildings often assist the parishioners of a congregation in burnishing their social credentials is one that I (Robert) stumbled upon long before I began studying the sociology of religion in any formal way. A religiously devout but also socially curious undergraduate, I paid visits to many of the more than a dozen Mennonite congregations

in the Harrisonburg, Virginia, area during my four years of undergraduate study at Eastern Mennonite University. Eventually, I discovered that
I could roughly predict the number of college professors attending a congregation based on the architectural form and interior design of the building.
Congregations that could boast an architecturally sophisticated building
with a thoughtful, acoustically tuned interior—of which there were only a
few—tended to attract a greater share of professors and administrators involved with the university, while those congregations with the tan-brick-
with-low-slung-roof-and-carport (not to mention the requisite beige
carpeting) that is a far more typical design of this mostly rural and suburban denomination tended to attract members from pink- and blue-collar
professions like farming, construction, and small business operation. In fact,
some of these church buildings were built without any assistance from an architect. These were "meetinghouses" in the truest sense of providing a simple
place to gather, and they were "American" in the sense of aiming to make that
space feel like a living room—that is, as comfortable, domestic, and inviting
as possible. Nor was it the case that congregations with more professors
and college administrators simply had more money with which they were
able to engage the services of architectural firms. College professors and
administrators at the poorly endowed university often earned less than their
small-business-owning co-religionists who seemed to prefer worshipping in
large, unsophisticated church complexes with sprawling fellowship halls and
multipurpose buildings. And even so, the congregations with the most educated parishioners seemed the most willing to spend their resources to build
stately structures that communicated refinement and good taste.

That social class shapes one's taste in buildings should not surprise us.
After all, French sociologist Pierre Bourdieu discovered, in his classic study of
French taste and social class (1984), that a preference for aesthetic properties
tends to be more pronounced among the higher social classes. In short, class
position, which is determined not merely by one's income level, but by educational attainment and occupational prestige, has consequences not only for
the kind of home one wishes to live in, but also for the kind of building within
which a religious person is willing to congregate. Religious buildings, especially within a single denomination, speak to the social class of those gathering inside them. Well aware of this, architects provide congregations with a
rare opportunity to define themselves socially, not merely theologically.

And yet, while architects of religious spaces operate in a similar environment as those who design non-religious structures and are subject to similar

pressures from clients wishing to define themselves and their tastes, we believe they also face at least two "problems" that are, if not unique, then uniquely important when compared with architects in general. The first involves what we might call "building a 'we.'" Architects who design religious buildings have a unique responsibility to help a group of individuals, most of whom bear no blood relation to each other, cultivate a sense of community and solidarity. Exactly how this can be accomplished depends not only on the artistic and cultural capacity of the architect, but also on her or his knowledge of the particular theological and liturgical traditions in question and an ability to translate those traditions into material form. In religious congregations that frequently share meals—for example, Muslim congregations that gather each evening during Ramadan—the design of the kitchen and dining space may turn out to be just as crucial as the design of the sanctuary. For it is in these spaces that bonds of community are created and solidified. In other traditions, the worship service itself is central, and in Catholic congregations, especially in majority-Catholic societies such as in Latin America, providing ample outdoor space immediately in front of or beside the church makes it possible to celebrate important holy days or life transitions. In any event, although architects of religious spaces are not the only ones tasked with helping a community to build a collective memory (Jones 2011), this objective takes on extra importance when one's "client" imagines itself not merely as a collective, but as single entity or even a "body."

The second "problem" faced particularly by architects of religious buildings involves that of designing a space that helps a group of people— whether corporately or individually—to experience a feeling of connection to transcendence. Here we think it worthwhile to point out that we understand "religion" to refer to a group of persons who are in some way *linked* to one another (thus the term "re-*ligio*," implying the *lig*aments that hold a physical body together) and who share some sort of commitment to an experience of or narrative about a Sacred Other. In point of fact, these "ligaments" of connection may go no further than a connection to a narrative tradition, or they may imply a group of people who meet regularly and share a sense of responsibility for each other and for the gathering. The point is simply that religious congregations imply linkages between people, as well as a relationship to a story about transcendence, even if those linkages may be weak and even when the connection to the story includes a good deal of skepticism. We agree with sociologist Nancy Ammerman's argument that "religious activity is recognized as such because it has something to do with things that are sacred, transcendent, or beyond the ordinary" (Ammerman 2007:225). Given such a definition, we believe that, in addition to contributing to a shared identity, architects of religious buildings uniquely share the burden of helping a group of persons relate, in some fashion, to a Sacred Other.

How such "helping" is done can take any number of forms. In a Christian church of the Orthodox tradition, a dome on which is depicted Christ Pantocrator provides parishioners the chance to marvel at a depiction of the all-powerful Christ reigning over the universe. In a Pentecostal church, such as those studied by the Mexican architect and theologian Daniel Chiquete in Sinalóa, Mexico, a sanctuary that allows worshippers to be physically close to the altar, rather than distant, gives them the opportunity to approach the space "where the action is" religiously and emotionally. Meanwhile, architects of neo-Pentecostal and evangelical megachurches, like the one who gave Robert a tour of her recently completed project, Ciudad de Dios in Guatemala City, often seek to provide worshippers the opportunity to experience an emotional connection to a sermon or a song by using theater-style lighting, seating, and sound, all of which maximize the experience of what is happening onstage while dampening the potential distractions coming from the seating area. Other traditions have very different modes of enhancing the experience of transcendence. Those with a well-developed tradition of sacred music place great emphasis—and abundant resources—in the service of acoustical design. The *masjid* or mosque must create an adequate, barrier-free space for kneeling in prayer (with a separation between men and women) and listening to the sung Quran. Meanwhile, in the Catholic tradition, a variety of pathways to enhancing an experience of transcendence has occupied architects over the centuries. Most familiar perhaps is the incorporation of geometric forms aimed at evoking awe and the incorporation of various nooks and chapels intended to make space for the veneration of saints and acts of devotion to a set of stories pertaining to the Bible and church tradition.

But Rome, with its abundance of elaborate churches, each one a "forest" packed with art and sculpture, is not the only Catholic architectural tradition. The Cistercian abbeys, virtually devoid of decoration—even stained glass was forbidden—aimed at bringing monks into a daily encounter with transcendence through a contemplative process of "interiorization." As architectural historian Terryl Kinder (2002:143) eloquently described it: "'Spectacular' is not a word one would normally use to describe [Cistercian churches]. The building was not meant to take one's breath away; quite the contrary, it was

intended to bring back the breath, slowly and evenly, to an internal quie-
tude. ..." Thus, the preferred "mode" for the experience of transcendence—in
this case, one of quiet meditation—can shape the architectural "medium" meant to facilitate it. This fact can lead two very different religious
traditions—for example, Zen Buddhism and Cistercian Catholicism—to develop surprising similarities in their architectural vocabulary.

In sum, even within a single tradition, various "pathways" toward facilitating an experience of, or connection to, transcendence can evolve and
can exist, while across traditions, similarities can develop due to parallelism
in modes of practice. The same principle is true for the means by which
architects of religious spaces must work to enhance connection *between*
congregants. Not all religious buildings, past or present, have been designed
by architects. Many congregations, especially in rural settings or with limited resources, have designed and built houses of worship without ever consulting a professional architect. Yet even these congregations often mimicked
a building style first introduced by an architect who strove to help a congregation interpret its tradition and its mission through its building. Thus,
architects of religious buildings have, for many centuries, played a formative
role in the global landscape by assisting religious communities as they realize
their aspirations in wood, stone, brick and glass. Nevertheless, as we will see
in the following chapter, some buildings used by congregations for religious
purposes were originally designed and erected for a very different religious
tradition or for no religious purpose at all. It is to these buildings that we
now turn.

6

Space Bending When Matter Matters

We have argued throughout this book that buildings have a formative capacity that shapes congregations that use them, even as buildings themselves are designed, built, and renovated—that is, they are shaped and reshaped—by the congregations themselves (with help from architects and sometimes with community input). From the congregation that conceives of a building that can communicate the grandeur of the Eternal to one that simply wants a better way to help its members feel well attended and "at home," religious building projects give congregations a means of tackling problems of both a practical and symbolic nature. Pushing further, we argue that religious buildings facilitate the gathering and entrainment of bodies for religious and community purposes (Collins 2004).

Not every congregation attempts to solve such problems by commissioning and seeing through the construction of a new building. Some congregations, after surveying their options and constraints, decide to take a preexisting building—one that was built for a different congregation, or that was built for a decidedly non-religious purpose altogether—and make it their own. Why would a congregation make such a choice? What are some of the implications of the choice for the community-building and worship experience of these congregations?

Repurposing for worship a building originally conceived, designed, and built for a very different community or for a non-religious purpose is hardly an exceptional practice. Across history, religious congregations have engaged in "space bending"—taking preexisting buildings and "bending" them toward their own needs, often, though not always, performing significant changes to the form of the structure as well as ritual forms of sanctification or symbolic "rededication" of the space. Early Christian church buildings were typically modified homes owned by middle-class converts to Christianity. As Jeanne Kilde (2008) has pointed out, such meeting places involved the adaptation of smaller rooms for baptismal rites and larger oblong rooms with a raised platform at one end for gathering the whole body.

Building Faith. Robert Brenneman and Brian J. Miller, Oxford University Press (2020). © Oxford University Press.
DOI: 10.1093/oso/9780190883447.001.0001

The Hagia Sophia in present-day Istanbul, Turkey, is perhaps one of the most well-known examples of a religious space originally designed for one religious tradition, but repurposed for another. Built as a Christian cathedral in 547, the church served the Orthodox tradition as the seat of the Ecumenical Patriarch of Constantinople for nearly 900 years (except for a short period in the thirteenth century when it was a Roman Catholic church) until the Ottoman Empire converted the building to a mosque in 1453. Christian rulers carried out similar acts of "religious repurposing" in places like Spain. For example, the Mosque-Cathedral of Córdoba, a massive and richly decorated structure built as a mosque in the late eighth century, was converted into a church in the thirteenth century by Christian rulers during the "Reconquest" of the peninsula. In the case of the Mosque-Cathedral, Christian rulers later converted a minaret to a bell tower and added a nave in obvious efforts to Christianize a space that was built for decidedly non-Christian purposes. Such efforts at "space bending" provide evidence that, even in antiquity, religious communities often found the work of other traditions to be so attractive and useful as to warrant adoption and adaptation.

Space bending can go even further and occur with buildings less obviously suited for religious gatherings. In this chapter we examine five examples of contemporary "space-bending" congregations—four in the United States and one in Guatemala—who have shown considerable flexibility and ingenuity in adapting a space to fit their particular needs. We start with four case studies that involve congregations that have taken buildings built for decidedly non-religious purposes—from a parking garage to a manufacturing plant to an army base to a high school—and retrofitted them to the needs of a worshipping community. We close with a case study of a congregation that took a page from the Ottomans by adapting a religious space initially designed for a different religious tradition for their own needs. Along the way, we seek to advance our larger agenda of shedding light on the multifaceted ways that buildings shape the congregations that gather inside them.

La Familia de Dios: If You Build Parking, They Will Come

Since its founding in 1990, Iglesia de Jesucristo La Familia de Dios (Family of God Church of Jesus Christ) has inhabited no fewer than six structures. One of Guatemala's largest megachurches, Familia de Dios plays the leading role in Guatemala's only Evangelical television station, Canal 27, the studios of which have been developed and hosted by the congregation from the beginning. The congregation, which currently meets in two spaces on opposite ends of the city, also owns a seminary with twenty full- and part-time faculty members and many more students. In 2018, I (Robert) was able to sit down with the director of the seminary, Dr. Rigoberto Galvez, who is also a minister in the church and part of a three-person team handling the six Sunday morning worship services held by the congregation. Perhaps the most remarkable feature of La Familia de Dios and its journey through various worship spaces is the fact that only one of the buildings it has inhabited in the course of its twenty-eight-year history was planned and built as a house of worship. Every other structure—from a former movie theater to a large tent to a former warehouse—was designed for other purposes. Just as remarkable is the fact that the religious building, a large megachurch worship space costing millions of dollars to construct and capable of holding several thousand worshippers at once, was home to the congregation for only about three years. Today the building sits empty, having been declared too dangerous to inhabit by the Guatemalan government after a landslide in 2012.

Dr. Galvez was quick to point out that the building itself is structurally intact and solid, having been built on a solid foundation and engineered to weather earthquakes. But the building sits at the foot of a small mountain that has been gradually populated by land squatters whose makeshift foundations and clearings have diminished the ability of the soil to absorb runoff, creating an erosion problem that eventually created the mudslide that flooded the perimeter of the church. Government institutions like CONRED (the National Emergency and Disaster Service), the Ministry of the Environment, and the local municipality of Mixco, the satellite city adjacent to Guatemala City, informed the church on a Monday that they would no longer be able to use the structure for worship services. This gave the leadership less than a week to determine where to meet the following Sunday. I expressed surprise that the congregation, having invested so heavily in building a structure of its own, had not pushed back against the government's decision to declare the structure uninhabitable, especially since no structural damage was apparent and the church had obtained a license to build on that piece of land. Dr. Galvez responded:

The government was worried that the mountain might erode further. . . .
But even before that, we had begun to notice a phenomenon that from

the beginning, really it was a mistake, humanly speaking, to build there. Because access was by way of the city of Mixco. The town of Mixco was small and had narrow streets, so it was hard for the brothers and sisters to get there. Mixco is a very religious town and Sundays they would sometimes close the streets [for Catholic religious festivals] and so we had to take an alternate route with very steep hills and so cars would get damaged. So our attendance was starting to decrease.

Galvez was admitting that, with just a few years of hindsight, the decision to build a large new sanctuary on the far outskirts of the city had already started to look a little less like the brilliant solution to its "problem" of having to hold multiple services every Sunday. Indeed, after three years of inhabiting the new sanctuary on the outskirts of Mixco, a satellite city adjacent to Guatemala City, the average Sunday attendance at Familia de Dios had fallen from about 7,000 worshippers to about 3,800. Thus, even before the mudslide, and the emergency it created, the leaders of the congregation had begun holding an additional Sunday morning service in a makeshift space closer to the center of Guatemala City and were planning to begin another service in the Hotel Camino Real, a five-star hotel in the business district of the city. Rather than fighting the decision to close the new building, the leaders made the decision to shift their attention to the hotel gathering and the unfinished structure closer to the city proper.

There was just one problem. Although the congregation had already purchased an expensive piece of land, conveniently located on the Roosevelt Highway, and much closer to the city center, the only *finished* building on that plot of land was an office building. After all, the goal of the purchase had been to expand the television studios. Next to the office building, the congregation had nearly completed a five-story parking garage. No matter. For the resourceful congregation, faced with the necessity of finding a space almost overnight for its thousands of members to meet for worship, the parking garage became the solution. The first floor of the basement, just below ground level, was chosen as the ideal space for worship. After all, in an "underground" church, sound technicians could turn up the volume on the PA system for a lively music experience without fear of complaints from the neighbors, as other megachurches have sometimes experienced in Guatemala City. Furthermore, parishioners arriving by private transportation had plenty of parking available and were able to park very close to the "sanctuary" itself. Of course, there were obstacles, both literal and figurative, that needed to be addressed in order to modify a parking garage for worship. Since sound ricochets off concrete, curtains were hung around the perimeter of the worship space and acoustic panels were installed on the ceiling. As can be seen in Figure 6.1, the many large columns were wrapped in fabric, and flat-screen televisions were attached to the back of each in order to ensure that even those sitting directly behind them could observe the speaker or the worship band on the altar. Indeed, when I (Robert) attended a worship service in the space in 2012, I was surprised by how quickly the "strangeness" of meeting in a concrete parking garage seemed to wear off.

In the end, Dr. Galvez described the mudslide as a blessing in disguise. Weekly attendance for the congregation has returned to between 6,000 and 7,000 worshippers showing up to at least one service each week, even though accommodating that many people means filling or nearly filling the 1,800-seat "auditorium" in the parking garage about four times each Sunday and requires considerable efforts at coordination by ministers, worship leaders, ushers, and many others. "The point is," remarked Galvez, "ease of parking made people happy. Parking is incredible because many times [other churches] haven't been able to grow because they lack enough parking." Of course,

Figure 6.1. Looking out from the edge of the stage in the parking-garage-turned-worship-space of La Iglesia de Jesucristo La Familia de Dios.
Photo: Robert Brenneman.

many Guatemalans do not own a car, including many of those worshipping at Familia de Dios, a congregation that has attracted many lower-middle class and working-class Guatemalans, but the location of the parking garage/sanctuary on a main thoroughfare makes it ideal for those arriving by public transit as well. In fact, the congregation has even managed to capitalize on its parking capabilities by renting parking spaces to employees of nearby businesses during the week. Dr. Galvez estimated that by renting between 100 and 150 parking spaces per day at twenty-five quetzals (approximately US$3.50), the congregation generates about US$250,000 annually in parking alone, which helps pay the $5 million mortgage taken in order to purchase the land.

Asked if the congregation's leaders dreamed of building a new space, Dr. Galvez mentioned the dream of building a 2,500-seat auditorium that would not be "improvised" but designed to the specific needs of the congregation and that, by accommodating more people, could help to cut down on the number of services required to accommodate the congregation. The idea would be to follow the lead of another, smaller Guatemalan megachurch called "Vida Real," which recently completed a building in another sector of the city. "And what did they build? The built a very practical building. Modern, acoustical, not expensive, flat, like a theater, but not graded, just flat. A metal structure with sheetrock walls and a platform like a theater, with [stage] curtains, lighting and all. . . . And they can hold 2,500 people. So that's the idea we have." Galvez explained further, making reference to a recent chapter of his published in a book on the future of the megachurch. "The era of the mega-construction is over. I might be wrong, obviously, but I think there won't be any more mega-constructions because it's too difficult to keep up facilities that large. That's why we don't aspire to a megachurch but instead to a medium church." Galvez went further to explain that the congregation expected to continue to meet in different places around the city, perhaps building a network of churches in the style of Willow Creek Community Church of suburban Chicago. The important thing for the congregation seems to be the ability to adapt quickly.

Church of the Resurrection:
Industrial Space to Anglican Worship

"Matter matters." I (Brian) heard this phrase several times while viewing the building of the Church of the Resurrection alongside the executive pastor of operations and generosity. This statement is not intended to refer solely to the sacramental nature of the church's worship—based on the Eucharist and Anglican patterns of worship—but also the way the congregation approaches its building. Multiple features of the church's interior hint at the importance of the physical structure. A prominent wall display titled "Building a Sanctuary of Transformation" explains the original construction of the building and the renovation by the church (with an accompanying three-page architectural tour handout). There are numerous works of art, plus plans in the works for artisans to craft large wooden doors for the main entryway to the sanctuary (since installed after my tour). Furthermore, the church believes the original architecture of the building gave glory to God even if it served manufacturing purposes.

Founded in 1954, Church of the Resurrection is part of the Anglican Church of North America after having left the Episcopal Church in 1993. Starting in 1990, the congregation met in settings that were not their own: a high school, a college chapel, and then another high school for seventeen years. The church now meets in a former manufacturing plant that they own in Wheaton, Illinois. In 1971, Plastofilm opened a facility designed by a student of Mies Van der Rohe, David Haid, and profiled in the *Chicago Sun-Times*. This was a rare industrial facility in Wheaton, a suburb 25 miles west of Chicago better known for its religious character, prohibition on alcohol sales until the mid-1980s, and the county seat in the second most populous county in Illinois.

Acquiring the building and renovating it to suit an Anglican congregation took some work. The building, shown in Figure 6.2, changed hands several times before becoming vacant in 2005. A parishioner, also a land developer, saw an advertisement for an auction for the building in late 2010. He asked the church whether he should purchase it, but the church said it did not have the money. Due to some problems with the building, the seller dropped the final price for the building and 4 acres to $400,000. The developer bought it, saying he could use it for his own ends if the church did not act, and the church was able to find the funds.

The church aimed to mold the building into who they were, a religious group interested in sacred and sacramental space as well as simplicity (but beauty within simplicity). Embodying these goals was not easy; one interior designer suggested installing drop ceilings and using primary colors. They renovated the majority of the building and opened the church offices in October 2012 and the sanctuary in December 2012. To highlight the opening

Figure 6.2. The south-facing exterior of Church of the Resurrection.
Photo: Brian J. Miller.

of the sanctuary, the congregation processed on foot from Glenbard West High School, their home for the previous seventeen years, to the former manufacturing plant.

I started to gain a better sense of how "matter matters" to the congregation in my visit to a regular Sunday service on a snowy winter morning. I parked in the lot across from the south entrance, noticed the freight train sitting on the tracks, and walked over to the former industrial building. The front-facing side of the church—running east-west roughly parallel to the railroad tracks that run through downtown Wheaton—is light brick on the first story and then glass windows outlined in black metal on the second story. The two-story entryway, relatively quiet this early on Sunday, has exposed ductwork on the ceiling and intersperses black metal features with cream colored walls. There are multiple tables set up for various ministries to feature their work, as well as a welcome table.

I entered the sanctuary through the largest of the three entryways in the back, walking through metal and glass double doors. Just inside, a baptismal font made of brass with a design made of pressed fingerprints sits on a tile

Jerusalem cross. There is a large candleholder behind the font. In line with the font and candleholder is a black stage with a simple altar and wood cross on it. The sanctuary is large: it holds roughly 925 seats in eight sections (four on the floor, four on risers in the back), has massive ductwork running in four lines from the back to the front, and has two large pillars in the back riser sections to hold up long beams that connect with a large truss just above the front of the stage.

I sat halfway up one of the back sections on risers. From a slightly raised perspective, I could see additional significant physical features of the sanctuary. The stage was indeed large; the width and depth dwarfed the two performers on bassoon and piano playing a prelude at stage right. Lighting in the sanctuary came both from regularly placed lights hanging down from the ceiling as well as plentiful early morning sunlight streaming through the long window running the whole length of the sanctuary on the south side. (While giving the sanctuary a more open feeling, the large window can be harmful: the church had recently purchased screens because sunlight had damaged dozens of the upholstered chairs in the sanctuary.)

The Anglican service, centered around the liturgy found in the Book of Common Prayer, started at 8:30 a.m. and people trickled in through multiple doorways (including from a children's area on one side where mothers with young children could participate in the service behind a large glass window) during prayer, song, and Scripture readings. With the singing of the doxology preceding the Eucharist, the musicians at stage right expanded in number. Joining four singers, a pianist, a cellist, and a choir of about ten people were a drummer (encased in a plexiglass enclosure) and a bassist. Additionally, the male singer at the far right started playing an acoustic guitar. To serve the Eucharist, the church has eight serving stations of bread and wine for attendees to access. The congregation sang four songs during communion. This provided enough time for the large congregation to make their way to the serving stations and back to their seats, while also providing the primary extended worship time in the service. By the third song, some attendees were standing and raising their hands, and the whole congregation was asked to rise for the final number. The singing from the congregation was strong. After the dismissal at 9:55 a.m., the postlude again featured the bassoon/ piano pairing that played before the service.

The sound was clear throughout, coming from two large stacks of seven speakers hung from the ceiling on each side of the stage, several small speakers on the stage for the first rows of the congregation, and three speakers high up on each wall perpendicular to the stage where the congregational singing, picked up on shotgun mics, was played back into the sanctuary.

As the church prepared for another service at 10:30 a.m., I wandered out of the sanctuary. I passed through the Rez Café. A long line of people waited for coffee and other treats from a setup featuring stainless steel appliances and a hip aesthetic. The seating area with tables and chairs was nearly full. People eager to get to the next service passed, others chatted, and still other headed off to classrooms. Children were present everywhere, and they had some space in a large room just beyond the café to run around.

Given the design of the building, if you enter the church from the east doors (rather than the south doors with the two-story narthex closest to the sanctuary), you might think it is a something other than a church. The all-glass entry opens to the Rez Café to the left—which, from my Sunday morning observations, appears to be a primary social space for the congregation—and a main black staircase straight ahead. If you take the stairs, you enter a loft-like suite with receptionists at the top of the stairs. Looking around, there are several large conference rooms—named "Acts 1" and "Acts 2"—as well as numerous offices and cubicles. My meeting with the executive pastor of operations and generosity started in his tall-ceilinged office with exposed ductwork.

During my tour of the church, I heard "matter matters" as well as two additional themes: enhancing the existing space, in addition to creating more space as the congregation needs. The plans for the main entry to the sanctuary illustrate how space can be enhanced to influence religious experiences. Outside the sanctuary entry are ten pieces of art made by church members depicting the ten readings from the Easter Vigil, a particularly important service of celebration for this congregation. The church is awaiting two carved wooden doors for the central entrance to the sanctuary, which would replace the black framed glass doors. The new doors will be made by artisans in Indonesia. Additionally, an archway will be installed above the new doors when they are ready. Both the doors and the arch will feature images of Christ. A special display, shown in Figure 6.3, shows the story of the building and its transformation.

The spacious former industrial facility offers more unfinished space if the congregation desires it. Due to limited funds, several large spaces (just under one-third of the building in total) were left relatively untouched with the initial renovations. The architects drew up a second phase of plans that could be enacted later. Even with a range of extra spaces for youth and children, as

Figure 6.3. Display wall, "Building a Sanctuary of Transformation," in a prominent place in the Church of the Resurrection.
Photo: Brian J. Miller.

well as a prayer chapel behind the sanctuary, a voluminous sacristy, plenty of seating outside the Rez Café, and an open gym space in the northeast corner of the building, more space could be helpful as the church expands and various ministries develop. For example, I heard about how a 200-seat wedding chapel could complement the spacious sanctuary that may be too big for many nuptials.

Transforming a place of industry and labor into a sacred space is not easy. Church of the Resurrection believes it has done so in such a way that both honors the building's original design as well as the congregation's faith tradition and current practices. Where once stood a symbol of American industry now stands a building intended to point people toward God.

The Islamic Center of Vermont:
From Horse Barn to Mosque

When the US Department of War approved the construction of a military fort for its Third Cavalry Regiment in 1894, it could hardly have imagined that one of the buildings in the massive complex of large red-brick structures would one day house a mosque. Perhaps even harder to fathom would be the notion that a horse barn—not any of the stately colonial mansions at the front of the complex—would provide such a sanctuary. But that is what took place. I (Robert) sat down with two lay leaders of the Islamic Center of Vermont in the upper floor of the building that they refer to as their *masjid*, or mosque. An undergraduate student of mine who belongs to the congregation had set up the interview for a Saturday evening on a blustery day in April. I entered the building, shown in both its historic and contemporary form in Figures 6.4 and 6.5, through a small addition at the front of the structure, where I was immediately confronted with a mound of shoes and floor-to-ceiling cubbies filled with shoes. I removed my own shoes and entered a hallway filled with fluorescent light and redolent with the smell of delicious dishes that were being served to members of all ages in a large room close to the entrance. In the hallway, a large poster provided instructions on how to pray properly, and at the end of the hall was a wide-open space also lit with fluorescent light fixtures embedded in a sea of white ceiling tiles. Wall-to-wall

Figure 6.4. A 1917 postcard with hand-colored photograph shows three of the stables built for the Fort Ethan Allen Cavalry Post in 1894 at a cost of $10,611.48 for each structure. The structure on the left is likely the one currently used by the Islamic Center of Vermont.

Photo: Fort Ethan Allen Museum. Used with permission.

Figure 6.5. Exterior of the mosque of the Islamic Society of Vermont.
Photo: Robert Brenneman.

carpeting was covered further with large oriental rugs. This space, the prayer room reserved for men, was mostly empty, as communal prayer was still more than an hour away. Most people were still enjoying the potluck. After I was introduced via my student liaison, my hosts led me to the second floor, where we took our seats on the floor, discussed the project, signed waivers, and began the interview. In addition to the student facilitator, my hosts were Nadim, a male former president of the society who migrated from Bosnia in the 1990s, along with Adeela, a female leader who is originally from India and now directs the Society's Sunday school program for children.[1] I asked them to explain how the community came to call this building home. Nadim explained: "This building was purchased in 1998 and the community was very small at that time. There were not many Muslims here, it was, you know, a few families around here, maybe let's say twenty or thirty families or something like that. . . . So between 1993 and 2008, that's the period that Muslims arrived here."

Adeela added, "Before the building was bought, what they did is some committee people had a house. They met in a house every Friday for prayer.

So they had thirty-five or forty people attending and maybe the men would go to somebody's basement or something like that."

Nadim pointed out that, in addition to meeting in the basements of members' homes, some members of the community would sometimes meet at the Chapel of Saint Michael Archangel at Saint Michael's College, less than a mile from the mosque: "Saint Michael's College allowed this because there was [sic] not many Muslims at that time, so maybe ten people would go to the chapel and pray in the chapel." When more Muslim families began arriving, many of them through the Refugee Resettlement Office located just a few blocks from the Center, the community began looking for a more adequate home—one that would allow them to have separate prayer rooms for men and women and that could provide some permanence as a meeting place. Eventually, the community learned of the space for sale: 5,000 square feet of unfinished warehouse space comprising the front third of a former horse barn in Fort Ethan Allen. The price was $180,000, a princely sum for the small band of recently arrived immigrants. Even more concerning was the fact that, as a Muslim community, a mortgage was out of the question since it involved paying interest. Nadim explained:

> It took a little while of time because when they started collecting money they used to go from home to home and come to knock on the doors and say, "Can you contribute for a building?" You know, "The building's going to cost $180,000," you know. "Can you chip in?" And they said, "Here is a hundred bucks or five hundred bucks or one thousand dollars." So that's how it started everything, going from home to home and you know talking to the Muslim people and saying, "We need the money. Can you contribute anything?" After a while, we collected $180,000 and then we purchased the building through the agency, and then start[ed] slowly, building everything, working inside—walls, sheetrock, carpet, painting. That was all of the work. Everybody chipped in, two hours, half a day, one day, working inside.

Since the upstairs area was in less disarray, the work began there. Carpeting was installed, a curtain was hung to provide separation for the sexes, and prayers began. Later, the arrival of more Muslims to the community prompted the congregation to focus its attention on the first floor, installing new windows, sheetrock, carpet, even electrical and plumbing work for restrooms and a kitchen. Eventually, the upstairs would become the space for women's prayer while the downstairs would house the kitchen, restrooms, and the men's prayer space. Nearly all of the labor for transforming and finishing the space was donated by members of the community. As Adeela explained: "Everyone was assigned to work on what they had experience with. You couldn't do what you didn't know how to do." Nadim added, "We have electricians, we have plumbers in the community [so they did that work] while everyone else did whatever they knew how to do." Women washed windows, took care of children, and prepared meals for the volunteers.

By the first decade of the 2000s, the space had been transformed and could serve as both a worship space and a space for celebrating meals, especially during the communal celebrations at Ramadan. But the community continued to grow, and in 2014 the congregation made the decision to purchase the rest of the building, this time at a cost of $750,000. According to Nadim:

> We had a general meeting again, we're talking, "Can we collect that money. What are we going to do? This is a chance because . . . this isn't easy for us to collect. . . . So we decide[d], "Yes, we're going to go for it you know." That was a new board and new president and they sat down as a team and they finally got a lawyer and they put down everything on paper you know and then finally it was signed by him, the lawyer, by our side.

Part of the reason for having a lawyer present was the need to draw up an agreement that would give the Society enough time to raise the full funds and thus avoid paying interest. A six-month plan was created, but when the community needed more time, the seller allowed for a three-month extension so that within less than one year, the Vermont Muslim community—a community that had grown to a size of approximately 250 women, men, and children—had raised three-quarters of a million dollars and was able to pay the full price of the remaining 10,000 square feet of the building. I asked my hosts if the option of finding a new piece of land on which to build a new building had ever been seriously discussed by the congregation.

NADIM: No. When we put all the cards on the table, the money was the number one issue. I mean, it was just the ideas from the people, but when we thought how much money it was going to cost us, then, maybe $1.5 million between the land and building, and it's going to take years and years to build. Some people said, "It's pretty obvious."

ADEELA: After twenty years, the people, they're used to being here. [They say] "This is *our* mosque."

ROBERT: This is what people know—where to come.

ADEELA: This is really a standard place too. But in terms of unity, this is the central place. We make it a community.

Summing up, Nadim added, "The main reason is the money. If I had two million, I would put it into starting from scratch. But the main reason is money. We don't have the money to start from scratch. There's this generation. Maybe a new generation, they're going to start."

When I asked Nadim to explain why starting from scratch would be better if the congregation had the money, he responded:

That would be much better because if you have a space, then you're going to put a fence around it, and you can have a park for kids to play. Maybe you can build a gym and during the winter you can play basketball, soccer in the gym, so you can have a complete center. Maybe you can have day care for the kids. So that's what I think, you know?

Clearly, the Islamic Society of Vermont, the state's only English-speaking mosque—a small group of Somali elders meets for prayer above a storefront in nearby Winooski—has made a bet on practicality. Not that the congregation has given up hope for the possibility of building at some point in the future. But for now, the leaders of the community seem satisfied with having a large space with which to work. Remodeling, which allows the congregation to save large sums of money by harnessing donated labor and advancing at their own pace, continues to proceed for the rear portion of the building, some of which is already being used for the thriving Sunday school program under Adeela's direction. Although it never came up in the interview, I wondered if perhaps the Islamic Society was attracted precisely by the nondescript nature of this building. After all, the structure is located off the main road in a cluster of late-nineteenth-century buildings that house college and medical school students, the Refugee Resettlement Office, Vermont Public Radio, and Vermont Public Television. In post 9/11 US society, there can be serious risks, both political and physical, to building structures that are "recognizably" Muslim.

As our interview came to a close, the scripture recitation, sung by a young woman in the next room, began to fill the space, amplified by a high-wattage

PA system. Thanking my hosts for their time and transparency, I followed them back downstairs, where kitchen cleanup was temporarily halted so that a plate heaped with lentils and curried rice could be prepared for me and sent home for my family. With that, the prayers began.

The Edge: Corporate Worship in a High School Auditorium

After a Sunday morning service of the Edge, I (Brian) stood on the high school stage talking with some of the leaders of the church. Kids ran around the stage and the voluminous backstage area, congregants lingered in the auditorium seats, and a few church members packed up music gear on the stage. Much of my conversation took place with Taylor, one of the church's elders and a regular drummer in the church's band. He told me that the church had just finalized plans to start holding Friday night music practices at a nearby church rather than meet one and a half to two hours before the Sunday services to practice. I knew from our earlier conversation that the church regularly schedules meetings throughout the week but because they do not own a building, they utilize houses, other church buildings, and for two years even made use of unused office space for prayer meetings in a building an attendee owned.

For Sunday worship, the Edge meets at Metea Valley High School. The Edge is a church in Aurora, Illinois, that proclaims on its website, "We pursue the perpetual edge where God's manifest glory incites a response from us, his children, through the power and work of the Holy Spirit." On a typical weekday, the school is home to over 2,800 students in the Indian Prairie School District serving suburban Naperville and Aurora, Illinois. Opened in August 2009, it is a large high school campus, surrounded by numerous subdivisions built in recent decades and located close to an interchange on Interstate 88.

Many religious congregations in the United States utilize buildings that they lease, rent, or borrow from secular organizations, including public school buildings. The Edge is one of these congregations. Since their founding in the 1990s, the Edge has never owned its own structure. This has not stopped church leaders from having regular discussions about acquiring their own building, but, even with their growth (now having between 150 and 200 attendees at their Sunday service), they continue to meet in the auditorium of this high-performing high school. To this point, leaders have looked at various options where they could make a building their own, but they choose to continue to worship in a high school. This has consequences for what the church can do and be.

Walking into the school on a snowy Sunday morning presented reminders of both the religious community as well as the school setting. Several men held the door open for me, and members of the congregation were drinking coffee and eating snacks in the two-story school lobby before the service began. It is a light space; the second story has semitransparent panels that brighten the wide hallways that run around the auditorium. The lobby has multiple reminders of the school: trophy cases, signs for different academic departments, windows for the main office, and even glimpses of lockers just down the hall to the right. There is one information table where I was greeted (and I grabbed a one-page guide for visitors) and several high-top tables nearby where parents gathered and kids ran around.

I entered the auditorium, shown in Figure 6.6, by the nearest door, with a bulletin in hand. It is a sizable space; a sign near the entrance says it has a maximum capacity of 930 people. A main walkway in the middle separates the floor seats in the front, with a second set of stadium seats in the back. The color scheme is gray—concrete blocks on the first half of the walls, acoustic panels on the top portions of the walls as well as mounted on the ceiling, and a large stage in the front. The lights were dimmed. A five-member band, casually dressed, was playing on the stage. From stage right to stage left, the band included a standing keyboard player, a female vocalist, a male guitarist who was also leading the singing, a bassist, and a drummer in the back with a more acoustic set of percussion instruments. While the service started at 9:30 a.m., it took a good five to ten minutes for the majority of attendees to leave their coffee and conversation and join the worship. The congregation skewed young and mostly white. There were a lot of children. In my khaki pants and tucked-in short-sleeve button-down shirt, I looked more formal than most.

The worship time with dimmed lights and words on a large screen behind the band proceeded for roughly half an hour. Several songs from Bethel Church—the evangelical music de jour from a congregation in northern California—went on for six to nine minutes in length, as the band regularly changed dynamics as they alternated between chorus and bridge and on and on. The auditorium provides ample opportunity for worshippers to spread out and some, like me, took advantage of seats further away from the main cluster of people. Yet, all attendees appeared to be engaged in the worship,

Figure 6.6. The auditorium of Metea Valley High School, viewed from the topmost seats stage left and with no curtains on the stage.
Photo: Brian J. Miller.

particularly in the front left section of the auditorium where there were more raised hands and movement to the music.

Pastor Steve, dressed in a blue plaid shirt, grey skinny pants, black Converse shoes, black knit hat, shoulder length straight hair, black glasses, and microphone over his ear, provided the sermon on prayer. He moved around the stage, but the platform's size would require significant movement for a preacher to cover fully. At 10:58 a.m., the band was asked to come back on the stage and Pastor Steve told a final story of a British hero of the faith who recorded over 10,000 answered prayers in his lifetime. The band played one more song. Short announcements followed, and the service was over at 11:13 a.m. The lights came back up, and recorded worship music played for the next thirty minutes or so. The band and others worked to clean up the stage, put everything on carts, and wheeled them through the backstage area, where they could be loaded through a large overhead door into a trailer. The kid's classrooms, down and around a corner from the auditorium in a single hallway, teemed with activity after the service as parents retrieved their kids and the families marched back to the front entry next to the school office. Slowly, the kid's workers packed up their items and wheeled them to the backstage area for loading. A Sunday that began at 7 a.m. with the unloading of the church's trailer would soon come to a close.

Meeting in the high school offers certain advantages to the congregation. Taylor said worshipping in the school offers the church flexibility. Conversations with other local church leaders highlighted the challenges that owning a building can present. This congregation is no stranger to using buildings that are not their own. The congregation started as a men's small group, meeting a couple of Saturday nights a month at a suburban church. They formally founded a separate congregation in 2010 and they met at the Hollywood Palms Movie Theater in Naperville. (This is a unique venue for a religious congregation: according to the theater's website, the three-story lobby is filled with palm trees from Miami and other tropical plants and the individual theaters have themed decorations such as the Witch's Castle from the *Wizard of Oz* and an Egyptian palace complete with the ark from *Raiders of the Lost Ark*.) That church started with about forty adults and ten kids and grew quickly. Needing more space, several attendees who worked at the local school district helped the church inquire about using different school buildings. They reached a month-to-month agreement to use Metea Valley—no long-term agreement has been signed—and the church first started meeting in the school in 2013.

At the same time, Taylor noted that the current arrangement presents challenges. Notably, the church never has complete control over the worship experience. For a congregation that considers corporate worship to be one of its hallmarks, meeting in a school auditorium is limiting. According to Taylor, the floor plan is not as conducive to the kind of intimacy and close worship they had when the small group first started meeting in the 2000s. While they do have a creative team at the church and they work to dress up the stage for special services (Easter, Christmas, etc.), the church has ongoing conversations about how to encourage community during the service. They once had a truss and lighting system for the stage, but it is difficult to set up weekly. They use some of the lighting and sound system of the school auditorium while also setting up their own sound equipment each week. Hearing these challenges described, I wondered: Can the leaders or the congregation truly be who they want to be on Sunday mornings because of a performing space that they cannot truly craft to be their own?

If they could craft a worship space and church from scratch, Taylor noted several important features they would desire. For the worship space, the lighting would be lower, they would have more control over higher quality music, and they would decrease the distance between the stage and the audience. A multipurpose space with stackable chairs and a truss system on the stage could provide more options to vary and customize the experience. They might seek out a unique building; the church had discussed finding an older or abandoned building in or near downtown Aurora in order to more fully integrate themselves into the community. Taylor says they will eventually need youth group space as their full kids' ministry grows older, and office space would be nice. These details suggest that some thought has already gone into how a building the congregation has more ability to shape could more directly connect to perceived needs.

For this younger and relaxed congregation, calling a high school home seems to fit: the church can benefit from the flexibility of not having to pay for or keep up their own building. At the same time, transitioning to being a more mature congregation, one that wants to fully shape the worship experience and provide suitable space for their growing kids, may mean committing to their own building. Perhaps having no permanent building is just part of the early steps of a newer congregation. Or, the choice to invest in goods other than a building may become a long-term feature of the religious group. For now, the stated goal in the welcome brochure of "seeking revival and transformation across Aurora as people encounter the love, power, and truth of Jesus Christ!" will continue to happen through regular Sunday worship services in a local high school.

Holy Transfiguration Antiochian Orthodox Christian Church: A Lutheran Building for an Orthodox Church

Stepping into the sanctuary of Holy Transfiguration and facing the front, Father Wilbur pointed out to me (Brian) the dominant image in the front of the church: the back wall behind the altar and the iconostasis that separates the congregation from the altar has a large image of Mary, the mother of Jesus, with a much smaller Jesus hovering in front of her midsection. Father Wilbur explained that it is not the size of the figures that matters—Mary is certainly larger, a comparison that can be disconcerting to Protestants—but rather the relationship between the two figures. Mary's hands are raised and open while Jesus's fingers are crossed. There are words painted on the wall around Mary: "more spacious than the heavens." This is the Theotokos, an important reminder of the incarnation that is at the core of the Orthodox faith.

This imagery resides in a church building that has only a few exterior signs that it is a unique architectural structure in Warrenville, Illinois. A suburb 30 miles southwest of Chicago, Warrenville has a working-class reputation and a sizable minority of Latino residents. On a corner lot, surrounded by homes on three sides and a baseball field across the street, sits an unassuming older brown house and a small church building. The sanctuary, long, with a pitched roof, and clad in white siding, sits just offset from the home in a structure originally built in 1946 for a Lutheran Church Missouri Synod congregation. Two exterior symbols recently installed on the Lutheran-looking structure give away the more unusual religious group that resides within: an icon of Jesus on the outside of the sanctuary and facing the street, as well as a sign over the main door of the sanctuary with an icon of Jesus and the words "My house is a house of prayer."

The transformation from a traditional, darker wood Lutheran church to an icon-filled, brighter Orthodox space required significant change. I had the sense in my conversation with Father Wilbur that the building was not just a receptacle in which worship and gathering could take place; everything about the interior could help shape an Orthodox understanding of God and the world. The congregation first worshipped at a local college, rented a space in a nearby suburb, bought a building several years later, and then purchased the Warrenville structure in 1999. A photo album in the church basement contains images of the original Lutheran building.

The Orthodox sanctuary is now quite different than it was for its previous occupants. The open altar of the Lutheran church has been replaced by an Orthodox altar behind a floor-to-ceiling iconostasis. The dark wood pews are gone, replaced by cushioned metal chairs in three sections sitting on oriental-looking rugs. There is now an open space between the iconostasis and the first seats, with a large chandelier hanging from the ceiling. The darker walls and ceiling are now gold and blue. The peaked roof is still there, though hanging from the center of the sanctuary is a large disc with the image of Jesus Christ Pantocrator, installed in September 2017. Behind the altar is not a cross but the Theotokos.

Still, the transformation is a work in progress. More funds from a fairly small congregation would be helpful for the priest and congregation to realize their vision. A memorial gift in the tens of thousands of dollars to change the building into an identifiable Orthodox church helped make possible some of the more recent changes. At the same time, a full transformation could be costly: one architect proposed a $7 million plan. The Christ Pantocrator that hangs above the congregation, shown in Figure 6.7, would traditionally be a dome in an Orthodox church. As Father Wilbur explained, the Orthodox dome suggests that God came down, while the peaked roof of Western churches suggests that God is up there. While the Pantocrator disc is not ideal, a Beirut iconographer said putting in the dome would not be worth it, and the church's efforts to look into a cupola for the front of the building produced costly estimates. In a few months following my visit, the church planned to add a five-foot-high gold cross to the top of the sanctuary facing the main street. Further down the wish list are other items that would require varying levels of efforts and funds to attain: new wood chairs for the sanctuary as the upholstered ones do not work well with all the candles they use, adding the "Holy, holy, holy" scene from Isaiah 6 to the ceiling, wooden doors for the main sanctuary entrance (rather than what Father Wilbur describes as doors that look like they belong in a dentist's office), expanding the narthex 25 feet out from the back of the church, and purchasing the house next door to serve as a home for the priest.

Entering the church on a crisp late-winter morning, the smell of incense was strong as I (Brian) walked up a half flight of stairs and turned to the right into the back of the sanctuary. There was a hazy glow: all the lights were on, including the chandelier in front of the iconostasis, the candles in front of all of the icons were aflame, and sunlight was coming through the translucent windows on both sides of the sanctuary. The majority of attendees were seated in the middle rear section, including the core group of singers just behind a music stand for the leader, and other attendees filled in around them as they arrived.

The Psalms service immediately transitioned into the Divine Liturgy at 10 a.m. and I was grateful for the service guide handed to me in the back. The priest entered with a red chasuble with gold trim while the deacon wore purple vestments. The Orthodox service bore some resemblance in order to a Catholic or Anglican service, but it had numerous unique features, including many sung prayers and liturgical elements, standing for the majority of the service (outside of the sermon), and significant periods when the deacon and priest were facing the altar and the Theotokos rather than the congregation. The service included a homily, coming forward for the bread and wine, and a veneration of a wooden cross placed on a table in front of the iconostasis.

Figure 6.7. The front of the nave of Holy Transfiguration Antiochian Orthodox Christian Church.
Photo: Brian J. Miller.

The congregation was white and featured some women with head coverings. Several small children played under supervision in a gated area in the back. After the service concluded around 11:50 a.m., the congregation headed to the basement under the sanctuary for their weekly meal together.

As I settled in for the drive home, several features of the building and its effects on the worship experience came to the forefront as I considered my experience. The lighting was consistent throughout the service, with no changes to brightness or which lights were used. Particularly compared to more austere or darker Protestant settings, the color palette and ornamentation stood out: the blue and gold surfaces alongside icons, wood, and red rugs provided a warm atmosphere. The sound included singing and speaking, with no amplification or instruments. It was not difficult to hear the clergy or congregation at any point. At multiple points, the congregation prayed or sang, while at the same time the priest and deacon offered spoken prayers in the front. The service had numerous repeated songs, as well as unique pieces led by a choir of three to eight members (it was difficult to tell exactly who was in the choir as the participants rotated at points, and several musical pieces explicitly featured cantors while most did not). The physical spacing of clergy and attendees did vary: the priest and leaders operated both in front and behind the iconostasis, and the congregation came forward twice. The incense added an olfactory element.

To try to embody the immanence of God that the Orthodox sanctuary is intended to present is indeed a project in what used to be a Missouri Synod Lutheran church. Compared to the two other sites I visited, Anglican and non-denominational evangelical places of worship, that worked with more blank or secular canvasses in terms of their buildings, the importance in the Orthodox congregation of a certain physical structure seemed to both constrain and enable possibilities for renovation of the building. On one hand, the former Lutheran structure required significant changes, and some alterations to fully develop an Orthodox building may be truly prohibitive given the starting structure. On the other hand, making incremental changes to a structure originally intended for a different religious group allows for deliberation about necessary or desirable changes at every step of the way. Father Wilbur summed up this tension when he described wanting to leave a legacy of a beautiful Orthodox building but done in an American style. This church building is likely to be a work in progress as its physical structure continues to shape and influence the worship of its Antiochian Orthodox inhabitants.

Learning from Space Benders

What can we learn from these five cases of congregational "space-bending"? One important lesson is that for some congregations, including some notably vibrant congregations, symbolism matters a lot less than one might think.

For the members of the Islamic Society of Vermont no less than for those of Guatemala's Familia de Dios, having adequate space to gather is far more important than having a space that communicates a theological message. The mosque in Vermont has neither dome nor minarets and looks nearly identical to the doggie day-care center and the landscape vendor sitting directly adjacent on either side of it. And yet, the society's members who made such significant financial sacrifices to purchase it, now call it home and refer to it as their mosque. Similarly, members of Familia de Dios eventually showed their preference for a convenient location above a religious building designed and built for worship. Furthermore, the Edge meets in a school that for most of the week provides little indication of serving as a worship space. Congregants from traditions as diverse as neo-Pentecostal Christianity and Sunni Islam and non-denominational American evangelicalism and in contexts as distinct as Guatemala and Vermont appear to value convenience and can even grow emotionally attached to a building that has little to offer aesthetically.

Additionally, congregations may often end up in another religious group's building or another kind of building altogether because of resource constraints. Building a new physical structure can be both time-consuming and expensive. The construction process involves decision-making on the part of the congregation about what they desire and want to commit to, working with possibly an architect, developer, and builder, raising funds, waiting for the structure to be completed, and then adjusting and tweaking the new building. The financial cost can be high, including significant mortgages or sacrifice on the part of the congregation. A long-term commitment is necessary in order to pay for and maintain the structure. Adapting an existing building to their own use can shorten the process of finding a suitable place to worship. Forgoing a new structure can lead to cost savings. The funds that otherwise might have gone into a new building could then be redeployed to other needs facing the congregation.

Of course, the fact that bending non-religious space toward religious uses *can* work in diverse contexts does not mean that doing so will necessarily work for every tradition or every context. Not every religious person would be eager to worship in an underground parking garage or pray in a renovated horse barn. But these congregations also show a remarkable resourcefulness that recognizes the potential for *transforming* space. Buildings do not have to begin as spaces for worship and religious experiences; they can become such spaces through the use of interior materials and equipment as well as the arrangement of bodies within that space. None of these five congregations made significant changes to the exterior or the footprint of the building, yet interior alterations could take the building down to its basic walls and roof and set up new conditions for which later social scenes would take place. Transforming interior space can transform experiences and consciousness. As the sociologist Randall Collins (2004) has argued, borrowing from Emile Durkheim (1995 [1903]) before him, something quite extraordinary can happen when many human bodies converge in one space, gathering in close proximity, with physical and aural barriers to outsiders, and sharing a mood and single focus of attention shaped by a mutual desire to celebrate and pay homage to something larger than themselves. In fact, gathering repeatedly under these conditions is part of what imbues a space with a sense of sacredness.

Still, it is worth noting that congregations that successfully use buildings they did not build can continue to dream of building a space of their own, one that is designed specifically to their own needs as a community. Thus, it seems that space bending is rarely the "first choice" of a religious community, but rather a pathway that is chosen by some congregations in certain situations as a "meanwhile" solution to a need for space.

It may seem obvious to state, but in order to renovate or alter an existing structure, a religious congregation needs to be able to find a building to rent or purchase. Not only do groups need to clear regulatory hurdles (see Chapter 4), there has to be a supply of structures that could be relatively easily modified for a new religious group to use. The next chapter approaches this issue: What happens to older church buildings, and how many of them are used by their original congregations or different congregations?

7

Aging in Place over Eight-Plus Decades

Adjacent to numerous University of Chicago buildings sits University Church.[1] The history page on the website for the church begins with its founding in 1894: "He gathered a few people together and formed a branch of the Christian Church (Disciples of Christ) in Hyde Park, directly next to the university" (University Church 2020). Featured in several architecture guides to Chicago, the church still sits in this same location at the northeast corner of S. University Avenue and E. 57th Street in Hyde Park. Noted Chicago area architect Howard Van Doren Shaw designed the medieval building and it was completed in 1923 (Greene 1998). The front page of the website (at the time when this chapter was first drafted in 2015) said the congregation is "a Christian community affirming the transformative power of God's love, which calls us individually and collectively to act for justice and to respect all creation" (University Church 2019). Yet, at the time, the website devoted little attention to the physical structure of the church. Even as the website listed "community & space" as one of its defining values, it was referring not to the physical space and building, but rather the social space the church provides: " 'You made me feel at home better than any other church I've experienced.' This is visitor feedback we take seriously as a multicultural congregation" (University Church 2015). Why, in a city almost obsessive about its architecture, would a church building constructed nearly a century ago by a noted architect and adjacent to one of the premier institutions of higher learning in the United States receive limited attention on the website of the congregation that has worshipped there for nearly a century? More recently, the updated website (June 2019) now features, as part of a rotating gallery of pictures, an image of an entry, which is connected to a 125th anniversary celebration.

Were we to take an 80-minute drive northwest to the small suburb of East Dundee, we would find Immanuel Lutheran Church. This Lutheran Church Missouri Synod structure has looked down on the Fox River for over a century from a location two blocks east of the waterway at the southwest corner of Main Street and Van Buren Street. The history page of the church's website tells of the congregation's founding in 1862 and says the current church

Building Faith. Robert Brenneman and Brian J. Miller, Oxford University Press (2020). © Oxford University Press.
DOI: 10.1093/oso/9780190883447.001.0001

building "was completed in 1886 at a cost of $25,000 and to this day continues to be our spiritual center and home" (Immanuel Lutheran Church & School 2014). The home page for the congregation has sizable images of the light brick, Gothic Revival church building and the red brick religious school. The history page contains a historic photograph of the church alongside numerous pictures of the school building and classes of children. The text on the history page describes the role of the building and congregation: "Immanuel Lutheran Church stands as a beacon of hope used powerfully by God to draw people closer to Christ" (Immanuel Lutheran Church & School 2014). What motivates a congregation with an average of 750 Sunday attendees in a small community of less than 3,000 residents to highlight their structure so prominently on their website?

Heading back to the city's southern suburbs on our tour of some of Chicagoland's older religious buildings, we find First Presbyterian Church of Homewood. This church in a third denomination, Presbyterian Church (USA), is located in a suburb roughly 25 miles south from the center of Chicago. The congregation's home page features two large images of the church building, one featuring members of the congregation on the front steps of the colonial structure and another without members. The history page tells of the first group of Presbyterians who formed in the community in June 1858 and soon built a simple structure. The page features images of two subsequent church buildings at the same location, one dedicated in 1915 and the second, "modeled after New England churches," which hosted its first service in 1958. Even with the emphasis on the changing buildings, the history page minimizes the importance of the structures: "Amid the history of buildings and structures, one thing has remained constant: the amazing, faithful people who ARE the church" (First Presbyterian Church of Homewood 2019). Unusually for the long-standing church buildings under consideration in this chapter, the building is not located on a street corner, and the church is flanked by and faces single-family homes in a variety of styles, including Cape Cods, ranches, and bungalows. In this congregation with over 150 years of history, how does a building constructed in the 1950s influence the actions of the congregation? See Figures 7.1, 7.2, and 7.3 for the websites of the three congregations discussed here.

That all three of these religious buildings are still at the same location as decades ago—albeit with changes, as exemplified by a new structure in Homewood or award-winning renovations in East Dundee (Cramer and Yankopolus 2006:159)—suggests that the buildings play an important role

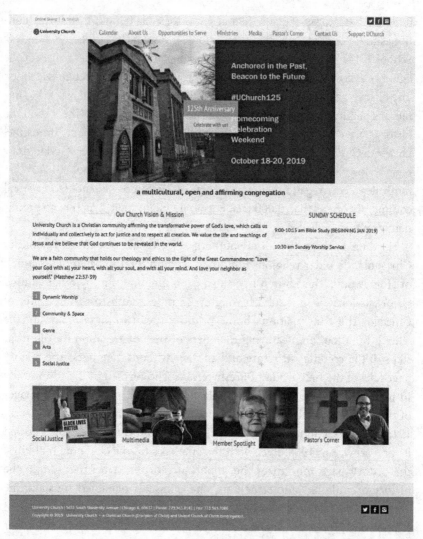

Figure 7.1. The home page for University Church, Chicago. The rotating stories at the top of the page highlight the identity of church and its various ministries. In this particular story about the 125th anniversary of the church, the stone building is featured.

Retrieved June 20, 2019, at http://universitychurchchicago.org/.

Figure 7.2. The history page for Immanuel Lutheran Church of Dundee. The page featured numerous images of older buildings alongside a written narrative. Retrieved January 22, 2016, at http://immanuel-ed.org/our-history/.

in the life of these religious congregations over a lengthy period. In this chapter, we argue that buildings matter in present moments as well as over time. Religious buildings shape current realities for religious groups with direct influences on practices and experiences, while also embodying historical methods and values. In the three examples to start this chapter involving older Chicago area congregations, their building could serve as an anchor, a calling card, a shaper of who they are and will be, or it could be a background characteristic or the material shell in which more important things happen. Put another way, a long-standing congregation or a new religious group looking to use an older religious building must contend with how the

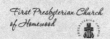

First Presbyterian Church of Homewood

HOME   ABOUT US   MEMBERSHIP   EDUCATION   OUTREACH   WORSHIP   FELLOWSHIP   CONTACT

History

Our History

First Presbyterian Church of Homewood

Our church dates back to 1858, when Homewood was already a railroad town (which was, at the time, called Thornton Station). A visiting preacher, in June of that year, planted the seed among a small group of individuals who slowly began to organize a congregation as First Presbyterian Church of Thornton Station.

A modest wooden building was eventually built to house the fledgling group, but over the next decade it suffered from lack of maintenance and the congregation dwindled, but did not die.

After the Civil War, prospects for our church began to improve. The village was renamed Homewood in 1869, and our name officially became First Presbyterian Church of Homewood between 1871 and 1873. During this time, parking problems arose – for member's horses, that is! Sheds were built as a solution. Also, a worship offering was just as likely to include a sack of potatoes, a crate of chickens or farm produce, as it was currency.

As the congregation grew, so did the need for a larger structure. In May, 1915, a new church building was dedicated to provide much-needed room. Interestingly, the building from the 1860's was moved and recycled – twice – first as an automotive repair shop, and later as apartments. The new church provided a beautiful room for worship, as well as space for the choir, church school and fellowship activities.

Over the next four decades, growth of our church mirrored the growth of our community. In October 1958, the current sanctuary, which was modeled after New England churches, held a worship service for the first time. Thanks to impressive fund raising efforts, improvements such as a pipe organ, air conditioning and elevator for handicap accessibility have been added - making a beautiful structure all the more appealing and hospitable for worship and reflection.

The need for more church school space was addressed in 1972, when the new Christian Education building was constructed. For all of the joy having this modern space in which to educate our youth provided, its construction necessitated the razing of the 1915 building.

This was a sad occasion for many, as it signaled the loss of an old friend, just as it was the beginning of a new and exciting period in our history.

Amid the history of buildings and structures, one thing has remained constant: the amazing, faithful people who ARE the church. Our leaders, both lay and clergy, have consistently ensured that First Presbyterian serves the needs of its members, as well as the community-at-large.

The mission and outreach activities of this congregation, well-documented in our 2008 published history, remain a core strength. It is an immense source of joy to all that we have touched lives not only in our village, but in remote parts of the globe as well.

For over 150 years, our congregation has responded to God's call, lifting hearts upward in worship, reaching hands outward in mission, and moving lives forward in faith in Jesus Christ. We prayerfully continue the journey, hoping to build a better world through our mission and ministry for the sake of the gospel.

A history book was written in 2008 for our church's 150th anniversary. Copies are available for purchase through the church historian, Phil Dillman. Contact the church office for more information at 708-798-0490 or fpchw@sbcglobal.net.

Please read about the history of the Presbyterian Church (USA). Click here and you'll be directed to their website.

Figure 7.3. The history page for First Presbyterian Church of Homewood. A written narrative accompanies six images of the church building, five exterior images and one interior shot, over the years.

Retrieved June 20, 2019, at http://www.fpchw.org/history.html.

building shapes worship and fellowship, even as changes can be made to the structure (as illustrated in the previous chapter with the Orthodox group transforming a Lutheran Church Missouri Synod building).

To address this continuity and influence of religious buildings and to build upon previous chapters that looked at religious structures under construction, this chapter asks two foundational questions: How do religious buildings fare over eight-plus decades in a changing American metropolitan region? Additionally, how do the congregations that used these buildings for decades present these structures on their websites? Answering both of these questions provides insights into the building energy for congregations that have made use of the same buildings for decades.

Few scholars have examined these dimensions of aging church buildings. Scholarship on broad trends in Protestant architecture, such as by religious studies scholar Jeanne Kilde (2002, 2008), historian Richard Kieckhefer (2004), and scholars Anne Loveland and Otis Wheeler (2003), highlight important changes across denominations and traditions. Separate denominations provided funds for church building, planning guides (as an example, the Lutheran Church Missouri Synod produced multiple documents; see The Committee on Church Architecture 1956; The Commission on Church Architecture 1965), and consultants, and similar architectural aesthetics thus could be repeated throughout regions or the entire country (Kilde 2002:72–74; Price 2013). Megachurches illustrate how even what looks like new architectural aims can incorporate traditional design as well as more modern aesthetics (Thumma and Travis 2007) that build on prior designs. As sociologist David Eagle notes, "Protestants had long built large, multi-purpose buildings that housed a host of religious and worldly services under one roof" (2015:601).

Outside of a comprehensive study of religious buildings in Cook County, Illinois, by geographers Wilbur Zelinsky and Stephen Matthews (2011), few have compared religious buildings within entire denominations in a large region, instead focusing on either geographic areas, many kinds of religious buildings, or case studies (Gallagher 2005; Vergara 2005; Konieczny 2009; Krieger 2009; Day 2014). Religious buildings played an important part of the suburbanization of religion; they offered new spaces in which congregations could worship, enhance community life, and establish a presence in the community (Diamond 2000; Diamond 2003; Miller 2017). These positive aspects of new suburban buildings also had consequences for older urban neighborhoods that congregations left behind: new religious groups and other organizations could utilize the older structures; some of the older religious buildings slowly fell into disrepair and some fell apart or disappeared; and these older structures could serve as reminders of white flight. Of course, a fragmented post-suburban landscape present in numerous American metropolitan regions today can render even relatively new central church buildings much less important than decentralized small groups that meet throughout the region (Wilford 2012).

To answer these important questions regarding the way religious buildings tend to "age in place," this chapter examines the fate of church buildings from four Protestant denominations—Presbyterian, Lutheran Church Missouri Synod, Seventh-day Adventist, and Disciples of Christ—in the Chicago region between 1936 and 2007–2016.

I (Brian) made use of three data sources to look at hundreds of churches in the Chicago region over eight decades. I started with addresses from a 1936 directory published by the Church Federation of Greater Chicago, a regional association of Christian denominations. I used a larger list of these addresses in an earlier project (Miller 2017) and realized I could use the historical address data to help look at the current condition of religious buildings. The decision to include these four denominations follows a simple logic: I wanted a reasonable number of congregations from denominations that reflect theological and liturgical variation but that nevertheless reside within the "mainstream" of Protestant Christianity during the twentieth century. Early English settlers founded what is now the Presbyterian Church (USA), a mainline Protestant denomination, while the Lutheran Church Missouri Synod is a more conservative branch of Lutherans (conservative Protestant rather than mainline Protestant) founded in 1847. The two other denominations are smaller in size: the mainline Protestant Disciples of Christ started in 1832, while the Seventh-day Adventists emerged in the mid-1800s. Given their founding dates, all four groups had opportunities to begin congregations and construct buildings in the Chicago region that grew rapidly in the second half of the nineteenth century.

Working with the 1936 addresses, I then used Google Street View to "visit" these same locations in 2015 and 2016 and to see what became of the religious building. In addition to the savings of time in not having to visit hundreds of church locations spread through an entire region, Street View often offered clear images of religious buildings from multiple angles (notwithstanding the occasional very full tree or blurry image). Using a screenshot of what Google Street View displayed for the address, I coded several pieces of information: (1) whether the church building is still standing;

(2) if the building still exists, whether the 1936 congregation still occupies the building, and if not, how the structure is used; and (3) several architectural features of the building, including the exterior material (red brick, light brick, stone, or wood/siding), whether a steeple and tower are present, and whether the building is located at a street corner.

For the locations where Google Street View showed the same congregation worshipping for over eight decades, I visited their websites and coded multiple aspects of the presentation. Did the front page feature the church building? If so, did it contain images of the exterior, the interior, or stained glass? Does the website have a history page with text or images telling the story of the congregation and/or building? If so, did this page have an image of the exterior or interior of the church? Examining website images was not always easy: Did the image look at the exterior or interior? Was the image meaningful regarding the building, or did the image contain a more generic image, such as part of a brick wall or an ordinary room, or was the emphasis clearly on the people present rather than the building or architectural features? The data in this chapter reflect the contents of the church websites between May and June 2015.

Two of the findings, in particular, help advance our argument regarding the effects of religious buildings on the social interaction and experiences of religious congregations. First, the varying rates of ongoing use of religious buildings by different denominations, as well as the presentations of the structures on the congregation's website, suggests the buildings and physical location have a stronger hold on some religious attendees and congregations compared to others. In other words, in at least some of the cases we studied, a religious building seems to serve the function of an "anchor"—steadying a congregation in time and space during decades of considerable social, religious, and demographic change. In more than a few cases, however, a congregation's building merely reflects a bygone religious past—the "ghosts of Christmases past" if you will—while the congregation has moved on. Our data suggest that evidence for such religious anchoring through a building is more common in some denominations than others. Second, how religious congregations present their structures on their websites provides insights into how they view and are shaped by their own buildings. While some congregations use the building to their advantage—as evidence of a historic tradition or as proof of decades of community involvement—others may intentionally leave the building off the website as they emphasize different features of the congregation. Together, the presence of congregations worshipping in the same buildings, plus engaging and vibrant displays of the buildings on their websites, can indicate an ongoing building energy that may mirror the excitement of new religious construction.

Patterns in Church Buildings over Time

Our analysis starts with the addresses of the 1936 churches to see whether the locations still have a church there, what architectural features that building has, and if the long-standing building is used by the same congregation. The Missouri Synod Lutherans led the way, with the highest percentage of 1936 buildings hosting the same congregations today, followed by Presbyterian and Disciples of Christ groups.

The Lutheran Church Missouri Synod denomination listed the most addresses in the 1936 directory: 166 church addresses across the Chicago region. At the time of this research in 2015 and 2016, Google Street View showed that 25 buildings were no longer standing and 36 structures were home to other uses (including other congregations). Overall, the same congregation is worshipping today at the 1936 address in 99 of the 166 cases (59 percent).

In the 1936 directory, the Presbyterians had the next largest number of congregations. The 1936 directory listed 120 congregations, and Google Street View showed 45 of the same buildings had the same congregations (47 percent of the 96 church buildings still standing at the 1936 address). The reduction came from 24 addresses having no church building and 51 church buildings having different uses today.

Compared to the Lutheran Church Missouri Synod and Presbyterian churches, the Disciples of Christ addresses in 1936 were much less likely to have a long-standing building and congregation at the same location. The 1936 directory listed 30 addresses, and today, 14 locations had no church building, 12 locations had other uses, and 4 locations (25 percent) had the same church as in 1936.

The Seventh-day Adventist congregations had patterns in between the three other groups. More of their buildings still stand today: 16 of the 21 addresses from 1936 still have a church building present. Yet, only 2 of those 16 locations (13 percent) are still home to the same Seventh-day Adventist congregation.

One plausible explanation for either destroyed religious buildings or religious buildings now hosting other uses involves white flight in response to an increase in non-white, particularly black, residents after World War II (Sugrue 1996; Hirsch 1998; Meyer 2000; Kruse 2005). All four denominations have some buildings no longer standing today within Chicago—though Presbyterians have higher rates—and roughly 80 percent of the church buildings given over to new uses today are located in Chicago. All four of these denominations were almost entirely white in 1936 when their addresses were included in the religious directory. Thus, their parishioners were undoubtedly among the numerous white religious groups leaving Chicago after World War II. Among the many groups that took flight from Chicago were Jews (Cutler 1996), Christian Reformed Churches (Mulder 2015), Catholics (McMahon 1995), and a variety of Protestant groups (Miller 2017), and evidence from other major Americans cities suggests that Catholics, Jews, and mainline and conservative Protestants moved to the suburbs in the postwar era (McGreevy 1996; Gamm 1999; Diamond 2000, 2003; Dochuk 2003; Doughtery and Mulder 2009). Although there is some evidence of conservative Protestant groups increasingly locating in large cities (e.g., Bielo 2011; Barron 2016), little work examines whether these congregations occupy the vacated buildings of once-existent religious congregations or build or adapt different structures.

In order to interrogate this explanation of white flight, we examined the ratio of still-standing, still-affiliated church buildings inside versus outside the city limits of Chicago for each denomination. The ratios show noticeable differences across these four denominations: Presbyterians had the highest percentage of no longer present locations within the city of Chicago. However, Disciples of Christ, Lutheran Church Missouri Synod, and Presbyterians had similar percentages of the locations given over to other uses located in Chicago. For Presbyterians, 16 of the 24 no longer existing buildings were in Chicago, and 36 of the 51 existing buildings with different uses were in Chicago. In other words, more than two-thirds of the vacated Presbyterian structures and more than three-quarters of the buildings that no longer belong to the denomination lie within the city limits, not the suburbs. Today, 7 of the 25 Lutheran Church Missouri Synod buildings that no longer exist were in Chicago, but 29 of the 43 buildings home to other congregations or put to other uses are in the city. Among the Disciples of Christ, 4 of the 14 buildings no longer in existence were located in Chicago, and 9 of the 12 existing buildings with new uses were in Chicago. For the Seventh-day Adventists, one of the 5 buildings no longer present were located in Chicago, while none of the 14 buildings with new uses was in Chicago.

Another factor that helps explain the number of 1936 congregations no longer worshipping at these sites is the declining membership figures of three of the four religious denominations. It is difficult for any religious group to maintain a large number of buildings—no matter how permanent their architecture or prominent their location—with declining attendance. Membership in the Disciples of Christ stood at about 1.6 million in 1935, peaked near 2 million in the late 1950s, and declined steadily to roughly 660,000 in 2009 (TheArda 2015a). Counting Presbyterian members is more difficult to trace due to mergers: the Presbyterian Church in the United States of America had 1.9 million members in 1935, while the Presbyterian Church (USA) had nearly 2.8 million members in 2009, down from nearly 3.8 million in 1993 (TheArda 2015b). Lutheran Church Missouri Synod membership declined less—over 1.2 million members in 1935, a peak of almost 2.8 million in 1971, and around 2.3 million members in 2009 (TheArda 2015c)—and across these four groups they had the most consistent locations. The Seventh-day Adventists grew over this period from about 150,000 members in 1936 to over one million members in 2010 (TheArda 2015d).

With the decline in members, the number of Presbyterian churches at these same addresses dropped significantly; 42 percent of the total 1936 church buildings still standing are now the home of different congregations. Yet, the majority of these Presbyterian buildings are still standing. More broadly, just over one-third of the 1936 buildings that are still standing house other congregations across these four denominations. This suggests that the structures were well-built and useful. Some still have stone-work over the doorways saying that they are Lutheran or Presbyterian churches. Additionally, they might be important resources for new religious congregations in urban and suburban contexts. Finding a decent building—particularly one with an established or well-located presence in a neighborhood—can be a difficult task for religious groups just starting out and trying to marshal resources. Many religious groups that are relatively new to the region (e.g., Zelinsky and Matthews 2011; Numrich and Wedam 2015), ranging from Missionary Baptist to Church of God in Christ, to Muslim congregations, can and have made old religious buildings new again. Thus, even if Presbyterian congregations left the community they once inhabited in 1936, their presence is still felt in the long-lasting structures. When sociologist Jay Demerath (1995) argued that mainline Protestants defeated conservative Protestants in the cultural battle in the United States, even with significant membership declines in mainline churches, this outcome also has a material component: the buildings of mainline congregations continue to influence religious and non-religious groups who experience these physical structures.

While Presbyterians were the only denomination of the four to have a majority of no longer standing churches located in Chicago, three of the four denominations had a majority of their churches put to other uses within Chicago city limits. Even if white flight helps explain the fate of a substantial number of these Chicago church buildings, others put to use even more church buildings after the congregation who worshipped there in 1936 left or folded. This reuse of church buildings could be the result of multiple factors, including a demand for real estate in Chicago and the consistent founding or arrival of new religious congregations who need a space in which to worship.

How did we know if the same congregation still occupied the same building? In many cases, we could see clearly visible church signs on Google Street View. Even in the Internet age, a vast majority of congregations have a sign along the nearest street or located on their façade giving their name, as well as extra information such as service times and perhaps the pastor. When a sign was not present or unclear, Google Maps sometimes identified the address as home to another congregation. For example, the 36 Presbyterian church buildings still standing yet home to other uses hosted numerous Baptist churches, a mosque, and an Orthodox church. New Life Community Church, a megachurch based in Chicago with now more than 20 satellite locations, meets in at least three of these long-standing church buildings (two Lutheran Church Missouri Synod, one Presbyterian). Across all four denominations, 80 percent or more of the 1936 church buildings were used for religious congregations. The other uses included care centers for children, community centers, offices, residences, and several that seemed to be boarded up.

We can sum up the locations and buildings from 1936 to recent years in the following way. Nearly 80 percent of the 1936 church buildings are still standing. While it is difficult to compare these figures to that of other religious groups in Chicago or elsewhere, this figure suggests that religious buildings have staying power. Lutherans and Presbyterians had higher percentages of buildings still present by the 2010s. Lutheran churches were also more likely to continue to occupy the same buildings seventy-plus years later. Presbyterians were more likely than the other three denominations to have abandoned their city buildings compared with their suburban buildings. Of the still-standing buildings inside Chicago city limits, roughly 70 percent for three groups were put to other uses.

Turning from the *locations* of congregations to their building's *architectural features*, we find smaller differences across the four denominations. Although no denomination built standardized structures, Presbyterians tended to favor red brick and stone compared to the other three groups, while the buildings of the other groups more often featured lighter brick or other options. Brick was the most common church exterior for all four groups, with stone comprising a sizable minority (nearly one-quarter). The data from the locations of these four denominations throughout the Chicago region corroborate Zelinsky and Matthews's (2011:71) finding regarding the strong preference for brick for churches in Cook County. However, the use of stone in these four groups was more prevalent than for all churches in Cook County in the first decade of the 2000s. None of the groups has many buildings featuring wood or siding exteriors, suggesting the religious groups preferred more permanent materials and facades.

A number of the 1936 churches across these four groups reflected neo-medieval auditorium designs or Gothic Revival architecture (Kilde 2002) with much smaller numbers built in Colonial Revival traditions or postwar variations. Regarding particular architectural features of the structures, the Lutherans and Seventh-day Adventists tended to build square towers at a higher rate than did the Disciples of Christ or Presbyterians. Across the buildings of the four groups, the locations of a tower or multiple towers could differ significantly: placed in the center of the front façade; a façade featuring two towers, one at each corner, with either the same heights for the towers or one significantly taller; or offset along the sides. Just over one-quarter of the buildings utilized steeples, with the highest rates coming on the Lutheran Church Missouri Synod structures. Additionally, a number of the Lutheran and Presbyterian buildings featured crosses at the peak of their facades. The still-standing buildings of these four groups appear to have higher rates of towers and steeples than found across religious buildings in Cook County today (Zelinsky and Matthews 2011:72). Lutheran and Presbyterian churches were very likely to be located on street corners, while Disciples of Christ were evenly split in such locations, and just under 40 percent of Seventh-day Adventist were on corners. These locations could indicate the importance of religious structures in the era in which they were built and/or deliberate efforts by congregations to secure visible property.

Seeing some of the typical architecture among these religious buildings helps illustrate these broad patterns. Figures 7.4 and 7.5 show two existing church buildings demonstrating traits of Gothic architecture, features regularly used by both the Presbyterian and Lutheran Church Missouri Synod congregations. The church building in Figure 7.6 illustrates the rarer and more modest wood church. Figure 7.7 provides an example of more modern architecture from a church building constructed after World War II to replace an earlier structure at the same location built around 1870.

Images of the still-existing Lutheran and Presbyterian buildings often suggest that the structures are well cared for and project a kind of permanence through their stone or brick exteriors and architectural features that harken back to previous centuries.

While Google Street View reveals the current state of the 1936 addresses, examining the websites for the congregations still present at the 1936 addresses provides additional insights into how congregations value and are influenced their buildings. Accounting for the online presence of church buildings helps provide a full look at the representation of the buildings as objects (Du Gay et al. 2013) and allows us to consider how the online presentation may feed back into experiences within such physical buildings. How do congregations still using these older religious structures present the buildings? Coding for several website features shows differences between the four groups.

Presbyterian, Lutheran, and Seventh-day Adventist congregations were likely to have a website (77 percent, 90 percent, and 100 percent, respectively) for their congregation. Among these web pages, roughly three-quarters featured the church building on the home page, and over three-fifths included information on the church's history and/or building on a separate page. When they displayed the church building on the home page, the photographs commonly involved an exterior image, while an interior shot was included a little less than 50 percent of the time. When the opening page of the website featured the exterior of the building, the image depicted of the church was often a broad shot of the front. Such an image can accomplish several goals: it can show a unique façade; it can show what someone passing on the street or sidewalk would also expect to see; and it shows off the primary entrance or public-facing part of the building. The images from the interior of the church commonly included either the front of the sanctuary, often emphasizing the altar, or a wider or overhead view of the entire sanctuary with the seating included. Lutheran Church Missouri Synod congregations were slightly more likely to depict stained glass windows.

The use of rotating images at the top of web pages made it easier for numerous congregations to have exterior, interior, and stained glass images all

Figure 7.4. Many church buildings, especially those inside the city proper, no longer belong to the congregation that built them. At the corner of Hirsch and Springfield in Chicago, the former home of Bethel Lutheran Church Missouri Synod now hosts New Life Christian Church—Humboldt Park.

Photo: Brian J. Miller.

Figure 7.5. At the corner of Western and Raynor in Joliet sits a neo-Gothic structure that has been home to First Presbyterian Church for over seventy years.
Photo: Brian J. Miller.

on their front page. Figures 7.8 and 7.9 show two examples of home pages featuring different aspects of the church building.

The emphasis on images of the church building on the front page did not carry over at the same rate to congregations providing information on their history or building. Of the 117 congregations with a website and still worshipping at their 1936 location, 73 sites (62 percent) contained a page devoted to their history or building. On such pages, the presentation could range from a simple narrative of the congregation and/or building(s) to very detailed records accompanied by information and images of buildings in which the church met. The majority of history or building pages featured an image of the church exterior (either showing the current building at an earlier date or showing a previously used structure) while a minority showed an interior image. Across the history pages, the images of the church buildings tended to take up less space than narrative text regarding the history of the congregation. (See Figures 7.2 and 7.3 at the beginning of the chapter for

Figure 7.6. Lakeview Seventh-day Adventist Church in the Chicago neighborhood of Roscoe Village is located on a residential block at 2318 W. Roscoe Street. The church occupies a relatively modest building with a small portico, light-colored siding, and a brick lower level.
Photo: Brian J. Miller.

history pages that provided a higher level of detail, utilizing text and images, regarding the congregation's history.)

That a majority of the history pages feature the church building may not be surprising given the longevity of the congregations and some of the structures. At the same time, a sizable minority of the history pages do not feature the building at all. University Church, described in the introduction to this chapter (and see Figure 7.1), is but one example. The history page is text heavy and describes different periods of the church, but makes only one reference to the building—and in passing, to describe how a quote from the influential third pastor of the congregation is "found on the sanctuary walls" (University Church 2020).

Summing up how these congregations presented their building on websites, the majority of the long-standing congregations have web pages, around three-quarters of main pages included an image of the church building, and a majority of the congregations in their 1936 buildings had a

Figure 7.7. An older church building sits next to a more recently constructed sanctuary at 5235 Fairview Avenue in Downers Grove. Formerly home to the First Presbyterian Church of Downers Grove (which, according to its Facebook page, celebrated its last Sunday in November 2018 after 93 years), the structure is now home to Saint Luke Presbyterian Church (which moved from another building in the suburb and had its first Sunday of worship in the building in August 2019).
Photo: Brian J. Miller.

separate portion of their website for their history or building with an image of the church building found on a majority of those pages.

The Influence of Long-Standing Religious Buildings

How can addresses for churches from 1936, Google Street View, and church websites better help us understand how religious buildings influence congregations and others? First, the stability of a number of these buildings and congregations, particularly for the Lutheran and Presbyterian churches, hints that buildings can help hold religious groups within particular

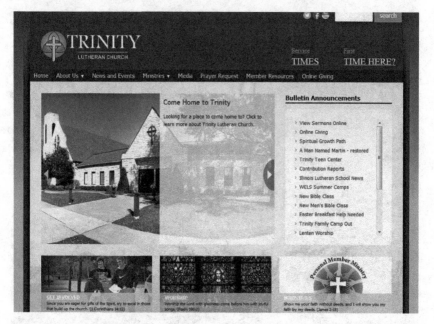

Figure 7.8. The home page of Trinity Lutheran Church of Crete highlights both the exterior façade of the church as well as important stained glass windows.
Retrieved March 17, 2017, at http://www.trinitycrete.org/trinitycrete/home.

communities. A building is an investment, a symbol, and a shaper of the congregation such that many congregations in these two denominations have stayed put over eight decades. Even among Protestants, who have weaker ties to their buildings and locations compared to Catholics (Gamm 1999), the building itself can help motivate religious groups to stay amidst other social forces like changing denominational or neighborhood demographics. It can be hard to leave a community even with pressure to do so, as historian Darren Dochuk's (2003) case study of a Baptist congregation in Detroit illustrates, and leaving a building with meaningful religious history could be similarly difficult.

Meanwhile, similarities in architecture can reinforce the continuity among many of these buildings and congregations. Even with differences in doctrine, history, social backgrounds, and locations throughout a large metropolitan region, related architectural features in church buildings unite hundreds of congregations. These similarities may be due to three factors. The churches standing in 1936 were built in a similar time period, from the mid-1800s to the early 1900s. Certain architectural styles, such as Gothic

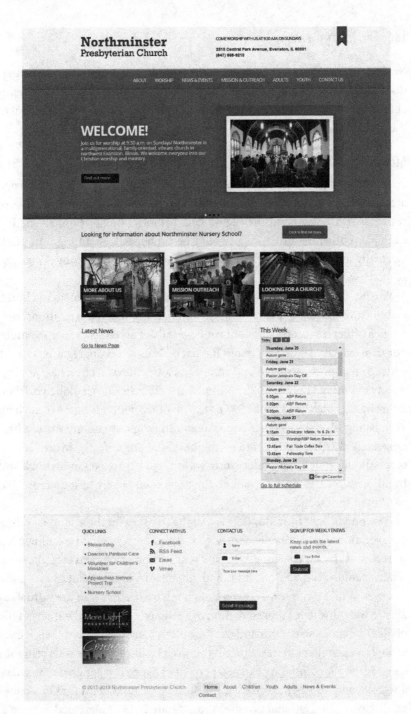

Figure 7.9. The home page for Northminster Presbyterian Church of Evanston features three dimensions of the church building: the interior of the sanctuary from the back, a view of the exterior from the front, and one of the stained glass installations.

Retrieved June 20, 2019, at http://northminpres.org/.

Revival, were popular across American denominations. Just as Robert discussed a building blitz in Guatemala, all of the buildings examined in this chapter were built during a time when Chicago's population as well as that of the region was growing rapidly.

Furthermore, all of these churches are located within the same region. This likely limits variation that could be due to regional styles of architecture. The church buildings in this study not only reflect 1936 styles, but also Chicago area and Midwestern approaches to religious structures. Different inflows of residents to Chicago and the region could inform architectural styles. For example, Lutherans in Chicago would be influenced by immigrants from Germany and other northern European countries, as well as by American aesthetics.

Finally, studying these four groups may be masking differences in church architecture that are dependent on denominations, religious traditions, theological differences, and different time periods of ascendency. For example, our data cannot tell us how many Baptist or Nazarene congregations in the Chicago region constructed and stayed in Gothic Revival churches, nor can we say anything about non-denominational churches or Catholic parishes. Zelinsky and Matthews (2011:97) note, "no other nation is home to such an astonishing diversity of creeds and organized religious communities, a heterogeneity mirrored substantially, if somewhat imperfectly, in the choice of a building style." A broader study within and across denominations and traditions as well as time periods and regions would likely turn up more disparities in architecture.

A second insight from this data is that the websites for these long-standing congregations provide evidence of how congregations view and are influenced by their own buildings. Long-standing religious buildings and even those no longer standing can take on additional dimensions with presentations on the Internet. While the average person does not have the ability to use virtual reality to walk through a representation of a religious building, the Internet life of older religious structures and congregations can both cement their legacy as well as open them to new interpretations. Having a website for a religious congregation is common; nearly 56 percent of American congregations have a website and 40.1 percent have a Facebook page, and congregations could easily have both (National Congregations Study 2015). Compared to the national figures regarding websites, the Lutheran, Presbyterian, and Seventh-day Adventist congregations exceed these figures, while the Disciples of Christ lag behind. But few researchers have examined these websites, particularly in connection with the religious buildings involved. The website may exist in the ether of the Internet, but these church websites regularly feature the physical building central to the congregation's worship and social interactions. The online lives of congregations are not just a bundle of individual attitudes and online interactions; they often continually refer to the buildings that shape religious practices and beliefs.

Placing the building on the website—as a majority of these long-standing congregations did—aids communication with visitors as the church makes a case for who they are. Presenting an image may help visitors identify the building, particularly those who scope out religious congregations online before attending. Going further, these older buildings could be of historical and aesthetic value in neighborhoods and communities that may be interested in historic preservation. Or, the older structures could be local landmarks, particularly the larger structures located at key intersections in changing neighborhoods and communities.

The use of the building on the website illustrates the importance of the structure for the congregation. Multiple images, as well as prominently highlighted features, hint at how meaningful the structure is to the religious group, influencing decades of community life, as well as a sacred space where worshippers encounter the Divine. One commission from the Lutheran Church Missouri Synod put it this way: "The church is the outward symbol of God's grace towards man [sic]" (Commission on Church Architecture 1965:39). Featuring an image of stained glass windows from the sanctuary presents a different internal understanding to the public than showing no image of the exterior or a broad image of a full sanctuary from the back.

Likewise, the minority of churches that did not acknowledge their building at all on their website may have done so intentionally. While many congregations may see the building as a source of cohesion and building energy because of tradition and a structured presence, other religious groups view it as an impediment, perhaps even a barrier, to visitors and the new work that is going on in the congregation. Roughly one-fifth of the Lutheran Church Missouri Synod and Presbyterian congregations did not feature the building on the home page, and nearly 40 percent did not highlight their church history on a separate page. Several reasons suggest themselves as probable causes. A lack of institutional memory may be at work. This could occur for a variety of reasons, including the leaving of key church leaders or lay members, a change in generations, church splits, or other ways that congregations can turn over in membership. Second, some congregations wish to express newness rather than history or tradition. This could be based on a reformer's impulse, or may reflect larger forces in American religion that emphasize independent congregations and spiritual individuals. Additionally, significant remodeling of the structure may have rendered the aged elements less visible or important. Finally, leaders of the congregation may hold a view of the church as the collection or group of people rather than a physical structure, or may wish to emphasize other elements such as the Scriptures or particular ministries. For the long-standing congregations that do not feature their building on their website, the edifice may not have the same influence, the same power, the same value.

In considering the influence of older religious buildings on religious groups, one final example illustrates a minority of cases among these four denominations in the Chicago region. On the edge of the Hermosa and Humboldt Park neighborhoods in Chicago and surrounded by residences in a multiracial setting sits an older church building at the northwest corner of N. Tripp Avenue and W. Wabansia Avenue. The red brick building features stained glass windows on the second floor, a sharply peaked roof, a square tower right on the street corner topped with a flat roof, and a prominent inscription in stone roughly half a story above the front entrance: "St. Markus EV. Luth. Kirke." St. Mark's Lutheran Church, a Norwegian congregation, dedicated the building in 1904 after the group formed in the 1890s (Moldstad 1905). Today, the building is home to Iglesia Communitaria "La Hermosa," which, loosely translated, means "The Beautiful Community Church." The home page of the La Hermosa features a description of the church as well as upcoming activities, all with a background image of desert and mountains. The only images of the century-old building are on the Galeria page; one image shows the sanctuary from the front and displays numerous stained glass windows along the side and back walls, chairs for seating, a small balcony, and a pleasant brightness both from the windows and light fixtures mounted between them.

This new congregation meeting in an old building highlights a common story in many American cities. Even when the original congregation is long gone, older buildings can continue to influence new religious groups. Yet, this chapter suggests that at least in these four Protestant denominations, there is some consistency in patterns to how many older church buildings remain as well as more uniformity in architecture within this region and time period of construction, who currently uses them, and how the buildings are presented online by the long-standing congregations. These findings suggest larger variability across religious groups in congregations staying in the same location across decades and differences in how various congregations depict their church building online.

This chapter takes a broader view of religious buildings across groups (over 300 structures built by four Protestant denominations within a large metropolitan region) and over time (eight-plus decades) in order to provide insights into how religious buildings shape congregations. Even within a city and suburbs undergoing significant physical and social change, a sizable majority of religious buildings in these denominations are still present, and just over half of the original structures are still home to the same congregation as in 1936. The findings suggest that these older buildings can continue to anchor congregations in particular places and that they are often important for congregational identity, as church websites frequently highlight the structures. Furthermore, the buildings now have online life as congregations present their older religious buildings to a broader audience and through a different medium than experiencing the building as an embodied visitor or worshipper. At the least, the still-standing structures attest to the physical, social, and religious activities of a religious group decades ago. At the same time, some of these buildings continue to shape and are shaped by their inhabitants and neighbors years after the foundation was laid. The congregations may be filled with different kinds of people, the neighborhood around the church building could have significantly changed, and the denominational and civil world in which the church operated has changed—but the church *building* continues. Brick, mortar, and stone are not eternal, but neither are they fleeting or transient. From the ancient megaliths of Stonehenge, to the towering Mayan temples still standing in Guatemala's rainforest, and even the neo-Gothic University Church of Chicago, long-standing religious buildings within both physical spaces and online realms attest to the lasting impact of the human tendency to build faith using stones.

8

Conclusion

> People have to have a place to do things together to keep them alive.
> —Member of the Tibetan Association of Vermont

In August 2015, *Seven Days*, Vermont's widely read weekly newspaper, ran a lengthy article about the Bhutanese and Tibetan communities in Vermont. The author noted that plenty of evidence exists to indicate that the Bhutanese and Tibetan communities are thriving in their new circumstances after migrating to the United States in the 1990s and early 2000s with help from the Vermont Refugee Resettlement Program. But leaders in both communities felt that something important was missing. The communities were nourishing an unfulfilled dream—they wanted to build a *temple of their own*. Said one member of the Bhutanese community: "If there is no temple in the community, the life of the people will be difficult and spiritually hollow" (Sari 2015). Not that the absence of a physical structure of their own had kept the Bhutanese from gathering for worship. At the time of writing, members of the Vermont Bhutanese community, which leaders estimated to number more than two thousand, were gathering weekly in a historic home owned by the Quaker Meeting of Burlington and adjacent to the Friends Meeting House. Prayers for peace, led by a priest, were followed with a *kirtan* session of celebratory singing. By 2018, due to the need for more space, the Bhutanese were gathering for worship and cultural events in the gymnasium of a shuttered Catholic elementary school next door to St. Joseph's, Burlington's co-cathedral. But they continued to look forward to a time when they could leave behind what one leader in the community referred to as the "spiritual homelessness" of existing without a place of their own. Despite the absence of a building, the community refers to itself as the "Vermont Hindu Temple."

The example of the Bhutanese of Vermont—most of the members of which have lived in Vermont for less than a single generation—illustrates the deep longing for a physical structure shared by so many religious (and cultural)

Building Faith. Robert Brenneman and Brian J. Miller, Oxford University Press (2020). © Oxford University Press.
DOI: 10.1093/oso/9780190883447.001.0001

communities around the world. After all, a physical structure can provide both an identifying material presence in the landscape of a local community as well as a space for gathering and worship. Without such spaces, congregations, with very few exceptions, are left dreaming of the day when they can "show and tell" their neighbors who they are. The fact that the Bhutanese have tended to gather in religious buildings built for and by other traditions—traditions which are now seeing numeric declines and squeezed budgets in many communities— underscores the continuing contribution of religious buildings to the ongoing multicultural experiment that exists in the United States.

I (Brian) live in a suburb known widely within the region and across the country for its religious organizations, congregations, and residents. Many of the local congregations worship in buildings that go back decades. At the same time, some of the patterns we found in this book play out on a regular basis. A few years ago, I enjoyed walking into the large sanctuary of a liturgical Protestant congregation just north of downtown who had made significant changes to the structure originally built by a large non-denominational congregation that moved to an adjacent suburb some years back. A Pentecostal congregation who built a structure on a busy corner on the northeast edge of town gave way to a Muslim group who kept all of the exterior the same, except for adding a crescent to the top of the white steeple and changing the name on the sign at the corner. Congregations meet in numerous public facilities, ranging from local schools to the Park District community center. In a suburb with a good amount of wealth and religious stability, the religious buildings matter tremendously as congregations seek structures that can both shape their encounters with the transcendent and fit within their financial constraints.

During a recent conference at St. John's University on the plains of northern Minnesota, I (Robert) had the privilege of joining the Benedictine monks for Sunday morning mass at the massive St. John's Abbey Church. Designed by the Hungarian-born Jewish architect and former Bauhaus instructor Marcel Breuer, the giant trapezoidal Abbey stands as a monument to the modernist impulse to privilege function over form. Seating, sight-lines, and acoustics improved exponentially compared to the original Abbey church with the help of innovations in engineering and materials. But the structure also points to the optimism and audacity of the post–World War II monks who kicked off the project in 1953 by contacting twelve of the world's most renowned *modernist* architects to invite them to propose a design for a new abbey that "will truly be an architectural monument in the presence of God" (Young 2014:25). Whether that dream was fulfilled or not surely depends not only on the observer's aesthetic taste, but also on the religious habits and preferences of the "beholder." Illtud Evans, a Dominican Friar and liturgical scholar, called the newly completed church "a triumph of intelligence and humility" (1961:517) even as other contemporaries, including many local Catholic leaders, saw only an "ecclesiastical garage" stripped virtually bare of religious art and artifact (Young 2014). Still, the church testifies to its particular moment in religious and cultural history. Completed in 1961, just a year before the sweeping liturgical reforms of the Second Vatican Council, the building bears the marks of a monastic community already pushing for worship reform and drawing inspiration from pre-modern architectural innovations by earlier Benedictines (Young 2014). Even today, nearly sixty years after the Abbey's consecration, the monks seem to embrace the audacity and simplicity of their gargantuan concrete-and-marble calling card. Building energy, it seems, has lingered.[1]

We started this book with a relatively simple question that sociologists have largely failed to address: How do religious buildings, the most material of structures, affect and shape the experiences of those who worship and visit? Sociologists have devoted a great deal of time to studying social structures, but very little effort has gone into examining how buildings affect the experiences of groups and individuals. Our attempt to answer this question took us to the places we know best: Chicagoland, Guatemala City, and Vermont. Despite their obvious differences, each of these regions features hundreds, if not thousands of "monuments" to the devotion and organization of a religious community—monuments that take the shape of a building made of brick, stone, concrete, wood, and even corrugated metal. Of course, as buildings, they are more than monuments because they do more than simply signify—they *facilitate*. This dual function of signifying and facilitating reveals the uniquely communicative and practical role of religious buildings.

Although it is difficult to summarize our findings in a neat and tidy conclusion, we are confident that at least five recurring patterns have emerged with enough frequency to be described as significant insights from our research. We discuss each of them in the following.

Building Energy

In Chapter 3 we defined "building energy" as the emotional energy arising out of the decision to embark on a building project. We consistently found excitement among religious congregations when they began exploring the possibility of acquiring, building, or making changes to structures in ways they felt would enhance the experiences had within that building. Actually embarking on a project *catalyzed* this excitement, magnifying and expanding it in congregations with both great and small amounts of resources. For many religious groups, acquiring a building of their own, one they could significantly shape, regardless of whether the initial structure was designed by that group, was an experience that proved deeply meaningful. Such a move was indicative of multiple markers of the congregations: permanence, a commitment of a body of believers to the continuation of their faith community, and the opportunity to create a space that could enable people to encounter the Divine.

This building energy often lingered throughout what could sometimes become a lengthy process. Reaching a consensus within a congregation about taking this sizable step takes time. Acquiring the money or loan to purchase land or a building or a mortgage takes time. Obtaining the permission of local authorities takes time. Developing plans of how to build or renovate takes time. Procuring the services of professionals to do the construction or renovation or, alternatively, utilizing the labor power of the congregation takes time. Moving into the structure, celebrating a new start, and then settling into and tweaking the space to the particular customs and purposes of the congregation take time. Yet, numerous congregations, including those in those study, found this to be a worthwhile process and had the building energy to see it through. While not all of the congregation and leaders had consistently high levels of enthusiasm throughout the process, nevertheless, a collective goal of a new or renovated building could be sustained for years. Additionally, while making key decisions during the building or renovating process may officially involve only a small number of people (clergy, lay leaders, professional architects and builders), the building energy was often palpable throughout congregations. Building projects such as the ones we studied are often for the whole congregation to support and benefit from. At the least, such projects may be departures from regular congregational life structured around worship services and auxiliary religious activities. At their best, building or renovation projects can prompt both individual and collective energy across a broad range of participants.

Evidence from websites of congregations who have worshipped in the same buildings for over seventy years suggests that multiple long-standing congregations hold their building as a key part of who they are today. Building energy can be supported and preserved for long periods of time. Maintaining an aging building is not an easy task: it requires resources, an interest and will in keeping the building in order, and a fairly stable set of attendees who stay in the same geographic area. Over time, the older building can become not only an asset that helps differentiate the congregation from others, but also a significant shaper of the religious experiences for multiple generations.

Tradition as Architectural "Toolkit" not "Straitjacket"

Architectural historians who study churches (e.g., Kinder 2002; Kieckhefer 2004; Kilde 2004) can describe architectural styles that are consistent across traditions and centuries. For example, both Kieckhefer and Kilde discuss the shift from Catholic church designs emphasizing an altar and intended to give attendees a sense of awe to Protestant styles that instead highlighted the spoken Word at the pulpit and the gathering of the congregation. Meanwhile, Kinder documents a Catholic Cistercian tradition in the churches and abbeys of Europe and North Africa that, while avoiding a single "style," still used simple lines and clean interiors devoid of color and excessive adornment in order to banish the "visual noise" that could threaten the silent meditation of the monks.

There is truth in describing such large patterns. On the whole, Catholic churches in the United States and Guatemala are easy to distinguish from low-church Protestant groups. At the same time, our cases across religious traditions in two national contexts suggest there is significant discussion and negotiation within these traditions about architecture. Depending on denominations and hierarchical structures, many congregations have at least some autonomy in designing a building that suits their congregation. Even in more hierarchical religious groups, congregations can and do have a say in the design process, especially at the point of deciding what kinds of design choices ought to be "on the table" for discussion. What often does not change within religious traditions are a limited number of key design elements that must be present. Few Protestant congregations could exist without a raised stage or a pulpit from which leaders or congregants could read and speak. Similarly, few Christian congregations could exist without physical design choices that ease the making of music and the projecting of sound, even though the question of how the sound will be projected, amplified, and controlled varies greatly. Muslim spaces must have an open space where attendees can kneel at prayer. An Orthodox structure needs a separate altar area in the front reserved for the clergy.

But how these basic design requirements are accomplished and what is included in addition to these basic requirements can take many forms. A Protestant church that practices baptism of all ages will have to decide if they need a font (located in the rear, the front, or somewhere else in the sanctuary), a tub or pool, or a design element that is forgone altogether in favor of a site outside the building. In a Catholic church, seating arrangements often become important. Will the congregation choose to have pews in one wing in front of the altar, pews in a cross shape on three sides of the altar, or a rounded structure that frees up the congregation to see more of each other? When a façade of an older building is to be protected, should it be kept in pristine original condition, or can it be significantly altered to align with the times (such as by removing the steeple or changing the material of the exterior walls)? Do the internal essentials need to be housed in a building clearly recognizable as a religious building, or is it fine if the exterior looks like a school, a store, or a parking garage?

One way to think about the interior and exterior design options available to congregations on the threshold of a building project is to borrow the "cultural toolkit" framework developed by sociologist of culture Ann Swidler (1986). In an influential article on the role of culture in shaping the action of individuals, Swidler argued that, rather than understanding culture as a set of "values" or "ends" that guide human action, a "toolkit" provides a better means of describing the "repertoire" of "habits, skills, and styles" (1986:273) from which individuals in a given society (or subculture) select a course of action. Such a view provides a more explicit role for the choices made by actors and groups, while avoiding the mistaken assumption that culture "determines" social action. And while Swidler makes no explicit reference to architecture in her description of "culture in action"—few sociologists of culture pay attention to architecture—it is by no means a giant leap to think of architectural style, especially when done by a religious group, as included among the many ways in which culture-in-action goes about "organizing experience . . . evaluating reality. . . [and] regulating conduct, and ways of forming social bonds . . . " (Swidler 1986:284).

In short, the image of a toolkit is an apt metaphor for describing the openness with which many congregations approach a building project. Rather than providing a "straitjacket" of architectural styles, most congregations select from a set of styles and design options with which they are familiar and to which they are drawn by their religious heritage, their prior experience, and their social class. Architects, like Ann Vivian, the Vermont designer of New

England religious spaces, advise congregations in effect by introducing them to a wider variety of styles and designs, which then allows them to "expand their toolkit" of style options. Subsequent to a completed building project, a congregation must learn how to employ the stylistic "tools" it has selected in order to communicate its identity and practice its faith.

Economic Constraints Shape Design Choices

If buildings matter, so do financial constraints. Perhaps this is an obvious pattern to highlight when discussing religious buildings: religious congregations are limited in what they can do with their buildings by the availability of money and other resources. But this emphasis on finances includes more than just the economic limitations placed on a congregation by its size and the class position of its members. Religious values regarding resources can also play a role. Prohibitions on usury require a large and growing Muslim community to exercise more patience than the typical Christian or Jewish congregation might have to employ before buying land and commissioning a new building. Furthermore, many religious congregations dream of larger or detailed structures but must face reality when it comes to paying for the building. Religious buildings are intended to promote religious experiences, but paying the bills can fundamentally shape how these experiences come to be. In effect, because they require congregations to make concrete decisions about resources, physical structures provide congregations with an occasion for putting to the test both their spiritual vision (i.e., What is most important to us?) and their ecclesial organization (How will decisions be made?).

However, we found that congregations exercised considerable ingenuity even when faced with serious economic limitations. Three sets of examples from our research stand out. The first is Mártires Seventh-day Adventist in Guatemala City, where, despite the small congregation, members went to great lengths to raise money to purchase land for their own church. Immediately afterward, the congregation came together to build the structure that could serve the group's needs. LeRoy Troyer recalled a similar situation when, after designing a modest but attractive sanctuary for a newly formed Mennonite congregation in South Bend, Indiana, in the early 1960s, members from nearby congregations sent teams of volunteers to help build the structure. Such "church raisings" have been common in rural areas and among congregations in which many parishioners possess skills from the building trades. We have little doubt that numerous congregations in the United States and abroad benefit from free or reduced labor to make their buildings a reality. A second case is that of the Edge in Aurora, Illinois. The congregation has met for years in a local high school. The stage and facility provide plenty of space and built-in lighting and sound systems. Yet, the leaders know that using a school limits their ability to shape worship and build community. For now, the congregation is choosing not to purchase land and build a structure and instead use a variety of buildings, including other churches and homes of members. While constructing a church (and raising money and taking out a mortgage) are signs of status, this group has its priorities elsewhere. Finally, not only did congregations adapt their buildings depending on their available resources, they could also grow accustomed to and see opportunities in what originally appeared to be an obstacle. A parking garage might not appear at first glance to be suitable for a church, but draping the walls with cloth fabric and filling the space with light and sound gave it the distinctive feel of a sanctuary. Similarly, a traditional Lutheran church building may not fit the worship of an Orthodox congregation, but modifying that space, and *using it*, week after week, allowed the parishioners to experience it as their own. A Muslim community in Vermont, by transforming a former US Army stable with sheetrock, carpet, and paint, came to discover in the long brick building that, as one parishioner described it, "This is *our* mosque." Such observations suggest that the regular gathering of practicants for worship within a particular structure can have the effect of imbuing that structure with a sense of sacredness—that is, a "set-apartness"—for those who worship regularly in it.

Nevertheless, most religious congregations in both Guatemala and the United States still prefer to construct a wholly new building when they have the opportunity. Even if their resources are limited, buying land and erecting a structure gives a congregation several advantages: they can guide how the land is used and the layout of the building (within the constraint of local zoning guidelines); they can be the first occupants and can customize the physical settings to their desires (and within their own constraints); and they have the pride of operating within a new structure. Yet, our own research suggests that congregations are also often quite flexible in worshipping in spaces not originally intended for religious groups, or altering religious buildings constructed by others. Several congregations we studied here had opportunities to leave what some might consider temporary spaces but chose not to.

Time Matters

The amount of resources possessed by a congregation at the construction or renovation of a building could have long-lasting consequences for subsequent worshippers. If a congregation has to construct a more intimate worship space early on, this could produce a preference for such spaces down the road (or spur a sizable expansion). Significant renovations made to a building may no longer be remembered several decades on, as new attendees come to see the space as normal. The future toolkit of possible alterations is likely impacted by the resource-constrained choices made earlier.

In terms of thinking about the life course of congregations and their buildings, congregations change over time as they shift from a new group to an established religious organization to possibly entering into decline and closing their doors. Their place of meeting is intimately tied to the congregation's activity and identity from beginning to end. At the beginning or middle of their life cycle, a new or renovated building can be a jolt of energy and point around which to coalesce. Building energy can be high. The effort expended to construct the new building is both exhilarating and exhausting. It is a key part of establishing a congregation within a community. The congregation has an opportunity to translate its theology and social practices into a physical structure while communicating the social class of its members through its size, choice of architectural style, and selection of materials and location. But buildings can also signal the decline or end of a congregation. When a structure is less than assiduously maintained, neighbors and community members draw conclusions about the waning vibrancy of the congregation. Declining membership affects the financial bottom line and what maintenance can be done. Some congregations do end, whether due to a limited number of members or a merger, or from an order from the denomination's headquarters. A few buildings—so far it remains relatively rare in the United States and even rarer in Guatemala—fall into ruin or are demolished.

Yet the end of the relationship between a congregation and its building has the potential to give new life to another religious organization or another organization in the community. Buildings can outlive their congregations and become sacred spaces for new groups. Both in the United States and Guatemala, an old building, particularly a well-built one in a key location, is a resource. As sociologist Eric Klinenberg (2018) has argued, religious buildings are an example of "palaces for the people"—physical spaces that provide the *social infrastructure* necessary for building community. Not every new church wants to construct an edifice on the outskirts of the community where land may be cheaper and they can erect a larger structure. Some want an older structure that has particular advantages yet can also be shaped to their uses.

Because of this potential for new religious uses, it is difficult to know from the outside how many religious congregations have significantly altered the interior of structures they did not originally construct. We pursued two methods that provided a glimpse into these older buildings: ethnographic work and looking at images on websites. Some buildings likely have layers upon layers of congregational history built into their structures as multiple groups have used the space. Religious buildings provide a kind of archaeological evidence: as communities change, particularly those in urban neighborhoods that have experienced white flight, higher levels of immigration, or gentrification, religious buildings continue to speak about the communities, practices, and social histories from which they sprang.

Going further, using the religious buildings of others provides possibilities for religious innovation. Congregations embedded in religious traditions often have certain building features in mind for their best or optimal worship and community experiences. When they utilize a building created by others, they might not be able to alter the structure in ways that they need to. They could persist in eventually finding a way to produce the alteration, or they may adapt to the new physical setting, perhaps unknowingly or unconsciously.

Alternatively, numerous established congregations grow old with their buildings. There is likely much variety in how much the original structure is altered, with numerous factors involved, including membership and attendance figures, available resources, and congregational priorities. Still, staying in the same location and in the same building (even if the older structure ends up as just a small part of what the building becomes) likely only highlights what we argue in this book: religious buildings shape religious experiences for individuals and congregations.

National Contexts Shape but Do Not Determine Local Building Vernaculars

One unique feature of our work is the cross-national comparison of religious buildings in the United States and Guatemala. These are two disparate societies: one the powerful behemoth of the Western Hemisphere, the other a small and ethnically diverse Central American country with historically steep pyramids of economic, political, and racial-ethnic inequality. Class differences are palpable, and these translate into not only the resources available for church buildings, but also expressions of religiosity. The two countries also have unique constellations of religious traditions, a key factor in how religious buildings are designed. While Guatemala is not without non-Western religious diversity, including a significant proportion of indigenous Mayan persons who practice Mayan spirituality alongside Catholic faith, it has only a tiny number of religious buildings not built for Christian congregations. Meanwhile, in the United States there are now more than two thousand mosques in use in the United States and nearly four thousand synagogues. Many other non-Western religious buildings abound, particularly in major cities and their metropolitan regions. At the same time, numerous patterns we saw in the church-building process held across these two national contexts. In both countries, congregations experienced building energy, encountered and addressed obstacles on their way to building a new building or renovating an old one, and some churches eventually fell into disarray while others housed congregations for longer terms.

A notable feature of comparing religious structures in these two spaces is that both countries draw on some common religious traditions and there is some transnational transmission of architecture. This is clearest in two examples. First, both countries have been influenced by the Catholic Church and its structures. While such influence has likely had a stronger effect in Guatemala beginning with the religious tradition of the colonizers, Catholic churches dominate numerous important locations in both countries. For example, a Catholic church sits on the central square of every Guatemalan city or town (adjacent to the main municipal building), and its façade provides a physical and cultural "backdrop" for major events both political and cultural. In the United States, cities and towns have rarely been oriented so strategically around a religious building from a single tradition. (Salt Lake City, with its massive Mormon Tabernacle at the center, is the exception rather than the rule.) But Catholic churches still abound in the United States; many of them, such as the Cathedral Basilica of Saint Francis in Santa Fe, mentioned in Chapter 2, provide important historical and cultural points of reference. As noted in Chapter 5, discussions about architecture within religious traditions can be quite vigorous, yet we suspect that Catholics from each country visiting Catholic churches in the other would find common elements they recognize.

Second, the rise of the megachurch among Protestants in the United States has had consequences for religious buildings in Guatemala. When Casa de Dios megachurch leaders decided to build a new campus, it was not only the Cirque du Soleil in Las Vegas that they visited for inspiration, but also Joel Osteen's Lakewood Church in Houston. Although we did not witness it in any of the particular cases we studied for this book, we suspect that architectural styles may follow immigrants to the United States as they acquire and build their own structures.

These two examples provide reminders that internal discussions about buildings among leaders of a congregation or within a denomination are situated within broader architectural practices and discussions. An Antiochian Orthodox congregation changing a Lutheran Church Missouri Synod church in a Chicago suburb must reconcile architectural elements from the United States, Lutheran homelands in Europe, and the eastern Mediterranean. An Anglican congregation can solicit carved doors from Indonesia. A Guatemalan Catholic church proposes a bell tower, hearkening to pre-modern European influence. Reconciling all of this with unique expectations about what religious buildings typically are within the United States and Guatemala requires work on the part of the religious group.

While our evidence is not enough to propose a grand theory of religious buildings that would hold across all countries and religious traditions, we do believe this work points a way forward for researchers interested in comparing religious traditions in different contexts. The globalization of religious buildings is well underway. The buildings may certainly look different—a Shinto shrine in Japan will differ from a Hindu temple in India and from an Anglican structure in central Africa—but physical structures may similarly shape religious adherents and groups. The architecture may reflect unique theologies, but all religious groups hope the physical arrangement of space both inside and outside their designated religious structures produces an effect on those who visit.

To produce those desired effects through physical structure, all religious groups pay attention to important building features: doorways and exits both to the building and particular interior spaces; the use of light and dark; how sound will be produced and reverberate; the verticality of the structure; surfaces ranging from ceilings to walls to floors; the expansiveness of interior space; and other particular designs that emphasize particular practices or responses. Religious groups may make specific decisions about each of these options, but they begin with similar building blocks or questions to guide their design. Congregations, under pressure to enhance the worship experience (thereby reducing desertion) through the cultivation of emotional energy (Collins 2004) work to create spaces that maximize an experience with the transcendent through exposure to the sights, sounds, and smells that represent divine presence for a given tradition.

Concluding Thoughts

When it comes to studying religious organizations in the sociology of religion in the United States, the unit of analysis is often the congregation. This makes sense: the group dynamics, the social milieu that is created, and the conflict and resolutions experienced by a group of people supposedly joined in a common religious community are fascinating. However, the emphasis on the social group can leave out the physical structures that undergird and shape the religious community. We argue that the building should not be an afterthought or an environmental variable. Rather, religious buildings are an essential part of understanding religious groups and religion as a whole. Even as these groups aspire to encounter the spiritual and Divine, the physical structures in which they worship and experience congregational life exerts both material and non-material influence.

We hope this book contributes to a burgeoning of research on religious buildings. There is good work in this field already, but we encourage scholars of religion to seriously consider physical structures as they analyze religious individuals, congregations, and organizations. In order to truly take structures seriously, we need to pay closer attention to the physical structures that shape social structures. Furthermore, studies of congregations should devote some energy to not just observing the structure in which a congregation worships, but also examining how that building—and the decisions that went into it—shape the group as they continue forward. Comprehensively examining congregations and religious traditions involves accounting for the physical structures that help shape their practices and beliefs. Paying more attention to religious buildings will help scholars address the materiality of religion, examine how congregations become a "we" rather than an aggregate of individual participants, better understand religious and congregational experiences, note the processes by which religious buildings arise and are sustained over time, and discuss the long-lasting effects of religious worship and gathering.

In closing, we experienced a phenomenon that many writers may experience: the more we analyzed religious buildings as sociologists, the more we noticed how they mattered. As I (Brian) sat in a church meeting in a former Plastofilm manufacturing plant or a high school turned church for a Sunday morning or looked at patterns of community responses to zoning requests from religious proposals, the buildings loomed more and more important. This was not just in the abstract from seeing data tables or thinking through field notes; there was a palpable, material experience in numerous congregations. As I (Robert) toured a parking-garage-turned-sanctuary, participated as a congregation built a small cement-block structure, and interviewed leaders in a local Muslim mosque, I had a similar experience: the building mattered in tangible ways to these congregations. Even for religious groups in which the building itself is de-emphasized or unornamented, the building both mattered to the congregation and stood out in our analyses. Almost all religious groups have a physical structure in which they worship and meet. Having sat in the pews, walked down the aisles, heard from the sound systems, and seen via simple and complicated lighting systems, we attest that those physical configurations shaped even us as researchers. How much more consequential these features must be for those who participate regularly in these communities of faith? Perhaps it should not have surprised us that the physical structures that gather human beings for encountering the Divine produce an emotional effect, even upon the casual visitor who arrives with a sharpened sociological imagination. After all, from Stonehenge to Tikal, from Angkor Wat to La Sagrada Familia (still under construction), and in Chicago, Vermont, Guatemala City, and around the world and for thousands of years, religious buildings have given human communities a place "to do things together to keep them alive." They are surely not the only such places, but they are the most ancient and, for the time being, they remain the most abundant.

Notes

Chapter 2

1. An earlier version of this chapter was published as: Robert Brenneman and Brian J. Miller. 2016. "When Bricks Matter: Four Arguments for the Sociological Study of Religious Buildings." *Sociology of Religion* 77(1):82–101.
2. We do not mean to imply that the Roman Catholic community that calls the Cathedral Basilica of Saint Francis home is not alive or active. All indications point to a diocese that continues to thrive more than a century after the church was completed.

Chapter 3

1. I have changed the names of interviewees in this chapter as an added safety precaution.
2. Multiple reports have surfaced recently alleging that some portion of the construction funds came from friends of the minister who have since been indicted for their participation in drug trafficking and are now serving time in a US prison (Barrientos 2018). Although Rev. Carlos "Cash" Luna has been called to provide testimony before a Guatemalan court, he has not been formally accused and continues to enjoy a strong reputation among many Guatemalan Protestants.

Chapter 4

1. An earlier version of this chapter was published as: Brian J. Miller. 2019. "'Would Prefer a Trailer Park to a Large [Religious] Structure': Suburban Responses to Proposals for Religious Buildings." *The Sociological Quarterly* 60(2):265–86.

Chapter 5

1. LeRoy Troyer passed away in December 2018, several months after our interview. He was eighty-one years old. I am grateful to his wife, Phyllis, for allowing me to sit with LeRoy for a delightful and inspiring conversation despite LeRoy's advanced age and failing health.
2. More recently, Yale showed appreciation toward classical architecture by hiring the prolific New York architect Robert M. Stern to be Dean of the School of Architecture from 1998 to 2016. Stern's tradition-inspired works are among the most popular examples of "new classicalism" in the profession today.

Chapter 6

1. The names of those interviewed have been changed except where noted, and some adjustments have been made to the language of the non-native speakers in order to improve readability.

Chapter 7

1. An earlier version of this chapter was published as: Brian J. Miller. 2018. "Still Standing after All These Years: The Presence and Internet Presentation of Religious Buildings in the Chicago Area, 1936–2016," *Visual Studies* 33(4):326–42.

Chapter 8

1. Private tours of the nave and the crypt by Benedictine brothers revealed a monastic community that believes that its abbey, despite the obvious divergence from traditional architectural vernacular, nevertheless represents the Benedictine values of simplicity and honesty.

Bibliography

Albright, Len, Elizabeth S. Derickson, and Douglas S. Massey. 2013. "Do Affordable Housing Projects Harm Suburban Communities? Crime, Property Values, and Taxes in Mount Laurel, NJ." *City & Community* 12(2):89–112.

Ammerman, Nancy Tatom. 1997. *Congregation & Community*. New Brunswick, NJ: Rutgers University Press.

Ammerman, Nancy. 2007. "Studying Everyday Religion: Challenges for the Future." Pp. 219–38 in *Everyday Religion: Observing Modern Religious Lives*, edited by N. Ammerman. New York: Oxford: Oxford University Press.

Ammerman, Nancy Tatom. 2014. *Sacred Stories, Spiritual Tribes: Finding Religion in Everyday Life*. New York: Oxford University Press.

Anacker, Katrin B., and Hazel A. Morrow-Jones. 2008. "Mature Suburbs, Property Values, and Decline in the Midwest? The Case of Cuyahoga County." *Housing Policy Debate* 19(3):519–52.

Archer, John. 2005. *Architecture and Suburbia: From English Villa to American Dream House, 1690–2000*. Minneapolis: University of Minnesota Press.

Association of Statisticians of American Religious Bodies. 2010. *2010 U.S. Religion Census: Religious Congregations & Membership Study*. Distributed by the Association of Religion Data Archives (www.theARDA.com).

Baker, Joseph O. 2010. "Social Sources of the Spirit: Connecting Rational Choice and Interactive Ritual Theories in the Study of Religion." *Sociology of Religion* 71(4):432–56.

Baldasarre, Mark. 1986. *Trouble in Paradise: The Suburban Transformation in America*. New York: Columbia University Press.

Barron, Jessica M. 2016. "Managed Diversity: Race, Place, and an Urban Church." *Sociology of Religion* 77(1):18–36.

Baumgartner, M. P. 1988. *The Moral Order of a Suburb*. New York: Oxford University Press.

Bellah, Robert N., Richard Madsen, William M. Sullivan, Ann Swidler, and Steven M. Tipton. 1985. *Habits of the Heart: Individualism and Commitment in American Life*. Berkeley: University of California Press.

Berger, Peter L. 1963. *Invitation to Sociology*. New York: Anchor Books.

Berger, Peter L. 1966. *The Social Construction of Reality: A Treatise in the Sociology of Knowledge*. Garden City, NY: Doubleday.

Bielo, James S. 2011. "City of Man, City of God: The Re-urbanization of American Evangelicals." *City & Society* 23(S1):2–23.

Bielo, James. 2018. *Ark Encounter: The Making of a Creationist Theme Park*. New York: New York University Press.

Biemiller, Lawrence. 2010. "Should Your New Buildings Look Old?" *The Chronicle of Higher Education*, May 16. Retrieved April 4, 2020, at https://www.chronicle.com/article/Should-Your-New-Buildings-Look/65488.

Bils, Jeffrey. 1996. "Naperville Neighbors in Conflict: Plans to Expand Mosque Unsettle a Neighborhood." *Chicago Tribune*, May 1. Retrieved December 29, 2015, at http://articles.chicagotribune.com/1996-05-01/news/9605010245_1.

Biondo, Vincent F., III. 2006. "The Architecture of Mosques in the US and Britain." *Journal of Muslim Minority Affairs* 26(3):399–420.

Bishops' Committee on the Liturgy. 1978. *Environment and Art in Catholic Worship.* Washington, DC: National Council of Bishops.

Blackburn, Yasmina. 2014. "Illinois Mosque Faces an Increasingly Common Zoning Problem." *Aljazeera America,* June 14. Retrieved September 1, 2016, at http://america. aljazeera.com/articles/2014/6/14/illinois-mosque-nomadic.html.

Blakely, Edward J. 2006. "Fortress America: Separate and Not Equal." Pp. 197–205 in *The Humane Metropolis: People and Nature in the 21st-Century City,* edited by Rutherford H. Platt. Amherst: University of Massachusetts Press.

Bogart, William T. 1993. "'What Big Teeth You Have!': Identifying the Motivations for Exclusionary Zoning." *Urban Studies* 30(10):1669–88.

Boswell, David, and Jessica Evans, eds. 1999. *Representing the Nation: A Reader.* London: Routledge.

Bourdieu, Pierre. 1979. "The Kabyle House or the World Reversed." Pp. 133–153 in *Algeria 1960.* New York: Cambridge University Press.

Bourdieu, Pierre. 1984. *Distinction: A Social Critique of the Judgment of Taste.* Cambridge, MA: Harvard University Press.

Brenneman, Robert. 2012. *Homies and Hermanos: God and the Gang in Central America.* New York: Oxford University Press.

Brown, Patricia Leigh. 1995. "Architecture's Young Old Fogies." *New York Times,* February 9. Retrieved April 4, 2020, at https://www.nytimes.com/1995/02/09/garden/ architecture-s-young-old-fogies.html.

Brown, Robbie, and Christine Hauser. 2012. "After a Struggle, Mosque Opens in Tennessee." *New York Times,* August 10. Retrieved October 24, 2016, at http://www. nytimes.com/2012/08/11/us/islamic-center-of-murfreesboro-opens-in-tennessee. html?_r=0

Cadge, Wendy, and Mary Ellen Konieczny. 2014. "'Hidden in Plain Sight': The Significant of Religion and Spirituality in Secular Organizations." *Sociology of Religion* 75(4):551–63.

Carlman, Susan Frick. 2015a. "Center Stage: Naperville Area Mosque Controversy Inspires Play." *Naperville Sun,* February 20. Retrieved December 29, 2015, at http:// www.chicagotribune.com/suburbs/naperville-sun/news/ct-nvs-mosque-knox-st-0220-20150219-story.html.

Carlman, Susan Frick. 2015b. "Locally Inspired Mosque Play's Company Launches City Residency." *Naperville Sun,* September 21. Retrieved December 29, 2015, at http:// www.chicagotribune.com/suburbs/naperville-sun/news/ct-nvs-mosque-play-st-0923-20150921-story.html.

Cather, Willa. 1927. *Death Comes for the Archbishop.* New York: A. A. Knopf.

Cetina, Karin Knorr. 1997. "Sociality with Objects: Social Relations in Postsocial Knowledge Societies." *Theory, Culture & Society* 14(4):1–30.

Chaves, Mark. 2004. *Congregations in America.* Cambridge, MA: Harvard University Press.

Chaves, Mark, and Philip S. Gorski. 2001. "Religious Pluralism and Religious Participation." *Annual Review of Sociology* 27:261–81.

Chen, Carolyn. 2002. "The Religious Varities of Ethnic Presence: A Comparison Between a Taiwanese Immigrant Buddhist Temple and an Evangelical Christian Church." *Sociology of Religion* 63(2):215–38.

Chicago Tribune. 1996. "Mosque's Revised Plans to Expand Raise Protest." *Chicago Tribune*, May 8. Retrieved December 29, 2015, at http://articles.chicagotribune.com/1996-05-08/news/9605080068_1_islamic-center-mosque-plan-commission.

Chicago Tribune. 2005. "Naperville Mixed-Use Site Faces Opposition." *Chicago Tribune*, August 5. Retrieved December 29, 2015, at http://articles.chicagotribune.com/2005-08-05/news/0508050266_1_gas-station-buildings-plans-show.

Chicago Tribune Editorial. 2011. "In Good Faith?" *Chicago Tribune*, February 17. Retrieved December 30, 2015, at http://articles.chicagotribune.com/2011-02-17/opinion/ct-edit-mosque-20110217_1_muslim-educational-muslim-leaders-mecca-mosque.

Ching, Francis D. K. 1979. *Architecture: Form, Space and Order*. New York: Van Nostrand Reinhold.

Chiquete, Daniel. 2006. *Silencio elocuente: Una interpretación teológica de la arquitectura pentecostal*. San José, Costa Rica: Universidad Bíblica Latinoamericana.

Churchill, Winston. October 28, 1943. "House of Commons Rebuilding." Commons Sitting of 28 October 1943. London, UK. Debate on the Floor.

Cilella, Jessica. 2012. "Bartlett Annexes Hindu Temple." *Daily Herald*, September 18. Retrieved December 29, 2015, at http://www.dailyherald.com/article/20120918/news/709189630/.

Cleary, Edward L. 1992. "Evangelicals and Competition in Guatemala." Pp. 167–196 in *Conflict and Competition: The Latin American Church in a Changing Environment*, edited by E. L. Cleary and H. W. Stewart-Gambino. Boulder, CO: Lynne Rienner.

Clingermayer, James C. 1996. "Quasi-Judicial Decision Making and Exclusionary Zoning." *Urban Affairs Review* 31(4):544–53.

Clingermayer, James C. 2004. "Heresthetics and Happenstance: Intentional and Unintentional Exclusionary Impacts of the Zoning Decision-Making Process." *Urban Studies* 41(2):377–88.

Collins, Randall. 2004. *Interaction Ritual Chains*. Princeton, NJ: Princeton University Press.

Collins, Randall. 2010. "The Micro-Sociology of Religion: Religious Practices, Collective and Individual (ARDA Guiding Paper Series)." State College, PA: The Association of Religion Data Archives at The Pennsylvania State University. Retrieved October 2, 2015, at http://www.thearda.com/rrh/papers/guidingpapers.asp.

Collins, Randall. 2013. "Does Nationalist Sentiment Increase Fighting Efficacy? A Skeptical View from the Sociology of Violence." Pp. 29–43 in *Nationalism and War*, edited by J. A. Hall and S. Malesevic. New York: Cambridge University Press.

Collins, Randall, and Mauro F. Guillén. 2012. "Mutual Halo Effects in Cultural Production: The Case of Modernist Architecture." *Theory and Society* 41(6):527–56.

The Committee on Church Architecture. 1966. *Architectural Guide for Church and School Building*. St. Louis: The Lutheran Church Missouri Synod.

Cragun, Ryan T., Stephanie Yeager, and Desmond Vega. 2012. "Research Report: How Secular Humanists (and Everyone Else) Subsidize Religion in the United States." *Free Inquiry* 32(4):39–46.

Cramer, James P., and Jennifer Evans Yankopolus, eds. 2006. *Almanac of Architecture & Design 2006*. Atlanta: Greenway Communications.

Crawford, Margaret. 1991. "Can Architects Be Socially Responsible?" Pp. 27–45 in *Out of Site: A Social Criticism of Architecture*, edited by D. Ghirardo. Seattle: Bay Press.

Cutler, Irving. 1996. *The Jews of Chicago: From Shltetl to Suburb*. Urbana: University of Illinois Press.

Daniels, Serena Maria. 2011a. "DuPage County Board Committee Backs Plan for Mosque." *Chicago Tribune*, February 1. Retrieved December 30, 2015, at http://articles.chicagotribune.com/2011-02-01/news/ct-met-mosque-willowbrook-committee-20110201_1_committee-backs-plan-muslim-educational-cultural-center-mosque.

Daniels, Serena Maria. 2011b. "DuPage County Approves Mosque Near Willowbrook." *Chicago Tribune*, March 22. Retrieved December 30, 2015, at http://articles.chicagotribune.com/2011-03-22/news/ct-met-dupage-mosque-0323-20110322_1_muslim-educational-cultural-center-mosque-unincorporated-residential-areas.

Daniels, Serena Maria, and Ted Gregory. 2011. "DuPage Board to Decide Today on Mosque." *Chicago Tribune*, February 7. Retrieved December 29, 2015, at http://articles.chicagotribune.com/2011-02-07/news/ct-met-suburban-mosques-20110207_1_new-mosque-muslim-educational-cultural-center-unincorporated-residential-areas.

Danielson, Michael N. 1976. "The Politics of Exclusionary Zoning in Suburbia." *Political Science Quarterly* 91(1):1–18.

Day, Katie. 2014. *Faith on the Avenue: Religion on a City Street*. New York: Oxford University Press.

DeFoster, Ruth. 2015. "Orientalism for a New Millennium: Cable News and the Specter of the Ground Zero Mosque." *Journal of Communication Inquiry* 39(1):63–81.

Demerath, N. J. 1995. "Cultural Victory and Organizational Defeat in the Paradoxical Decline of Liberal Protestantism." *Journal for the Scientific Study of Religion* 34(4):458–69.

Diamond, Etan. 2000. *And I Will Dwell in Their Midst: Orthodox Jews in Suburbia*. Chapel Hill: University of North Carolina Press.

Diamond, Etan. 2003. *Souls of the City: Religion and the Search For Community in Postwar America*. Bloomington: Indiana University Press.

Dickinson, Greg. 2015. *Suburban Dreams: Imagining and Building the Good Life*. Tuscaloosa: University of Alabama Press.

Dochuk, Darren. 2003. "'Praying for a Wicked City': Congregation, Community and the Suburbanization of Fundamentalism." *Religious and American Culture: A Journal of Interpretation* 13(2):167–203.

Doughtery, Kevin D., and Mark T. Mulder. 2009. "Congregational Responses to Growing Urban Diversity in a White Ethnic Denomination." *Social Problems* 56(2):335–56.

Du Gay, Paul, Stuart Hall, Linda Janes, Anders Koed Madsen, Hugh Mackay, and Keith Negus. 2013. *Doing Cultural Studies: The Story of the Sony Walkman*. Los Angeles: Sage Publications.

Durkheim, Emile. 1995 [1912]. *The Elementary Forms of Religious Life*. Trans. Karen E. Fields. New York: The Free Press.

Eagle, David E. 2015. "Historicizing the Megachurch." *Journal of Social History* 48(3):589–604.

Eiesland, Nancy L. 2000. *A Particular Place: Urban Restructuring and Religious Ecology in a Southern Exurb*. New Brunswick, NJ: Rutgers University Press.

Estadística, Instituto Nacional de. 2018. "Tema / Indicadores." Guatemala City: Instituto Nacional de Estadística Guatemala. Retrieved June 13, 2018, at https://www.ine.gob.gt/index.php/estadisticas/tema-indicadores.

Fegelman, Andrew. 1984. "Du Page Blames Economics for 'Gap' in Housing." *Chicago Tribune*, January 20, p. 21.

Finke, Roger, and Rodney Stark. 2005. *The Churching of America, 1776–2005: Winners and Losers in Our Religious Economy*. New Brunswick, NJ: Rutgers University Press.

First Presbyterian Church of Homewood. 2019. "Our History." Retrieved June 20, 2019, at http://ww.fpchw.org/history.html.

Fischel, William A. 2004. "An Economic History of Zoning and a Cure for Its Exclusionary Effects." *Urban Studies* 41(2):317–40.

Freedman, Sam, and Tom McNamee. 1979. "Du Page Remains Unmoved." *Suburban Trib*, December 3, Sec. 1 pp. 1, 6.

Freund, David M. P. 2007. *Colored Property: State Policy and White Racial Politics in Suburban America*. Chicago: University of Chicago Press.

Frey, William H. 2015. *Diversity Explosion: How New Racial Demographics Are Remaking America*. Washington, DC: Brookings Institution Press.

Gallagher, Sally K. 2005. "Building Traditions: Comparing Space, Ritual, and Community in Three Congregations." *Review of Religious Research* 47(1):70–85.

Gamm, Gerald H. 1999. *Urban Exodus: Why the Jews Left Boston and the Catholics Stayed*. Cambridge, MA: Harvard University Press.

Gans, Herbert. 1967. *The Levittowners: Ways of Life and Politics in a New Suburban Community*. New York: Pantheon Books.

Garrard-Burnett, Virginia. 1998. *Protestantism in Guatemala: Living in the New Jerusalem*. Austin: University of Texas.

Garreau, Joel. 1991. *Edge City: Life on the New Frontier*. New York: Doubleday.

Giaimo, Michael S., and Lora A. Lucero, eds. 2009. *RLUIPA Reader: Religious Land Uses, Zoning, and the Courts*. Chicago: American Bar Association.

Giddens, Anthony. 1994. *The Constitution of Society*. Cambridge: Polity Press.

Gieryn, Thomas F. 2000. "A Space for Place in Sociology." *Annual Review of Sociology* 26:463–496.

Gieryn, Thomas F. 2002. "What Buildings Do." *Theory and Society* 31(1):35–74.

Gillespie, Mary. 1982. "HOPE Enjoys Good Progress in Fair Housing for Du Pagers." *Suburban Sun-Times*, October 22, Sec. W, p. 3.

Goff, Lisa, and Mark Miller. "A Swaggering County Skims the Cream, but Reckless Growth Imperils Its Future." *Crain's Chicago Business*, April 28, 1986, pp. 19–22, 24–35.

Goldsborough, Bob. 1999. "Churches Want to Expand Beyond Pews." *Chicago Tribune*, February 16. Available at http://articles.chicagotribune.com/1999-02-16/news/9902200003_1_church-building-expansions-parking-lot.

Goldsborough, Bob. 2010a. "DuPage Rejects Islamic Center." *Chicago Tribune*, January 13. Retrieved December 29, 2015, at http://articles.chicagotribune.com/2010-01-13/news/ct-met-islamic-center-rejected-01132010_1_irshad-learning-center-parking-and-late-night-services-islamic-center.

Goldsborough, Bob. 2010b. "Lawsuit Claims Bias in Rejection of Proposed Islamic Center." *Chicago Tribune*, April 8. Retrieved December 29, 2015, at http://articles.chicagotribune.com/2010-04-08/news/ct-met-0409-islamic-suit-20100408_1_irshad-learning-center-dupage-county-board-religious-bias.

Goldsborough, Bob. 2011a. "Small Mosque Easily Wins Approval from DuPage." *Chicago Tribune*, July 5. Retrieved December 29, 2015, at http://articles.chicagotribune.com/2011-07-05/news/ct-met-dupage-mosque-0703-20110705_1_small-mosque-islamic-prayer-center-traffic-studies.

Goldsborough, Bob. 2011b. "DuPage Board Oks Mosque, Community Center Near Lombard." *Chicago Tribune*, September 13. Retrieved December 30, 2015, at http://articles.chicagotribune.com/2011-09-13/news/chi-dupage-board-oks-mosque-community-center-near-lombard-20110913_1_mosque-dupage-board-community-center.

Goldsborough, Bob. 2012. "DuPage Board Rejects Dome and Minaret for Mosque Near Willowbrook." *Chicago Tribune*, March 13. Retrieved December 30, 2015, at http://articles.chicagotribune.com/2012-03-13/news/chi-page-board-rejects-dome-and-minaret-for-muslim-educational-cultural-center-of-america-mosque-near-willowbrook-20120313_1_muslim-educational-cultural-center-dome-and-minaret-mecca-officials.

Gooren, Henri. 2001. "Reconsidering Protestant Growth in Guatemala, 1900–1995." Pp. 169–203 in *Holy Saints and Fiery Preachers: The Anthropology of Protestantism in Mexico and Central America*, edited by J. Dow and A. Sandstrom. Westport, CT: Praeger.

Gottdiener, Mark. 1994. *The Social Production of Urban Space*. Austin: University of Texas Press.

Greeley, Andrew. 2001a. "A Cloak of Many Colors: The End of Beige Catholicism." *Commonweal*, November 9, 2001, p. 4.

Greeley, Andrew. 2001b. *The Catholic Imagination*. Berkeley: University of California Press.

Green, John C., and Mark Silk. 2011. "The Religion Gap Abides." *Religion in the News* 13(2):8–9, 26–27.

Greene, Virginia A. 1998. *The Architecture of Howard Van Doren Shaw*. Chicago: Chicago Review Press.

Gregory, Shirley Siluk. 1996. "Deadlock on Mosque Expansion: Naperville Council Tables Issue to June 4." *Chicago Tribune*, May 24. Retrieved December 29, 2015, at http://articles.chicagotribune.com/1996-05-24/news/9605240081_1_islamic-center-council-member-worship.

Griswold, Wendy, Gemma Mangione, and Terence E. McDonnell. 2013. "Objects, Words, and Bodies in Space: Bringing Materiality into Cultural Analysis." *Qualitative Sociology* 36:343–64.

Guggenheim, Michael. 2010. "The Laws of Foreign Buildings: Flat Roofs and Minarets." *Social & Legal Studies* 19(4):441–60.

Guggenheim, Michael. 2013. "Unifying and Decomposing Building Types: How to Analyze the Change of Use of Sacred Buildings." *Qualitative Sociology* 36(4):445–64.

Hackworth, Jason, and Kirsten Stein. 2012. "The Collision of Faith and Economic Development in Toronto's Inner Suburban Industrial Districts." *Urban Affairs Review* 48(1):37–63.

Hamilton, Marci A. 2005. *God vs. the Gavel: Religion and the Rule of Law*. New York: Cambridge University Press.

Harvey, Daina Cheyenne. 2010. "The Space for Culture and Cognition." *Poetics* 38:184–203.

Hendrick, Rebecca. 2004. "Assessing and Measuring the Fiscal Health of Local Governments: Focus on Chicago Suburban Municipalities." *Urban Affairs Review* 40(1):78–114.

Hirsch, Arnold R. 1998. *Making the Second Ghetto: Race and Housing in Chicago 1940–1960*. Chicago: University of Chicago Press.

Hirt, Sonia A. 2014. *Zoned in the USA: The Origins and Implications of American Land-Use Regulation*. Ithaca, NY: Cornell University Press.

Holt, Douglas. 1998. "Huge Hindu Temple to Take Root in Northwest Suburbs." *Chicago Tribune*, October 31. Retrieved December 29, 2015, at http://articles.chicagotribune.com/1998-10-31/news/9810310061_1_temple-pramukh-swami-maharaj-sect.

Howe, Justine. 2018. *Suburban Islam*. New York: Oxford University Press.

Iannaccone, Laurence R. 1991. "The Consequences of Religious Market Structure: Adam Smith and the Economics of Religion." *Rationality and Society* 3(2):156–77.

Ihlanfeldt, Keith R. 2004. "Exclusionary Land-Use Regulations within Suburban Communities: A Review of Evidence and Policy Prescriptions." *Urban Studies* 41(2):261–83.

Immanuel Lutheran Church & School. 2014. "Our History." Retrieved January 22, 2016, at http://immanuel-ed.org/our-history/.

Imrie, Rob, and Emma Street. 2009. "Regulating Design: The Practices of Architecture, Governance and Control." *Urban Studies* 46(12):2507–18.

Imrie, Rob, and Emma Street. 2011. *Architectural Design and Regulation.* Chichester, West Sussex, UK: Wiley-Blackwell.

Jacobs, Jane. 1961. *The Death and Life of Great American Cities.* New York: Random House.

Jasso, Guillermina, Douglas S. Massey, Mark R. Rosenqzeig, and James P. Smith. 2005. "Immigration, Health, and New York City: Early Results Based on the U.S. New Immigrant Cohort of 2003." *FRBNY Economic Policy Review* 11(2):127–51.

Jenco, Melissa. 2011. "Naperville to Annex Land Meant for Mosque: Islamic Group Agrees to Work with Wary Neighbors." *Chicago Tribune,* December 21. Retrieved December 29, 2015, at http://articles.chicagotribune.com/2011-12-21/news/ct-met-naperville-annex-1221-20111221_1_annex-land-annexation-agreement-islamic-center.

Jia, Lile, Samuel C. Karpen, and Edward R. Hirt. 2011. "Beyond Anti-Muslim Sentiment: Opposing the Ground Zero Mosque as a Means to Pursuing a Stronger America." *Psychological Science* 22(10):1326–35.

Jones, Paul. 2011. *The Sociology of Architecture.* Liverpool, UK: Liverpool University Press.

Kaika, Maria. 2010. "Architecure and Crisis: Re-inventing the Icon, Re-imag(in)ing London and Re-branding the City." *Transactions of the Institute of British Geographers* 35(4):453–74.

Kaika, Maria. 2011. "Autistic Architecture: The Fall of the Icon and the Rise of the Serial Object of Architecture." *Environment and Planning D: Society and Space* 29:968–92.

Keetch, Von G., and Matthew K. Richards. 1999. "The Need for Legislation to Enshrine Free Exercise in the Land Use Context." *U.C. Davis Law Review* 32:725–53.

Kieckhefer, Richard. 2004. *Theology in Stone: Church Architecture from Byzantium to Berkeley.* New York: Oxford University Press.

Kilde, Jeanne Halgren. 2002. *When Church Became Theatre: The Transformation of Evangelical Architecture and Worship in Nineteenth-Century America.* New York: Oxford University Press.

Kilde, Jeanne Halgren. 2008. *Sacred Space: An Introduction to Christian Architecture and Worship.* New York: Oxford University Press.

Kinder, Terryl. 2002. *Cistercian Europe: Architecture of Contemplation.* Grand Rapids, MI: Eerdmans.

Kingdom Impact Center. 2016. Retrieved September 28, 2016, at http://www.kicministries.org/.

Klinenberg, Eric. 2012. *Going Solo: The Extraordinary Rise and Surprising Appeal of Living Alone.* New York: Penguin Press.

Klinenberg, Eric. 2018. *Palaces for the People: How Social Infrastructure Can Help Fight Inequality, Polarization, and the Decline of Civic Life.* New York: Crown.

Kneebone, Elizabeth, and Alan Berube. 2013. *Confronting Suburban Poverty in America.* Washington, DC: Brookings Institution Press.

Konieczny, Mary Ellen. 2009. "Sacred Places, Domestic Spaces: Material Culture, Church, and Home at Our Lady of the Assumption and St. Brigitta." *Journal for the Scienttific Study of Religion* 48(3):419–42.

Kraftl, Peter, and Peter Adey. 2008. "Architecture/Affect/Inhabitation: Geographies of Being-In Buildings." *Annals of the Association of American Geographers* 98(1):213–31.

Krieger, Martin H. 2009. *Urban Tomopgrahies*. Philadelphia: University of Pennsylvania Press.

Kruse, Kevin M. 2005. *White Flight: Atlanta and the Making of Modern Conservatism*. Princeton, NJ: Princeton University Press.

Lang, Robert E., and Jennifer B. LeFurgy. 2007. *Boomburbs: The Rise of America's Accidental Cities*. Washington, DC: Brookings Institution Press.

Larson, Magali Sarfatti. 1993. *Behind the Postmodern Façade: Architectural Change in the Late Twentieth-Century America*. Berkeley: University of California Press.

Latinbarómetro. 2014. "Las religiones en tiempos del Papa Francisco." Santiago, Chile: Corporación Latinbarómetro.

Latour, Bruno. 1993. *We Have Never Been Modern*. Cambridge, MA: Harvard University Press.

Law, John. 2009. "Actor Network Theory and Material Semiotics." Pp. 141–58 in *The New Blackwell Companion to Social Theory*, edited by Bryan S. Turner. Malden, MA: Wiley-Blackwell.

Law, John, and Annemarie Mol. 1995. "Notes on Materiality and Sociality." *The Sociological Review* 43(2):274–94.

Laycock, Douglas, and Luke W. Goodrich. 2011. "RLUIPA: Necessary, Modest, and Under-Enforced." *Fordham Urban Law Journal* 39:1021–72.

Li, Wei. 2009. *Ethnoburb: The New Ethnic Community in Urban America*. Honolulu: University of Hawai'i Press.

Loewen, James W. 2005. *Sundown Towns: A Hidden Dimension of American Racism*. New York: The New Press.

Logan, John R., and Harvey L. Molotch. 1987. *Urban Fortunes: The Political Economy of Place*. Berkeley: University of California Press.

Lord, Steve. 2015a. "Church Renovation Sparks Grant Idea from Aurora Alderman." *Aurora Beacon-News*, August 12. Retrieved December 29, 2015, at http://www.chicagotribune.com/suburbs/aurora-beacon-news/news/ct-abn-aurora-grant-st-0813-20150812-story.html.

Lord, Steve. 2015b. "Aurora Looks at Work at Several Developments." *Aurora Beacon-News*, December 7. Retrieved December 29, 2015, at http://www.chicagotribune.com/suburbs/aurora-beacon-news/news/ct-abn-aurora-work-st-1208-20151207-story.html.

Loveland, Anne C., and Otis B. Wheeler. 2003. *From Meetinghouse to Megachurch: A Material and Cultural History*. Columbia: University of Missouri Press.

Low, Setha. 2003. *Behind the Gates: Life, Security, and the Pursuit of Happiness in Fortress America*. New York: Routledge.

Luhrmann, T. R. 2012. *When God Talks Back: Understanding the American Evangelical Relationship with God*. New York: Alfred A. Knopf.

Lutheran Church—Missouri Synod Commission on Church Architecture. 1965. *Architecture and the Church*. St. Louis: Concordia.

MacLeod, Suzanne. 2013. *Museum Architecture: A New Biography*. New York: Routledge.

Manchir, Michelle. 2012. "Islamic Center Files Lawsuit against DuPage County." *Chicago Tribune*, August 16. Retrieved December 29, 2015, at http://articles.chicagotribune.com/2012-08-16/news/ct-tl-west-chicago-islamic-center-suit-20120816_1_prayer-center-prayer-services-federal-lawsuit.

Marshall, Alex. 2019. "Glass, Golden Flames or a Beam of Light: What Should Replace Notre-Dame's Spire?" *New York Times*, May 10, 2019. Available at https://www.nytimes.com/2019/05/10/arts/design/notre-dame-spire-designs.html

Marti, Gerardo. 2014. "Present and Future Scholarship in the Sociology of Religion." *Sociology of Religion* 75(4):503–10.

Massey, Douglas S., Len Albright, Rebecca Casciano, Elizabeth Derickson, and David N. Kinsey. 2013. *Climbing Mount Laurel: The Struggle for Affordable Housing and Social Mobility in an American Suburb*. Princeton, NJ: Princeton University Press.

McDonnell, Terence E. 2010. "Cultural Objects as Objects: Materiality, Urban Space, and the Intepretation of AIDS Campaigns in Accra, Ghana." *American Journal of Sociology* 115(6):1800–52.

McElmurry, Kevin. 2007. "Alone Together: Gendered Worship in the Seeker Church." PhD dissertation, University of Missouri.

McGreevy, John T. 1996. *Parish Boundaries: The Catholic Encounter with Race in the Twentieth-Century Urban North*. Chicago: University of Chicago Press.

McGuire, Meredith B. 1990. "Religion and the Body: Rematerializing the Human Body in the Social Sciences of Religion." *Journal for the Scientific Study of Religion* 29(3):283–99.

McLean, Fiona. 1998. "Museums and the Construction of National Identity: A Review." *International Journal of Heritage Studies* 3(4):244–52.

McMahon, Eileen M. 1995. *What Parish Are You From? A Chicago Irish Community and Race Relations*. Lexington: University Press of Kentucky.

McNeill, Donald. 2009. *The Global Architect: Firms, Fame and Urban Form*. New York: Routledge.

MECCA. 2018. "The Mecca Center." The Mecca Center. Retrieved August 9, 2018, at http://meccacenter.org/

Mehler, Neil H. 1990. "Wheaton Zoning Deal Urged." *Chicago Tribune*, August 8. Available at: http://articles.chicagotribune.com/1990-08-08/news/9003060587_1_parking-deck-parking-spaces-variations.

Meyer, Stephen Grant. 2000. *As Long as They Don't Move Next Door: Segregation and Racial Conflict in American Neighborhoods*. Lanham, MD: Rowman & Littlefield.

Miller, Brian J. 2016. "A Small Suburb Becomes a Boomburb: Explaining Suburban Growth in Naperville, Illinois." *Journal of Urban History* 42(6):1135–52.

Miller, Brian J. 2017. "Growing Suburbs, Relocating Churches: The Suburbanization of Protestant Churches in the Chicago Region, 1925–1990." *Journal for the Scientific Study of Religion* 56(2):342–64.

Moldstad, Rev. John A. 1905. "St. Mark's Evangelical Lutheran Church." Pp. 528–29 in *A History of the Norwegians of Illinois*, edited by A. E. Strand. Chicago: John Anderson.

Moon, Dawne. 2004. *God, Sex, and Politics: Homosexuality and Everyday Theologies*. Chicago: University of Chicago Press.

Moreno, Sylvia. 2006. "Hurting for Tax Revenue, Town Ponders a Freeze on Churches." *Washington Post*, August 19. Retrieved October 11, 2016, at http://www.washingtonpost.com/wp-dyn/content/article/2006/08/18/AR2006081801056.html .

Mulder, Mark T. 2015. *Shades of White Flight: Evangelical Congregations and Urban Departure*. New Brunswick, NJ: Rutgers University Press

Murphy, Kevin D. 2011. "The Historic Building in the Modernized City: The Cathedrals of Paris and Rouen in the Nineteenth Century." *Journal of Urban History* 37:278–96.

National Congregations Study. 2015. "Explore the National Congregations Study Data." Retrieved June 22, 2015, at http://www.thearda.com/ncs/frequencies.asp.

Neitz, Mary Jo. 2004. "Gender and Culture: Challenges to the Sociology of Religion." *Sociology of Religion* 65(4):391–402.

Nichols, Aiden, O.P. 2015. "Contemplating the Kingdom: The Need for Re-Iconization in Our Own Time." *Sacred Architecture Journal* 28:11.

Numrich, Paul. 1998. "A Pentecostal Megachurch on the Edge: Calvary Church, Naperville, Illinois." Pp. 78–97 in *Tending the Flock: Congregations and Family Ministry*, edited by K. Brynolf Lyon and Archie Smith, Jr. Louisville: Westminister John Knox Press.

Numrich, Paul D. 2000. "Change, Stress, and Congregations in an Edge-City Technoburb." Pp. 187–212 in *Public Religion and Urban Transformation: Faith in the City*, edited by Lowell W. Livezey. New York: New York University Press.

Numrich, Paul D., and Elfriede Wedam. 2015. *Religion and Community in the New Urban America*. New York: Oxford University Press.

Packer, Robb. 2006. *Doors of Redemption: The Forgotten Synagogues of Chicago and Other Communal Buildings*. North Charleston, SC: BookSurge.

Padoongpatt, Tanachai Mark. 2015. "'A Landmark for Sun Valley': Wat Thai of Los Angeles and Thai American Suburban Culture in 1980s San Fernando Valley." *Journal of American Ethnic History* 34(2):83–114.

Park, Robert Ezra. 1925. *The City*. Chicago: University of Chicago Press.

Pels, Dick, Kevin Hetherington, and Frédéric Vandenberghe. 2002. "The Status of the Object: Performances, Mediations, and Techniques." *Theory, Culture & Society* 19(5–6):1–21.

Pelaez, Severo. 1998 [1970]. *La patria del criollo*. Ciudad de Mexico: Universidad Autònoma de Mèxico.

Pendall, Rolf. 1999. "Opposition to Housing: NIMBY and Beyond." *Urban Affairs Review* 35(1):112–36.

Pew. 2006. "Spirit and Power: A 10-Country Survey of Pentecostals." Washington, DC: The Pew Forum on Religion and Public Life.

Pew Research Center. 2011. "Muslim Americans." Pew Research Center. Retrieved December 30, 2015, at http://www.people-press.org/files/legacy-pdf/Muslim%20American%20Report%2010-02-12%20fix.pdf.

Pew Research Center. 2014. "Religion in Latin America: Widespread Change in a Historically Catholic Region." Washington, DC: Pew Research Center.

Pew Research Center. 2015. "America's Changing Religious Landscape." Pew Research Center. Retrieved December 30, 2015, at http://www.pewforum.org/files/2015/05/RLS-08-26-full-report.pdf.

Pew Research Center. 2017. "U.S. Muslims Concerned about Their Place in Society, but Continue to Believe in the American Dream." Pew Research Center. Retrieved March 2, 2018 at http://assets.pewresearch.org/wp-content/uploads/sites/11/2017/ 07/09105631/U.S.-MUSLIMS-FULL-REPORT-with-population-update-v2.pdf.

Pew Research Center's Forum on Religion & Public Life. 2012. "Controversies over Mosques and Islamic Centers across the U.S." Retrieved October 3, 2016, at http://www.pewforum.org/files/2012/09/2012Mosque-Map.pdf.

Placek, Christopher. 2012. "Once-Approved Willowbrook Mosque Now in Peril." *Daily Herald*, June 13. Retrieved February 8, 2016, at http://www.dailyherald.com/article/20120612/news/706129634/.

Preda, Alex. 1999. "The Turn to Things: Arguments for a Sociological Theory of Things." *The Sociological Quaterly* 40(2):347–66.

Price, Jay M. 2013. *Temples for a Modern God: Religious Architecture in Postwar America*. New York: Oxford University Press.

Purcell, Mark. 2001. "Neighborhood Activism among Homeowners as a Politics of Space." *Professional Geographer* 53(2):178–94.

Putnam, Robert D., and David E. Campbell. 2010. *American Grace: How Religion Divides and Unites Us*. New York: Simon & Schuster.

Rakatansky, Mark. 1995. "Identity and the Discourse of Politics in Contemporary Architecture." *Assemblage* 27:8–18.

RECI. 2014. "Kingdom Impact Center Purchases Building in Aurora." Press Release, June 12. Retrieved December 29, 2015, at http://www.reciusa.com/resources/PR/2014/6-2014/PR%201631%20Plum%20St%206-12-14.pdf.

Reichmann, Werner, and Anna-Lisa Müller. 2015. "The Secrets of Architecture's Actions." Pp. 2–23 in *Architecture, Materiality and Society: Connecting Sociology of Architecture with Science and Technology Studies*, edited by Anna-Lisa Müller and Werner Reichman. New York: Palgrave Macmillan.

Riedel, Barnaby B. 2009. "The Character Conjuncture: Islamic Education and Its Social Reproduction in the United States." Ph.D. dissertation in comparative human development, University of Chicago.

Rothwell, Jonathan T., and Douglas S. Massey. 2010. "Density Zoning and Class Segregation in U.S. Metropolitan Areas." *Social Science Quarterly* 91(5):1123–43.

Ruez, Derek. 2013. "Partitioning the Sensible at Park 51: Ranciere, Islamophobia, and Common Politics." *Antipode* 45(4):1128–47.

Rugh, Jacob S., and Douglas S. Massey. 2014. "Segregation in Post-Civil Rights America." *Du Bois Review: Social Science Research on Race* 11(2):205–32.

Ruzich, Joseph. 2010a. "MECCA Champions Willowbrook Mosque." *Chicago Tribune*, August 18. Retrieved December 30, 2015, at http://articles.chicagotribune.com/2010-08-18/news/ct-x-w-0818-willowbrook-mosque-20100818_1_mosque-mecca-sunbulli.

Ruzich, Joseph. 2010b. "Proposal to Ban Religious Facilities in Unincorporated DuPage Draws a Crowd." *Chicago Tribune*, August 26. Retrieved December 29, 2015, at http://articles.chicagotribune.com/2010-08-26/news/ct-met-dupage-zoning-meeting-0827-20100826_1_islamic-center-zoning-proposal-islamic-group.

Ruzich, Joseph. 2011. "DuPage Zoning Panel Opposes Plan for Mosque Near Willowbrook." *Chicago Tribune*, January 14. Retrieved December 29, 2015, at http://articles.chicagotribune.com/2011-01-14/news/ct-met-mosque-debate-20110114_1_unincorporated-residential-areas-zoning-proposal-muslim-educational-cultural-center.

Sanchez, Robert. 2012. "DuPage Rejects Height Waiver for Mosque." *Daily Herald*, March 13. Retrieved February 8, 2016, at http://www.dailyherald.com/article/20120313/news/703139723/.

Sari, Kymelya. 2015. "Bhutanese and Tibetans in Vermont Seek Own Community Centers." *Seven Days*. Retrieved October 1, 2018, at https://www.sevendaysvt.com/vermont/bhutanese-and-tibetans-in-vermont-seek-own-community-centers/Content?oid=2819351.

Schmadeke, Steve. 2013. "Federal Judge Reverses Ruling on Islamic Center." *Chicago Tribune*, March 31. Retrieved December 29, 2015, at http://articles.chicagotribune.com/2013-03-31/news/ct-met-muslim-center-20130331_1_irshad-learning-center-federal-judge-reverses-county-board.

Schmidt, Stephan, and Kurt Paulsen. 2009. "Is Open-Space Preservation a Form of Exclusionary Zoning? The Evolution of Municipal Open-Space Policies in New Jersey." *Urban Affairs Review* 45(1):92–118.

Self, Robert O. 2005. *American Babylon: Race and the Struggle for Postwar Oakland.* Princeton, NJ: Princeton University Press.

Sewell, William H., Jr. 1992. "A Theory of Structure: Duality, Agency, and Transformation." *American Journal of Sociology* 98(1):1–29.

Shlay, Anne B., and Peter H. Rossi. 1981. "Keeping Up the Neighborhood: Estimating Net Effects of Zoning." *American Sociological Review* 46(6):703–19.

Singer, Audrey, Susan W. Hardwick, and Caroline B. Brettell, eds. 2008. *Twenty-First-Century Gateways: Immigrant Incorporation in Suburban America.* Washington, DC: Brookings Institution Press.

Skiba, Katherine. 2012. "Walsh Says U.S. Government Was Too Politically Correct to Prevent Fort Hood Massacre." *Chicago Tribune*, August 10. Retrieved March 1, 2018, at http://articles.chicagotribune.com/2012-08-10/news/ct-met-joe-walsh-muslims-0810-20120810_1_congressman-walsh-fort-hood-army-psychiatrist

Sklair, Leslie. 2017. "Iconic Architecture and the Rise of Globalizing Cities." *Brown Journal of World Affairs* 23(2):127–37.

Sklair, Leslie. 2010. "Iconic Architecture and the Culture-Ideology of Consumerism." *Theory, Culture & Society* 27(5):135–59.

Smith, Christian. 2010. *What Is a Person? Rethinking Humanity, Social Life, and the Moral Good from the Person Up.* Chicago: University of Chicago Press.

Smith, Christian, Brandon Vaidyanathan, Nancy Tatom Ammerman, José Casanova, Hilary Davidson, Elaine Howard Ecklund, John H. Evans, Philip S. Gorski, Mary Ellen Konieczny, Jason A. Springs, Jenny Trinitapoli, and Meredith Whitnah. 2013. "Roundtable on the Sociology of Religion: Twenty-three Theses on the Status of Religion in American Sociology—A Mellon Working-Group Reflection." *Journal of the American Academy of Religion* 81(4):903–38.

Smith, Dennis. 1991. "Coming of Age: A Reflection on Pentecostals, Politics and Popular Religion in Guatemala." *Pneuma* 13(2):65–81.

Smith, Gerry. 2009. "Islamic Center Foes Try New Tack: To Thwart Planned Move, Critics Cite Possible Iran Link." *Chicago Tribune*, November 22. Retrieved December 29, 2015, at http://articles.chicagotribune.com/2009-11-22/news/ct-met-naperville-islamic-center-11222009_1_irshad-learning-center-mahmood-ghassemi-islamic-center.

Smith, Gerry. 2010. "DuPage County to Consider Controversial Zoning Change." *Chicago Tribune*, August 22. Retrieved December 29, 2015, at http://articles.chicagotribune.com/2010-08-22/news/ct-met-dupage-church-zoning-20100822_1_zoning-proposal-irshad-learning-center-zoning-laws.

Smith, Ronald W., and Valerie Bugni. 2006. "Symbolic Interaction Theory and Architecture." *Symbolic Interaction* 29(2):123–55.

Sorkin, Michael. 1991. *Exquisite Corpse: Writing on Buildings.* New York: Verso.

Stevens, Garry. 2002. *The Favored Circle: The Social Foundations of Architectural Distinction.* Cambridge, MA: MIT Press.

Stewart, Beverly. 1989. "Church Outreach, Suburban Zoning Often at Odds." *Chicago Tribune*, February 24. Available at http://articles.chicagotribune.com/1989-02-24/news/8903080127_1_church-and-state-shelter-one-night-church-outreach.

Stoll, David. 1991. *Is Latin America Turning Protestant: The Politics of Evangelical Growth.* Berkeley: University of California Press.

Stroik, Duncan G. 1999a. "Environment and Art in Catholic Worship: A Critique." *Sacred Architecture Journal* 2(1):5.

Stroik, Duncan. 1999b. "Vocatio Architecti." *Sacred Architecture Journal* 2(1):2.

Stroik, Duncan. 2009. *The Church Building as a Sacred Place: Beauty, Transcendence, and the Eternal.* Chicago: Hillenbrand.

Sugrue, Thomas J. 1996. *The Origins of the Urban Crisis: Race and Inequality in Postwar Detroit.* Princeton, NJ: Princeton University Press.

Swasko, Mick. 2011. "Naperville Panel to Reconsider Proposed Mosque Site; Islamic Group Seeking to Have City Annex Land." *Chicago Tribune*, November 2. Retrieved December 29, 2015, at http://articles.chicagotribune.com/2011-11-02/news/ct-met-naperville-mosque-proposal-1102-20111102_1_naperville-panel-mosque-site-annexation.

Swidler, Ann. 1986. "Culture in Action: Symbols and Strategies." *American Sociological Review* 51:14.

Taracena, Arturo, G. Gellert, E. Castillo, T. Paiz, and K. Walter. 2002. *Etnicidad, estado, y nación en Guatemala, 1808–1944.* Guatemala: ASIES.

Taylor, Graham Romeyn. 1915. *Satellite Cities: A Study of Industrial Suburbs.* New York: D. Appleton.

Temkin, Jody. 2001. "Houses of Worship Grow with Population: Islamic Center Joins Churches, Synagogue as City Diversifies." *Chicago Tribune*, June 10. Retrieved December 29, 2015, at http://articles.chicagotribune.com/2001-06-10/news/0106100341_1_church-building-islamic-center-church-basement.

TheArda.com. 2015a. "Christian Church (Disciples of Christ)." Retrieved June 22, 2015, at http://www.thearda.com/Denoms/D_1071.asp.

TheArda.com. 2015b. "Religious Groups: Reformed/Presbyterian." Retrieved June 22, 2015, at http://www.thearda.com/denoms/Families/F_91.asp.

TheArda.com. 2015c. "Lutheran Church-Missoui Synod (LCMS)." Retrieved June 22, 2015, at http://www.thearda.com/denoms/D_887.asp.

The Commission on Church Architecture of The Lutheran Church—Missouri Synod. 1965. *Architecture and the Church.* St. Louis: Concordia.

The Committee on Church Architecture. 1966. *Architectural Guide for Church and School Building.* St. Louis: The Lutheran Church—Missouri Synod.

Thumma, Scott, and Dave Travis. 2007. *Beyond Megachurch Myths: What We Can Learn from America's Largest Churches.* San Francisco: Jossey-Bass.

United States Conference of Catholic Bishops. 2000. *Built of Living Stones: Art, Architecture, and Worship.* Washington, DC: United States Conference of Catholic Bishops.

University Church. 2015. Retrieved June 22, 2015, at http://universitychurchchicago.org/.

University Church. 2019. Retrieved June 20, 2019, at http://universitychurchchicago.org/.

University Church. 2020. "University Church: A Brief History." Retrieved April 5, 2020, at http://universitychurchchicago.org/about/history/.

Vale, Lawrence. 2008. *Architecture, Power, and National Identity.* New York: Routledge.

Vergara, Camilo José. 2005. *How the Other Half Worships.* New Brunswick, NJ: Rutgers University Press.

Villagrán, Ximena. 2016. "Guatemala: Por cada templo católico habría hasta 96 evangélicos." *Soy 502.* Retrieved May 28, 2019, at https://www.soy502.com/articulo/cada-iglesia-catolica-hay-6-evangelicas-registradas.

Wagner-Pacifici, Robin, and Barry Schwartz. 1991. "The Vietnam Veterans Memorial: Commemorating a Difficult Past." *American Journal of Sociology* 7(2):376–420.

Warner, Stephen. 2007. "Presidential Plenary." Paper presented at the Annual Meeting of the Society for the Scientific Study of Religion, November 3, 2007, Tampa, FL.

Weber, Max. 1978. *Economy and Society: An Outline of Interpretive Sociology.* Edited by Guenther Roth and Claus Wittch. Berkeley: University of California Press.

Wellman, James K., Jr. 1999. *The Gold Coast Church and the Ghetto: Christ and Culture in Mainline Protestantism.* Urbana: University of Illinois Press.

Wellman, James K., Jr., Katie E. Corcoran, and Kate Stockly Meyerdirk. 2014. "'God Is like a Drug . . .': Explaining Interaction Ritual Chains in American Megachurches." *Sociological Forum* 29(3):650–72.

Wiggins, Ovetta. 2003. "No Master Plan for Houses of Worship." *Washington Post,* November 20. Retrieved October 12, 2016, at https://www.washingtonpost.com/archive/local/2003/11/20/no-master-plan-for-houses-of-worship/1086256e-5512-471b-a708-35f86fd00266/.

Wilford, Justin G. 2012. *Sacred Subdivisions: The Postsuburban Transformation of American Evangelicalism.* New York: New York University Press.

Williams, Peter W. 1997. *Houses of God: Region, Religion, and Architecture in the United States.* Urbana: University of Illinois Press.

Williams, Roman R. 2010. "Space or God: Lived Religion at Work, Home, and Play." *Sociology of Religion* 71(3):257–79.

Williams, Roman R., ed. 2015. *Seeing Religion: Toward a Visual Sociology of Religion.* New York: Routledge.

Winchester, Daniel. 2008. "Embodying the Faith: Religious Practice and the Making of a Muslim Moral Habitus." *Social Forces* 86(4):1753–80.

Yaneva, Albena, and Liam Heaphy. 2012. "Urban Controversies and the Making of the Social." *Architectural Research Quarterly* 16(1):29–36.

Yates, Jon. 2001. "Hindus Build Monuments to Their Faith: A Growing and Affluent Indian Population Fuels Temple Boom." *Chicago Tribune,* January 19. Retrieved December 29, 2015, at http://articles.chicagotribune.com/2001-01-19/news/0101190379_1_temples-hindu-indian-community.

Young, Victoria. 2014. *Saint John's Abbey Church: Marcel Breuer and the Creation of a Modern Sacred Space.* Minneapolis: University of Minnesota Press.

Zelinsky, Wilbur, and Stephen A. Matthews. 2011. *The Place of Religion in Chicago.* Chicago: The Center for American Places.

Zukin, Sharon. 1991. *Landscapes of Power: From Detroit to Disney World.* Berkeley: University of California Press.

Index